Make The Bullies Pay
and help us lower our
Suicide Rate

Written by: Dawn Perucca

Make the Bullies Pay and Help Us Lower Our Suicide Rate

Written by Dawn Perucca

Contents

MAKE THE BULLIES PAY AND HELP US
LOWER OUR SUICIDE RATE

SOCIAL MEDIA HAS CAUSED OUR SUICIDE RATES TO INCREASE

Between 2001 and 2020, the suicide rate in the U.S. has climbed 33%. Americans are more than twice as likely to die from killing themselves than they are likely to die from someone else killing them.

Online bullying has been increasing dramatically since 2006. That is about the same time our suicide rated started increasing dramatically. Bullying is a bigger problem now than it has ever been before. Some people get bullied in person and online. Since it is easier for bullies to bully online than it is in person, bullies are doing more bullying now than they ever have before.

Homicides get a lot of attention. We read about homicides in the headlines in newspapers. Lots of news stories report homicides. Lots of television shows feature homicides, political figures talk about homicides, police stations have large budgets that are allocated for homicides. Suicides are rarely reported in newspapers or on the news. Very few television shows or movies discuss suicides. Police stations do not have large budgets set-aside to investigate suicides.

I hardly ever hear anyone talk about suicides. Even when I have been doing research about suicides, I have found lots of articles and reports about how bad this problem is but nothing I have read has offered any solutions. It seems like no one has any idea what the remedy is.

I have some ideas that I think would be very helpful, but I am not sure how I can get people to listen to me. I am not a celebrity. Perhaps, I need to hook-up with a celebrity who can help me spread the word. I am planning to do radio interviews all over the United States to advertise my 2 books about bullying once I have books printed and ready to send. It would be nice though, if my idea about BULLY BOXES and BULLY MANAGEMENT CLASSES could be implemented a lot sooner than that. I explain, in detail, in the next chapter of this book about my idea for having BULLY BOXES being legally required to be placed in the bathrooms at all schools, churches, libraries and large corporations where people work so it would be easy for the people who are being bullied or victimized in some way, to report the bullies. These BULLY BOXES would be locked. They would be in a place where anyone could drop a note inside a secure box that would report who has been treating them badly and that they need help. The notes would be retrieved from all the BULLY BOXES regularly, by authorized people only.

I have also listed lots of solutions to bullying in the final chapter of this book, but I really think my 'BULLY BOX' idea could help save a lot of lives.

Also, a report about how many suicides have occurred within the United States between the years 1981 and 2020 reported the following statistics:

- 1981   28,000 suicides
- 1986   31,000 suicides
- 1991   31,000 suicides
- 1996   31,000 suicides
- 2001   31,000 suicides
- 2006   33,000 suicides
- 2011   40,000 suicides

- 2016   45,000 suicides

- 2017   47,000 suicides

- 2018   48,000 suicides

- 2019   48,000 suicides

- 2020   46,000 suicides

I do not know why the suicide rate was lower during 2020 than during 2019. The Corona Virus Pandemic probably affected it.

THE TOP 15 REASONS PEOPLE COMMIT SUICIDE ARE:

1. Mental illness
2. Traumatic experience
3. Bullying
4. Personality disorders
5. Drug addiction / Substance abuse
6. Eating disorders
7. Unemployment
8. Social Isolation / Loneliness
9. Relationship problems/ Genetics / Family history
10. Philosophical desire / Existential crisis
11. Terminal illness/ Chronic pain/ Financial problems
12. Prescription drugs

During 2016, the Top 10 leading causes of death made-up about 74% of all the deaths that year. The Top 10 causes of death that year were:

1. Heart Disease
2. Cancer
3. Unintentional injuries
4. Chronic Lower Respiratory Complications
5. Stroke
6. Alzheimer's Disease
7. Diabetes
8. Influenza and Pneumonia
9. Kidney Disease
10. Suicide

Some statistics on bullying and suicide are as follows:

It is the 3rd leading cause of death among young people.

During 2016, it was the 2nd leading cause of death among people who were between 15 and 34 years old.

During 2016 there were more than twice as many suicides as there were homicides.

For every suicide among young people, there are at least 100 suicide attempts.

More than 14% of high school students have considered suicide.

Almost 7% have attempted it.

Bully victims are 2 – 9 times more likely to consider suicide than non-victims, according to studies done at Yale University.

A study done in Britain revealed at least half of suicides among young people are related to bullying.

10- to 14-year-old girls are at an even higher risk for committing suicide.

ABC News reported about 30 percent of students are either bullies or victims of bullies.

ABC News also reported about 160,000 kids stay home from school every day because they are trying to avoid being bullied.

Some warning signs that may be a clue that a young person is considering suicide.

Acting depressed

Ongoing sadness

Withdrawal from others

Losing interest in their favorite activities

Trouble with sleeping

Trouble with eating

Talking about death or dying

Showing an interest in death or dying

Participating in dangerous activities

Substance abuse

Self-harm

Giving away favorite possessions, then, saying goodbye to people

Telling someone they can't handle things anymore

Making comments that things would be better without them

Some ways to help someone who is considering suicide

If someone tells you they are considering suicide, take them seriously and get them help immediately.

Keep weapons and medications away from them.

Parents should encourage their children to talk about bullying. Some of them do not want to admit they have been victims of bullying.

Parents should insist on having access to their children's friends on social network.

Parents should have open communication with their children about bullying.

Parents should ask their children if anyone has been bullying them through text messages.

If parents see a serious bullying problem, they should talk to their school authorities about it.

Parents may also contact local Police or local Attorneys to get some help regarding bullying.

Parents should care about their kids' emotions. They should make sure they are not so strict and rigid that they are making their children feel miserable all of the time.

Parents should make sure they are not so uninterested in their children's lives that their children believe no one in the world really cares about them.

Within the United States, the 5 states that have the highest suicide rates are:

Montana...............................28.9 / 100,000

Alaska...................................27.0 / 100,000

Wyoming..............................26.9 / 100,000

New Mexico..........................23.3 / 100,000

Idaho....................................23.2 / 100,000

Within the United States, the 5 states that have the lowest suicide rates are:

New York..............................08.1 / 100,000

New Jersey............................08.3 / 100,000

Massachusetts........................09.5 / 100,000

Maryland...............................09.8 / 100,000

Connecticut...........................10.5 / 100,000

It is believed that some of the reasons the states that have a high suicide rate tend to be states that have easy access to firearms, mental illnesses, substance abuse and poor access to medical care for mental illnesses.

It is believed that some of the reasons the states that have a low suicide rate tend to be states that have easy access to medical services, reduced obesity, reduced smoking, economic stability and high funding for public healthcare.

Significantly more men commit suicide than women, at every age.

19.3% of all suicides come from men and women who are above the age of 85.

19.2% of all suicides come from men and women who are between 45 and 64.

11.6% of all suicides come from males and females who are teenagers.

The suicide rates among nationalities are:

14.7% White people

10.9% Native Americans

06.3% Hispanics

05.9% Asians and Pacific Islanders

05.5% Black Americans

The methods people use to commit suicide are:

49.9% Firearms

26.7% Suffocation

15.9% Poisoning

07.5% Other methods

According to a survey that was conducted by the Cyberbullying Research Center, (www.cyberbullying.org), during 2016, 5,707 students who lived within the United States were surveyed. The students were between the ages of 12 – 17 years old. The results from that survey reported that 33.8%

of those students had been cyber-bullied at some time during their lifetime. The results from the rest of the survey were intended to measure how much each student had been cyber-bullied during the previous 30 days. Those results were:

16.9% Were cyber-bullied.

22.5% Had received mean or hurtful comments online.

20.1% False rumors about them had been posted online.

12.7% Mean names or comments with a sexual content were posted about

them online.

12.2% Someone threatened to hurt them online.

11.9% Threatened to hurt them through a cell phone text.

11.1% Mean or hurtful pictures were posted of them online.

10.3% Someone else pretended to be them online.

10.1% Mean names or comments about their race or color were posted online.

7.4% A mean or hurtful video of them was posted online.

7.1% Someone created a mean or hurtful web page about them online.

25.1% One or more of the above situations happened to them 2 or more times.

IDEAS I HAVE REGARDING HOW WE CAN DECREASE BULLYING AND OUR SUICIDE RATE

I believe a lot of the people who have Aggressive Personality Types were born with those tendencies. Research shows that people who have Aggressive Personality Types can also develop those personality tendencies when they spend their childhoods in certain environments. Regardless of how their aggressive tendencies became so dominant, MRI scans of the brains of the people who have these abrasive personalities always prove that the frontal lobe of these people's brains is not within the normal range. The area of their brains that controls empathy and compassion is dramatically under-active. Many of these people have personality disorders that have never been diagnosed.

I also believe that the people in this world who have sensitive personality types are more likely to be bullied and they are likely to be people who are not good at standing-up for themselves. These people especially need to have a lot of different ways they can signal for help when they are being treated so badly that they can't stand to keep living the life they have been living. I have listed a lot of phone #'s at the end of this book that people who are being treated horribly can call if they need help but the people who are being bullied or are likely to attempt suicide typically do not call these phone #'s.

I do not understand why victims of bullies usually do not get help from anyone until they attempt suicide. They should have lots of ways they can get help way before they get to that point.

One of the reasons it is more difficult to report the perpetrators these days is because most people have caller ID now. Sometimes, people do not want to call for help because they do not want the person on the other end of the line to know who is calling and they do not want the person who answers the phone to be able to detect their location with the GPS technology that exists today. It is also hard to send an e-mail to try to get help without people being able to find-out who just sent the e-mail. Sometimes people want to be able to get help anonymously and they do not know how to do that.

Most people do not realize they can send anonymous letters through the mail to various authorities to get the perpetrators to stop doing their evil tactics.

One of the things that helped me figure-out ways to help the people who are getting bullied and the people who are likely to commit suicide came from the following story.

I learned quite-a-bit when I was doing phone interviews with people and doing searches on the internet to learn more. One of the things I learned that I think every school should be using was that there was a school that figured-out that they had some students who had trouble with having meltdowns. That school gave those children something yellow to hand to their teacher when they felt like they were about to become angry and something red to hand to their teacher when they felt like they were about to have a full-blown tantrum. This school discovered that those kids knew they were about to have an outburst, they just did not know how to not have the outburst. Once those kids had yellow and red objects to hand to their teachers. Their teachers got them the help they needed right away. They knew that if one of those children was handing them the yellow or red object, that child needed to be escorted to a quiet room, immediately. Once the child was in the quiet room, they could sit with a kind companion and talk, or they could stay there by themselves if they needed to get calmed down. That strategy worked well.

I thought this was an excellent example of how problems could be stopped from happening, instead of waiting until a problem occurs, then punishing and blaming people. Our society needs to have lots of different ways to prevent problems from happening.

I think the same sort of strategy could work for the people who are overly distressed from bullies. Some of the people who are getting bullied, are not having tantrums and they are not telling other people what they have been enduring. Some of those people are keeping all their frustrations inside their head. Extroverts are a lot more likely to talk about what they are thinking. Introverts usually keep most of their thoughts to themselves. If no one knows they are at the point where they cannot take it anymore and they do not want to keep living, no one can help them. I think these people who keep most of their thoughts to themselves need to be taught that they should seek help if they are feeling overwhelmed.

All young people need to be taught what they should do if they are being bullied. There needs to be easy ways for the victims to report the bullies. There must be discreet ways the victims can tell someone, who can help them, exactly who the bullies are and what they have been doing. Sometimes the victims are afraid to report the problem because they think the bullying will become worse if they do report it.

I think every school in the world should be required to have BULLY
BOXES. These BULLY BOXES would be very much like a suggestion box.
Anyone would be able to drop a note into these locked boxes. The BULLY
BOXES should be placed somewhere where they are not in view of any
security cameras. Perhaps the BULLY BOXES could be installed inside of
restrooms. There should be instructions on the outside of the box that
explain, anyone who is being bullied should write down or type-out their
story and place their story into this box. It should explain that they should
name the bully or the bullies. The BULLY BOXES could even have pre-
printed check lists near them, that people could check-off then fill-in the
perpetrator's name. The person who is reporting the bully may list the name
of the bully or the names of the bullies. They would not need to report who
they are. They would not need to sign the paper. The victims should be
allowed to report bullying that has been happening on school grounds or off
school grounds. Each school would have some designated adults (for
example, school counselors or school psychologists) who would have a key
to this box. The people who have the authority to open these boxes and read
the notes would then be required to investigate every report.

Since a lot of kids are home-schooled these days, the kids who are home-schooled should also drop a note in a BULLY BOX. I think there should also be BULLY BOXES at churches and libraries so those kids would have opportunities to report bullies anonymously.

If it was required by law that all schools, churches and libraries have a BULLY BOX installed in their bathrooms. Then, there would be one more way that anyone who is being abused could let someone know they need help. For example, the note could say something like, "I was raped by my uncle, and I am afraid to tell my parents. His name is Clyde Brady, he is in his 30's. He lives in Rockford, IL, he drives a white pick-up truck and his license plate # is??????." Maybe this girl, would drop a note in a BULLY BOX but would never tell her parents something like this. I think more people would report their situation if they knew they could report it privately. Anyway, I think the BULLY BOXES would help a lot of different people escape their dangerous situation.

Sometimes kids get treated horribly by one of the parents in their home and the other parent in the home has no idea how horribly their child has been getting treated from the other parent. Sometimes the parents know their relationship is a mess, but they think their kids will be better off, if they just keep living together as a family.

KIDS NEED TO HAVE EASY AND SAFE WAYS THEY CAN REPORT THAT THEY ARE BEING BULLIED AND THEY CAN'T STAND LIVING THE WAY THEY HAVE BEEN LIVING.

I think a lot of the insensitive people in this world really have no idea how much damage they do to the sensitive people, and they need to be educated and stopped.

The people who are given access to the notes inside the BULLY BOXES should be people who have been thoroughly trained regarding how to interact with the bullies. They should have a network of people who they can get to help them interact with the bully, try to get the bully to behave decently and they should be educated regarding what they should do if the bully refuses to cooperate.

As of right now, bullying causes an unbelievable # of people to commit suicide and the victims of bullying typically have no idea how they can get the bullies to stop bullying them. I think BULLY BOXES would give them an option that could help them get the bullying stopped.

I also think there should be BULLY MANAGEMENT CLASSES. These classes would be like anger management classes. People who are caught bullying people should be required to attend these classes. The people who instruct these classes would be thoroughly trained regarding how to learn why that person was bullying then decide if that person needs help because they have been getting treated badly too, or if that person needs education regarding how to treat others much kindlier, or both.

If our Government made the BULLY BOXES and the BULLY MANAGEMENT CLASSES a requirement, there would be expenses incurred to make this happen, but I think, in-the-long-run, our government would save a lot of money overall because fewer people would end-up in juvenile detentions centers and in jails. I think many of the people who are living a destructive life would get help early-on, then be able to improve their behaviors dramatically. I also think if all the bullies in our society were forced to learn how to behave better, they would become better parents and their children would benefit dramatically too. I think the BULLY BOXES and the BULLLY MANAGEMENT CLASSES would have a positive domino effect. Why must we wait until after a crime has happened to search for a remedy?

Bullying and suicides are a major crisis that is becoming increasingly worse over time. People should be talking about this topic and trying to find solutions. Newspapers should be reporting these kinds of stories. Television News Stations should be reporting these types of stories. Politicians should be addressing this problem and trying to find solutions. Police Stations should be allocating funds to spend on these types of problems.

When I was doing phone interviews with people, at least 3 of the people I interviewed told me they have had a hard time with getting security guards and their local police to help them with the problems they had been having with bullying.

THE DEFINITION OF BULLYING:

Repeated aggressive acts causing an imbalance of power between the perpetrator and the victim. Unfortunately, we face bullying as we go about our daily lives. Sometimes the bullying we encounter is subtle and we do not realize we are being bullied. The following stories that I collected when I was interviewing people about bullying describes lots of examples of subtle and not so subtle bullying.

THIS GIRL, WHO HAS TOURETTE'S SYNDROME, WAS BEING BULLIED IN PERSON AND ONLINE

The person who I spoke with on the phone this day is someone I have never met before. Her daughter has Tourette's syndrome. I will be referring to her daughter as VICTIM # 1. I had never even heard of her. One of my friend's asked her if she would be interested in telling me her story and letting me include her story in my book. My friend gave me her phone #.

This Mom, who was anxious to stand-up and fight for her daughter, has the ESFP Personality Type according to the Myers-Briggs Personality Test she took after I asked her to take it for me.

The ESFP Personality Type is known as 'The Entertainer, The Promoter, The Realist and the Performer.'

People who have the ESFP personality type tend to be playful, and fun-loving.   These people tend to live in the moment. They try to enjoy life to the fullest. They try to focus on the positive. They tend to be warm and friendly without having any hidden agendas. Being capable of understanding and meeting the emotional needs of other people tends to be one of their greatest gifts. These people do not like to be bored. They love to interact with other people. They tend to not try to control others. But they also do not want to have other people try to control them. If you try to control them; they will probably disappear from your life. These people tend to be very good listeners. More women have this personality type than men.

Her daughter has the ISTJ Personality Type.

The ISTJ Personality Type is known as 'The Inspector.'

People who have this personality type tend to be hard workers. They tend to be reserved, quiet and calm. These people tend to be wise and logical. They tend to accumulate a lot of information in their memory. They tend to be very accurate and patient people. They tend to be thorough. They tend to be self-sufficient and comfortable with being alone. These people need to have time alone to be able to recharge. These people tend to make most of their decisions based on logic, not on emotion. They are ruled by their heads, not their hearts. They tend to be more concerned with facts, than with protecting people's feelings. These people tend to have a strong work ethic. They usually like to use lists and schedules. They are organized and they like to be prepared for things ahead of time.

The people who have this personality type are likely to be physically and mentally organized, highly intellectual, great at planning for things ahead of time, people who can remain calm during tense situations, good at having committed relationships, love traditions, they tend to be well-respected in their communities, they love memorizing details and facts.

I told her a little bit about myself. She was anxious to start telling me her story. She told me, she personally had been bullied a little when she was young. She told me she had dark circles under her eyes and some people had accused her of using drugs. That was about the extent of her bullying experiences from her childhood.

When her daughter was 6 years old, she was diagnosed with Tourette's Syndrome.

She told me that Tourette's Syndrome is strongly misunderstood by the public, partially because of the media's portrayal of it. She told me only about 10% of the people who Tourette's Syndrome use Cuss words when they have tics.

I did some research about Tourette's Syndrome so I could better understand it and be able to explain it.

When someone has Tourette's Syndrome; they might have involuntary twitches, called tics. The presence of vulgar vocal tics is called Coprolalia. The presence of vulgar motor tics is called Copropraxia. Only about 10% of Tourette's Patients have vulgar vocal tics. About 9 out of 10 of the people who have T.S. do not use swear words. Tourette's is not a swearing disease.

One person who has Tourette's explained the tics as being like blinking. She said, you can delay blinking a little bit but once you do blink, you will probably blink more because you delayed the blinking. She also said, delaying the tic causes the person who has Tourette's to feel pain, stress and discomfort. She also said, if she tries to suppress tics too long, she will have a tic attack. Tic attacks can last 15 minutes to several hours. A severe tic attack can cause the person who is experiencing the attack to need to be rushed to the hospital and sedated until the tics calm down. During a severe tic attack, the Tourette's Patient can hurt them self or be in severe danger.

People who have Tourette's can pick-up tics from things they see or hear, like television or the radio. People who have T.S. do not choose what their tic will be. Random phrases they start saying are not a direct reflection of what they are thinking or feeling. Although tics can be triggered by what is going on around them, most tics are completely random.

People who have T.S. may say inappropriate things at inopportune times but some of their tics are positive phrases.

T.S. is a neurological disorder, not a psychological disorder.

If someone who has T.S. tries to change their vocal tic to be more appropriate for their audience, that causes distress for the individual who has T.S., then that person will be likely to keep ticking until the tic is satisfied. When someone who has T.S. becomes embarrassed by their symptoms, their symptoms tend to become worse.

T.S. affects the brain in that it causes a lack of inhibitory control. Most of us have a filter in our brain that keeps us from blurting-out things we know we should not say. T.S. patients' filters do not work properly. T.S. patients tend to have abnormal dopamine levels, serotonin levels and other neurotransmitter inefficiencies. They are also likely to have oddities in their basal ganglia.

Among the people who have T.S.; not everything they blurt out is words. Sometimes, their vocal tics are chirping noises, coughing, throat clearing or humming sounds.

Their non-vocal tics may be eye blinking, tugging at clothes, or distinct movements of their head or neck.

I saw a video of Victim # 1 online. She is a very attractive girl. She looks like she is completely normal. She did have some minor facial tics.

Her Mom told me when her daughter was in the 4th grade; 2 of the boys at her school started bullying her and it got to be bad. When her daughter was in the 5th grade, there was 1 boy at school who was bullying her.

Her daughter had been attending a private Montessori School when this was happening. She told me it was a small school. She decided to take her daughter out of this school and place her in the public school before she entered the 6th grade. This was the 1st time her daughter had attended a public school.

Once her daughter was attending the public school; she got punched in the stomach and someone threw a rock in her face that almost blinded her.

This Mom reported these incidents to the Principal of the school. He did almost nothing about the situation. Years later she learned the parents of the boy who threw the rock at her daughter's face were good friends with the Principal.

Next, her daughter started attending the Junior High School. Soon after that, this Mom became disappointed with some of the things her daughter had been doing online. She told me the things her daughter had done were typical online behaviors for a 12-year-old girl. She was trying to keep her daughter safe and teach her daughter how to be safe online. She banned her daughter from using social media for a while.

Soon after that, this Mom was on Instagram. She noticed her daughter had liked one of her photos. Since she had banned her daughter from using Instagram months before this; she called her ex-husband and asked him if he had given their daughter permission to use Instagram again. He told her he had not given their daughter permission to use Instagram again.

This Mom asked her daughter, "Why are you using Instagram again, since we told you not to use it for a while?"

Her daughter responded, "I haven't been using Instagram."

Before too long, this Mom realized someone had stolen about 35 pictures from her Instagram page and created a fake account. The online account appeared to be her daughter's account. The bully who created this account wanted people to believe this account was owned and operated by Victim # 1.

The bully who was operating this account was sending nasty messages to 6 of Victim # 1's friends. The messages she was sending were filled with lots of profanities. They were also sending messages to the recipients that said things like, 'You are not popular, you are hated, you should be killed, you are a *#@_ (! &), +^#!%^, and a *%@_*($!. Next, Victim # 1's friends started calling her and asking her why all this was happening.

Victim # 1 was in shock that anyone would do something like this.

Once Victim # 1's Mom learned this was happening. She screen-shot it and placed that photo on her account. She also reported these events to her local Police Department. When all this was happening; Social Media was still new enough, that there were not that many laws in place yet that could protect the victims of online bullying.

This local Police Department told Victim # 1's Mom she would need a subpoena or a search warrant for them to get involved; but even then, there would be nothing they would be able to do, because Victim # 1 hadn't been harassed directly. At that time, there were no laws in that state that banned people from stealing someone's identity and impersonating them online. These Police Officers told her there was nothing they could do to help protect her child from this type of a crime. The Police Officers told her. The people who received the online hate messages could get a subpoena or a search warrant because they had received messages that had profane language and they could prove they were harassed. They said their stories would fall under that State's Laws about cyber-bullying.

This Police Department also told this Mom, "You will need to contact Instagram directly and ask them to close this account." She was able to get this account closed; but she told me, doing that was a difficult task because many social media sites were created in other Countries. They are being operated by other Countries and the people who live in the United States have absolutely no power over these sites.

When this Mom announced, 'I really want to find out who created this account.' This task was very difficult. She was desperate to learn who had done this to her daughter. A Media Reporter from her local news team interviewed her. During the middle of June, on a Wednesday night, this story was aired on her local news station. The type of story she was telling was something that had not really been aired on TV that much yet because Social Media was still kind of a new phenomenon. Good Morning America saw the interview she had done with her local News Team. They invited her to be interviewed on Good Morning America. Soon after their local interview, she and her daughter were both interviewed by Good Morning America.

This Mom told me her story is not that alarming now; but when this happened to her daughter, this story was alarming because most people had never heard of this sort of thing happening before.

Since their story was getting National attention all-of-a-sudden. The State she was living in was embarrassed that they did not have any laws in place that could protect someone who is being impersonated online yet. Suddenly some people started to feel the pressure to create some new laws. This State felt like they had just received a big black eye because this story had suddenly become National News. All-of-a-sudden, a Subpoena was issued that would allow these local Police to try to discover who had created this fake online account. These local Police did figure-out who had created this account. The Bully was a 12-year-old girl. Her parents had gotten a divorce and the new father figure who had moved into their home was a train-wreck. This girl's home life was less than ideal. This girl was a good athlete and appeared to have some friends.

Victim # 1's Mom told me she did not want to ask this girl for an apology, because there would be absolutely no meaning or value behind doing that. She really wanted this girl to learn from this experience and try to do better in the future. She thinks this girl should have had to do some Community Service. She believes this girl is insecure and jealous.

Currently, Victim # 1 is a Junior in High School. She has not been getting bullied anymore. She and her Mom try not to dwell-on the events that happened several years ago. They do not want to live their lives as Victims.

She told me most young people do not know how to handle their frustrations. She remarked, "We are not born knowing how to handle pain or how to express it. Lots of kids are never taught positive ways to behave when they are feeling stressed-out."

She also told me kids are being exposed to inappropriate things at much younger ages now than they were before there was social media. She told me there are so many inappropriate ads that pop up when a curious 8-year-old boy does a search online for penis. She remarked, he will suddenly be bombarded with ads for porn. She said parents need to teach their kids things at a much younger age now than they did before there was Social Media because kids are getting exposed to adult issues at much younger ages now. It is now extremely important that we teach our kids how to be resilient.

Most Parents think Cyber-Bullying involves people sending negative messages to other people on Social Media. Most Parents do not realize Cyber-Bullying can be someone creating fake accounts about another person; then the Bully sending nasty messages from the fake account and convincing other people the nasty messages are being sent from the person they created the fake account for.

When parents forbid their children from using Social Media; their children can still be bullied online if someone creates a fake account about them and bullies' people through the fake account.

If someone discovers a fake account has been made about them or one of their friends or family members; some of the things, they should do include.

1. Find-out if bullying is illegal in the State, they live in. If it is, report the bullying incident to their local Police. Perhaps the State you live in has laws against impersonating someone online. If the State you live in does have that, get a Subpoena or a Search Warrant to help learn who created the fake account.

2. Have an in-depth conversation with the victim and discover if there is anything you can do to help that person. Listening to their story may be one of the things that victim is needing. Try to find out if they know who could have created the fake account.

3. If a school age child is the one a fake internet account was made about; contact that child's school. They should be informed. If a fake account was created about one of the children at a certain school; it will be likely that fake internet accounts have been created about other children at the same school.

4. If there are no laws in the State, you live in that can protect someone from being impersonated online; try to congregate lots of other parents / adults in your area and get new laws created that will help protect people from being impersonated online.

She told me she had been watching all the movies there are about bullying because this happened to her daughter. She told me about a movie she had watched that is about bullying and she told me I should watch it. The name of the movie is, 'A girl like her.' That night I did an online search for this movie, and I watched it online. I cried more during this movie than I have ever cried while I've watched any movie.

This movie is about a High School that is ranked very high Scholastically. One of the girls in this movie was being bullied so badly that her guy friend named Brian gave her a tiny video camera to wear. It looked like it was a piece of jewelry. She did not want to wear it because she was worried that if anyone discovered she was videotaping them, she would get bullied even more. She made this boy promise he would never show this video footage to anyone. He agreed that only she and he would look at the video footage. She wore that tiny camera for 6 months and she video-taped her bully attacking her verbally and physically frequently during that time.

I am going to list specific things the Bully in this movie, Avery, did to the Victim, Jessica. I realize these events were all scripted and were not something that happened in real life. However, this movie was created with the intent of trying to accurately depict bullying that does happen in the real World. I think if you have never witnessed bullying like this, you will be shocked that this sort of thing does happen. In this movie, 'A Girl Like Her' Avery did the bullying that is listed below. Some of these messages, Avery said to Jessica directly. Some of these messages, Avery texted to Jessica.

Avery communicated to Jessica:

1. You make my life miserable just by being here and I am gonna make your life miserable too.
2. Seriously, Jessica, if you disappeared the World would be a better place.
3. Just go end yourself.
4. Nobody likes you.
5. UGLY
6. Go die please.
7. Go F yourself, Jessica, you stupid B
8. B
9. Why did not you text me back? I thought we were friends. I was so nice to you.
10. Nice outfit today; Who picked-it-out? UR Grandma? Oh, wait, she is dead, LOL B.
11. Watch it, Jessica
12. Whore, whore, whore, whore, whore, whore, whore, whore, I have been practicing my spelling.
13. Everyone hates you but no one more than me.
14. Oh, you need to go to class, you need to go to class? I do not give a F if you need to go to class.
15. . Did you get to class? Did you get to class?
16. . What's-up UGLY?
17. You are so UGLY!!!
18. You suck so bad!!!
19. Go kill yourself.

20. Everybody hates you.

21. How come you are so pretty? – SIKE

22. Later Freaks

23. Die Jessica Burns

24. Ha Ha Ha Ha Ha, your life is worthless, and you need to just end it.

25. You are a disrespectful little Cunt. Did you know that?

26. I am opening your locker for you, what are you 5? Do you enjoy the cute little decorations? Who decorates their locker like this? (Avery then ripped Jessica's decorations out of her locker.)

27. How is my little Bitch doing, Good?

28. Go home and crawl under a rock.

29. What are you doing in my bathroom? Nothing to say? No? Well, your restroom is down there with all the rest of the little Bitches. Did you get that? Are you understanding me? Do you have nothing to say?

30. She is not a fighter, is she?

31. Do you understand me? You are gonna go back to your little bathroom that you love so much. (She then, shoved her into one of the bathroom stalls.)

32. Do it already.

33. 1,2,3 DIE – GO DO ITTTTT

34. You are so ugly and weird.

35. You are still here?

36. You are so ugly and short.

37. Just end it

38. Go die please

39. Be a good friend and kill yourself.

40. Ugly B

41. I F'ing HATE YOU!!!!!!!!!

After Avery completely emptied Jessica's locker, she shoved her into the empty locker and said, "Oh, wow, you have no clothes, Oh, what are you

42. gonna do? That is so sad. Put the world out of its misery and disappear you F'ing waste of space.

43. F-off

44. Go to sleep and do not wake-up

45. You suck

46. You do not belong here, OK?

47. (After Avery's friends knocked Jessica over), Avery said, "I am sorry, I'm so sorry, It is fine, really. Sorry, I did not mean to. Next, she acted like she was going to help Jessica up by reaching out her hand toward her. As soon as Jessica almost grabbed her hand, Avery pulled her hand away and said, "Yeah, right." Then she walked away.

48. You are a F'ing bitch.

49. Someone pushed Jessica into Avery. Avery turned around and asked, "Did you just push me, Jessica?" Jessica responded, "No." Avery then shoved Jessica, then turned around and walked away. Then, Avery said, "Why do not you just kill yourself, seriously, Jessica, if you disappeared, the World would be a better place.

50. Go kill yourself; we all want you to.

51. I have a funny feeling that she thinks everything will get better from here on out.

52. Oh, well, well, well, It is Jessica Burns

53. Do you think I am just gonna get bored with you and forget about you? That's not the case because I F'ing hate you.

54. Do you smell anything? Next, she grabbed Jessica by the wrist and
dragged her into the shower and turned the water on.

55. I need to kick your F-ing A.

After video-taping this bullying for 6 months, Jessica was sitting on
the floor in one of the hallways of the High School one day. She was crying
because Avery has just bullied her one more time. She told Brian:

"I can't do it."

"I can't be put-up with it anymore."

"I'm tired."

"I can't, I can't do it."

Brian responded, "I'm so sorry" He hugged her.

"I just do not know how much more of this I can take." Jessica told
him.

Brian responded, "That's why we have all this film, Jessica, we have
all this footage."

Jessica told him, "It is embarrassing; I am not going to show it to
anyone. It is gonna get worse. It is never gonna end. It is never gonna end. It
is never gonna get better. I feel like I have no way out."

Eventually, Jessica, the victim in this movie decided, she could not
take it anymore. She swallowed a bottle of pills and ended-up in a coma. Her
parents had no idea she had been enduring bullying. When some of her
teachers were interviewed, they said she was quiet and reserved and she had
not been communicating to them that anything had been going on.
Immediately, lots of the students at the school were talking about Jessica
swallowing a bottle of pills and ending-up in a Coma. Some of them knew
that a girl named Avery had been treating Jessica badly. Avery had 4 girl

friends who she hung around with all the time. All 4 of those girls were present in all the videos Brian's camera had captured. All 4 of those girls knew how Avery had been treating Jessica.

When Jessica went into a coma; Brian did not come forth and announce that he knew why she had tried to commit suicide. He did not tell anyone that he had 6 months-worth of video footage that documented Avery bullying Jessica. He did not even visit Jessica at the hospital for quite-a-while. Eventually, he decided he would show some adults the video footage he had even though he had promised Jessica, he would never show it to anyone.

Because this event happened at this school; a Female Investigator was sent to this school to investigate and try to figure-out why this happened. The Female Investigator eventually convinced Avery to let her interview her and video tape her at school and inside her home. The Investigator convinced Avery she would be following her around because she wanted to learn what a popular girl's life is really like. This Investigator brought her video cameras into Avery's home. That was where it was obvious that everyone in this home despised the Mom, including the Dad. There was constant tension inside this home. This Mom was constantly criticizing and belittling everyone in this family. Avery said she gets good grades at school because she is in a big hurry to get out of this house.

Some examples of the dialogue that took place inside this home during this movie are as follows:

The Investigator told the Mom, Kassie, "You have a very nice kitchen." Kassie responded. My husband paid a lot of money for it when he had a job."

Avery is trying to lose weight, so she always wants to eat lots of vegetables.

She is still reeling from the time she did not make it on the Pom-Pom Squad. She came home that night and said, "You know what it is, I am too fat." I attribute her not making the team to that Psycho Coach who was giving her a lot of attitudes about the way she treated the other kids on the Pom-Pom Squad.

This is Josh, our Son, who recently graduated from High School, narrowly. His favorite thing to do is play video games. College is not interesting to him.

When Josh told his Mom, "Please stop with that." Kassie responded, "It is alright, It's your one minute of fame. You might as well suck it up."

You know you guys might consider not eating before Avery gets down here. That is obnoxious, Avery, Chop Chop!!!!!!!!

Kassie also said, "Let us get started. I made sure you got a lot of vegetables and a lot of protein because I know that you said you are worried about your weight. Avery responded, "Thank you for sharing that. It is so polite of you." Kassie responded to Avery, "You're welcome."

Kassie asked her son, "What did you do today, Josh?" Josh responded, "Not much, I played the blah, blah, blah video game." Kassie responded, "I hear that is a pretty popular game to play for kids your age, and also for 13-year-olds."

Kassie asked Avery, "Why do not you tell us why your friends are filming us while we dine on this excellent Cuisine?"

Avery responded, "I do not know, Mom, because they like me."

Kassie responded, "Do you think it is because you are a beautiful, talented and intelligent young lady, and that is the reason you were selected for this prestigious opportunity?"

The husband then said, "Kassie, leave her alone, will ya?"

Kassie responded to him, "Are not you proud of our daughter, do not you think this is a great opportunity for her?"

Avery responded, "Stop, just stop, cut the B.S., just stop, just stop, let's just eat, let's just eat, let's just eat."

The husband said, "Let's just have dinner."

Kassie replied, "We are just having fun here. Can't we have fun occasionally?"

"Give her a break, Let us have our dinner. That is what we are here for," the husband said.

Kassie responded, "Well, maybe when you learn how to lighten-up we can do that. We can have dinner and have fun at the same time."

Avery responded, "Seriously, please stop."

Kassie stated, "Well, it is exciting that they are here. I am glad we can all eat and be involved in this film about you. I am very proud of you; very proud of you."

The Husband then said, "I'll tell ya what," then he stood-up, grabbed his plate; then he walked out of the room.

Kassie asked, "Where are you going?"

"Game time, you know where I'll be," the husband remarked.

Kassie announced, "I just wanted a peaceful dinner with our family, and this is what I get?"

Initially, Kassie said to her husband, "Look at you are watching TV, lying there on your A with your frickin' clicker and not contributing anything to this household."

On another evening in this household, Avery rolled her eyes, then said, "OK, this is a typical night in the Keller household, there is fighting in our home every night." She then started video-taping her parents fighting.

Kassie also said to her husband, "Wash your hands, cuz, men do not wash their hands after they go to the bathroom. When I go to the bathroom; I like to wash my hands after I take a piss, Jesus Christ."

The Husband responded, "I'm on it, I'm on it." He continued to lie on the bed.

Kassie spoke to him, "While we're on to what we're on; are you on to getting a job this week; or is that gonna go another 2 months?"

The husband responded, "Yeah, I got an appointment with my friend Jerry on Wednesday."

Josh noticed Avery was videotaping their parents. He asked her, "What the H do you think you are doing? Are you kidding me; what the H are you doing? Are you taping them? What are you doing?"

Avery responded, "Yes, I am taping them, stop asking me questions. Get out of my face. It is none of your F'ing business, Josh."

Josh responded, "This is family business. Is this a joke?"

Avery responded to him, "Is this family business? Oh my God, go back to playing video games, loser, yes."

While Josh and Avery were arguing, Kassie and their Father had been arguing in the background non-stop the entire time.

Josh said to Avery, "You're such a B."

Avery responded to him, "Oh, I am a B, B, is that the most creative thing you can come-up with to say? Hey, why do not you try going back to school."

Josh told Avery, "Grow-up."

Avery responded to him, "Grow-up? Really, you are how old, and you dropped-out of College and still live at home, yes, grow-up?"

Kassie screamed in the background, "I do not know what else I can do."

Avery then announced, "Not only do my parents' fight; my brother is a F'ing douche bag. Oh, so yes, that is my night."

This school had a meeting that invited parents to attend so they could try to find solutions to the bullying that had been happening in their school. One of the parents stood-up and announced: Usually the parents who show-up at our school meetings are the parents of the kids who are doing well. He also stated, the Mental Health of the bully's needs to be addressed too. We will never stop the bullying unless we find some method of getting inside the heads of the bullies and finding some way to bring healing to them. He said, 'Hurt people, hurt people.' The bullies are likely to be victims who are hurting too. The bullies need help. If you do not teach the bullies proper ways to behave; the bullying will never stop.

The Principal of this school organized a meeting with Avery and both of Avery's parents after the 4 girls Avery had been hanging around with documented specific bullying Avery had done to Jessica. All 4 of those girls signed that document. Those 4 girls wanted to document that information so they would not be blamed for doing all the stuff Avery had done. Those girls had witnessed all the bullying and did help Avery with some of it.

Once The Principal, Avery and Avery's parents were all sitting at a table together in a closed room; the Principal stated, "I have a statement here that says you are the cause of the bullying that was done to Jessica. He also stated, "We are here to find-out the complete story. I am giving you a chance with your parents here to tell us your side of the story because I know there is always 2 sides to every story.

Avery responded while she looked at the piece of paper, "I did not do any of this stuff."

At this point, Avery did not know yet, that Jessica had been videotaping all the bullying Avery had done to her and Brian had already presented all those videos to the authorities.

Avery continued, "Stop, I did not do any of these things. I did not, let us see; I did not harass her; I did not send her multiple mean things; I was not mean to her relentlessly.

The Principal held-up the paper and asked her, "You did not do any of these things?"

Avery responded, "No, I did not do any of those things. I did not harass or bully Jessica."

The Principal then asked, "If you say that, then why would your friends put this on paper and put their names on it? This is serious. This is not just, "Oh Jeez stuff."

Avery responded, "I am not joking around about this. Obviously, I know it is serious, but I did not do any of those things."

The Principal responded, "This isn't something I can just pass-off because you said, "I did not do anything, do you understand that?" There will be consequences for your actions and part of the consequences are that you must take responsibility for the things that you do."

Avery then told him, "Yeah, OK, so maybe I joked around with Jessica. Maybe, I joked around with her, just like those girls did. I was just joking around with her. Maybe I took it a little bit too far. Maybe it hurt her feelings. I do not know. It is not my problem that this girl can't handle a joke. Everyone blew it way out of proportion. That is not true. None of that is true." She said, as she pointed to the page.

Kassie said, "You know he is bullying you right now, by trying to get you to admit to something you did not do."

Avery stated, "Mom, I know."

The Principal responded, "I am not bullying. I am asking questions to find out answers."

Kassie responded, "My daughter is being thrown under the bus by these girls for something that you know Damn well happens in schools everywhere across America."

Avery stated, "OK, OK, we understand. I did not do anything. Everyone understands I did not do anything."

The Principal stated, "I do not understand that you did not do anything. What I understand is that I have a very serious situation here that I must take care of, and I want to know everyone's point-of-view including yours, so that proper actions can be taken."

Kassie asked, "Did the bullying put her in a coma or did she put herself in the Coma by swallowing the pills?"

Avery responded, "Yeah, that is an actual logical point, thank you, and I am telling you I did not do anything. OK, I joked around with her. Seriously, this is such B.S. Now, I am seriously done with this if that is what you wanna hear that I am sorry for joking around with her, then I am very sorry for joking around with her. I am so terribly sorry that I did not know that this girl does not know how to take a F'ing joke. Sorry, a freaking joke, I did not know that somebody cannot take a joke.

Seriously, like grow the hell up, grow the hell up. Take a joke. I am so sorry, I am sorry. I must get to class, cuz I am a very good student." She then left the room.

Soon after that meeting, she posted a very angry video. In her video, she angrily stated, "I did not do shit, he called my parents in there and tried to embarrass me it's like, honestly." This is my way of getting to explain without people interrupting me or telling me I am lying. This is the only way for me to put out there the way that I feel. Everybody here at school is blaming me for this stupid-ass Jessica Burns B.S. I am so sick of everyone turning against me and blaming me for what happened. This girl did this to herself. I did not tell her to go and do what she did. No one told her; she made that decision. For all those girls and they know who they are. You have F'd with the wrong girl.

Soon after Avery posted this video, the female investigator approached her and asked her nicely to take down the video. Avery agreed to take down the video.

At the end of this movie, the female investigator who had been interviewing Avery showed-up at Avery's home and showed her the video footage she had of Avery bullying Jessica. Of course, Kassie really tried to watch the video with Avery and the investigator. Avery finally convinced her Mom to let her watch it with the investigator alone. Avery finally cried and acted like she was sorry it happened. She admitted she was a bully. She said she has never had anyone to talk to her entire life. She said her Mom has never talked to her; she just criticizes her all the time. Childcare experts say parents should give their children positive reinforcement versus negative reinforcement at a ratio of about 4 / 1, always more positive reinforcement than negative reinforcement. Childcare experts say children do need to have some negative reinforcement. Avery said she would rather get negative attention than no attention at all. Avery said her friends are not real friends. She said the only person who had ever been a real friend to her was Jessica and she admitted she had turned against Jessica. At the end of the movie, Jessica does die. Avery then acted like she was sorry that Jessica had died, and she acted like she was sorry she would never be able to apologize to her.

The female investigator promised Avery she would get her lots of help.

The Mom of Victim # 1 thought this was a great Movie. She contacted the Lady who Directed this movie, directly. She even arranged to show this Movie at her Local Town Hall. About 200 people showed-up to watch this movie and about $6,000.00 was donated to help this cause because this event was arranged.

I have done a lot of research about bullying. After I saw this movie; I did more research about bullying. I want to understand why some people bully.

One of the sites I found was a site that was posting the results they gathered after they had interview roughly 9,000 people on the topic of bullying. This survey asked lots of personal questions. When the results were being analyzed, the interviewed were placed in 3 separate groups. Group 1 was the people who had never bullied anyone. Group 2 was people who had bullied other people once, twice or a few times. Group 3 was people who had bullied people frequently.

Among these people who had been surveyed, 14 % said they had bullied someone. Among those who had bullied; these results proved that most of them had experienced some type of traumatic experience during the past 5 years before they bullied. Some of those traumatic experiences were, 1.

Their parents or guardians split-up, 2. One of their relatives had died. 3. They had gained a brother or a sister.

These people who were interviewed had answered lots of questions about if they had bullied, why did they do it.

The results from this survey proved that we all respond to stress in different ways. Some people have learned how to do positive things to try to recover from enduring stress. Some of us use meditation, exercise, listening to good music, communicating with healthy people, dancing, watching great movies, getting involved with doing hobbies that they love to do, etc. to feel better. Some of us, however, never learned how to use positive activities to learn how to recover from enduring stress.

These test results reported that among the people who had bullied frequently; those people tended to use negative behaviors to relieve their stress. Many of those people tended to use bullying, violence or alcohol abuse to try to recover from their stress. Some people never learned any positive ways of responding to stress.

THE MOST COMMON REASONS PEOPLE BULLY

Among the people who had bullied; these are the most common reasons these people bullied, according to this report:

LOW SELF-ESTEEM:

Some people try to avoid negative attention directed at them by focusing their attention on other people. Lots of people spend lots of time comparing themselves to other people instead of focusing on their own beauty.

THEY'VE BEEN BULLIED:

Research shows that people who have been bullied will be twice as likely to bully others than people who have not been bullied.

DIFFICULT HOMELIFE:

The people who bully are extremely likely to have come from homes where there was lots of violence, arguments & hostility. Their parents did not have much time to spend with them. They are more likely to come from large families than small ones. They are also likely to come from homes where at least one of the parents in their home is not their biological parent.

LOW ACCESS TO EDUCATION:

Some people have never been taught that hate-based conversation is not appropriate. It may be the norm in the environment they grew-up in.

FAMILY ISSUES:

When people grow-up in homes that are not warm and loving and/or they are not allowed to communicate and express their wants and needs. Or, if the home they grew-up in had a lot of punishing. Those people will be likely to become bullies.

A BULLY'S PERSONAL HISTORY:

Children who experience lots of social rejection or academic failure will be likely to become bullies.

THEY CRAVE HAVING POWER:

Some people desperately crave having power, purpose and control over other people. These types of people want the victim to become self-critical. They deeply need to feel like they are more important than all the people around them. They feel they need to belittle others so they can feel like they are more important. Those people tend to race to be in positions of power. Frequently, however, the people who are placed in positions of power, are not properly trained to be able to handle that position and do not have the leadership skills that are necessary to be able to handle the position of power properly. Those people tend to be people who do not know how to motivate people to do things any other way than by being mean to them or to bully them.

PROVACATIVE VICTIMS:

Sometimes the victims are annoying one way or another without trying to be annoying. The Bully is someone who has little patience and is not willing to tolerate the annoying behaviors. The Bully lacks compassion, empathy and coping skills. This kind of bully lashes out because they feel like they were provoked.

CULTURAL CAUSES OF BULLYING:

Sometimes bullies are glorified in some Cultures. They are given more power and money because they are bullies. Some of the people who witness that think they need to bully people so they will be able to have power and money.

INSTITUTIONAL CAUSES:

In some environments there is a low standard regarding how people should treat each other. Some of the people in that environment will think they should bully too.

SOCIAL ISSUES:

Sometimes people get more Social Recognition when they behave negatively than when they behave positively. Acting out usually gets noticed more than behaving courteously. Some people love attention and choose to act obnoxiously, just so they can get attention.

During 2005, the United States Government reported about 28% of students get bullied.

Among those students who reported they had been bullied. These students reported they had endured the following types of bullying:

13% were made fun-of, called names or insulted

12% were the subject of rumors

5% were pushed, shoved, tripped or spit-on

5% were excluded from activities on purpose

During 2016 a report done by the National Center for Education reported the locations school-related bullying occurred were:

42% hallway or Stairwell at school

34% inside the classroom

22% in the cafeteria at school

19% outside on the school grounds

10% on the school bus

9% in the bathroom or in the locker room

43% of the bullied students said they did report the bullying to an adult at the school.

About 57% of the bullying stops when a peer of the victim intervenes.

The victims in this study that surveyed around 9,000 people asked the subjects who had been bullied; "Why do you think you were bullied?" Most of the responses were in the following categories:

Physical appearance, race/ethnicity, gender, disability, religion and/or sexual orientation.

This study also revealed: Among High School students who are bullied, 15.5% are Cyber-Bullied and 20.2% are bullied on School Property. During 2007, about 18% of students had been Cyber-bullied at some point in time. During 2016, 34% of students reported having been Cyber-bullied at some point in time. Among teens who had reported having been bullied, 90% of them reported they had also been bullied off-line. Among people who have been Cyber-bullied, about 40-50% of them are aware of who the perpetrator is. Among these people who were surveyed, 81% of them thought bullying online is easier to get away with than bullying in person. This survey also revealed that females are about twice as likely as males to get bullied online.

SOME OTHER REASONS BULLIES BULLY

Bullies love power.

They want immediate power.

They want to oversee everyone and everything all the time.

They want to be the ones who make all the decisions.

They are so determined to be the one who has the most power that they will do whatever it takes to gain power.

They love to control and manipulate people because they always want everyone to know they are in charge and no one else is allowed to be more important than they are.

They are willing to do whatever it takes to become the one who is King or Queen of the Castle.

Power is more important to them than what anyone thinks of them.

While they are trying to gain power; they do not care about whether they hurt anyone emotionally or physically.

Anytime a bully is awake; they are trying to prove to everyone, all the time, that they are very important.

Most bullies want lots of attention. They are attention-seekers. They want to gain the attention of all the people around them.

Bullies want to be always in the spotlight.

Bullies want to attack anyone who is a threat to them.

Bullies are used to walking all over people.

Bullies fear being laughed at.

A bully's biggest fear is to be dethroned from power.

Bullies constantly need to make themselves feel strong by making others feel weak.

Bullies do not care about how they make other people feel.

Many Bullies are very envious of the personal possessions of others.

Bullies tend to be people who are very selfish and greedy.

Bullies are likely to come from homes that did not have much involvement with Religion.

Bullies frequently come from families that did not have 2 of their biological parents living in the home they were living in.

Bullies are at high risk for alcohol and substance abuse.

Bullies are at high risk for mental health problems like depression, anxiety or hostility.

Many bullies were not good at schoolwork and are embarrassed by that.

Many people have historically believed that bullies bully because they have an inferiority complex or because they were bullied. Studies have proven that is not always the case. Sometimes bullies are overly self-confident and so Narcissistic and Self-centered that they really think they are more important than everyone else.

Bullies typically think they should have more of everything than anyone else.

Bullies typically think their children should not have their own wants and needs. They think their children should fulfill all their needs and they should accomplish all the things they wanted to accomplish but did not.

Bullies truly believe other people's lives should revolve around them.

They frequently are so self-absorbed that they do not even understand that they are so annoying that most people do not want to have anything to do with them.

HOW DO BULLIES DECIDE WHO THEY ARE GOING TO BULLY?

If you are smart, competent and self-assured and you like to improve things, fix things, find solutions, challenge the status quo, correct injustice or create art. Bullies will not like that. Bullies will feel like you are showing everyone you are more competent than they are if you show people that you can improve things, fix things or create things. Bullies will see you as competitor and they will try to find fault with you immediately.

Bullies do not like the people who are good at what they do. They do not like people who are intelligent, determined and creative.

Bullies do not like people who are popular and well-liked.

Bullies do not like people who have physical features that attract attention.

Since Bullies are used to being able to walk all over people; they will attack you right away if you stand-up for yourself.

Bullies are typically willing to fight people dramatically longer and more intensely than other people are willing to fight.

If you are an interesting person. You will be likely to be bullied. Bullies will not like it if you get more attention from people than they do.

Bullies like to bully people who appear to be people who will not be able to fight back. They want to win every battle.

Bullies like to attack people who are different. They typically do not have much of an imagination and they tend to be people who think they should be making all the rules and everyone else should follow their rules and think and act the same way they do. They do not understand that every human being is different, and every human being is supposed to be different.

Instead of encouraging people to become the best person they can be. They want to belittle others so they can feel like they are Superior to everyone else.

Bullies like to prey on people who have a sexual orientation that is different than their sexual orientation.

Bullies also do not like people whose Religious or Cultural beliefs are different than their Religious or Cultural beliefs.

Bullies like to target people whose race is different than their race.

Bullies are likely to target people who have a passive, submissive, meek or quiet communication style. The bully usually assumes that person will not confront anyone, fight back or report them.

Bullies tend to target people who appear too not be confident. They like to prey on people who do not give eye contact and are nervous.

Bullies like to attack people who appear to be loners or only have a few friends. If someone does not hang out with a group of people, the bully will think that person will be an easy target.

Bullies tend to prey on nice people. They think they will not fight back. Nice people are frustrated all the time that bullies target them. They are cooperative, and they do the things they are supposed to do. No one has any good reason for being mean to them; yet bullies love to give them a hard time.

Workplace bullies like to attack the individuals who are liked by their Supervisors and praised for their performance.

Workplace bullies also tend to focus on people who are new to the workplace.

Workplace bullies are likely to target inexperienced, older or handicapped employees. They are also likely to attack people who have an illness or a disability.

Bullies are likely to act out when they are not asked to be a part of a clique.

Bullies also like to attack people who are fair, honest, ethical and have strong morals and integrity. Bullies realize they do not possess those same traits and they are very jealous of those people.

Bullies like to attack people who are whistle blowers. They hunt down the people who expose fraudulent or unethical practices.

Women are bullied more frequently than men.

Seventy percent of all bullies are men. Sixty-five percent of their targets are women.

When women do bully, sixty-seven percent of their targets are women.

WHY ARE SOME PEOPLE MEAN?

Egos tend to be the reason for a lot of mean behaviors. When someone feels like they are unattractive, they are likely to announce that other people are less attractive than they are. If they are self-conscious about their intelligence level; they will be likely to try to find people who are less intelligent than they are to pick-on. If they think they are not always as kind as they should be, they will be likely to try to accuse other people of being unkind. It is also common for people who are likely to waste time while they should be working to find the people who are hard workers to criticize. They will want to prove that those people are not really that good of a worker after all. All the things I just described are examples of how some people like to criticize other people to make themselves feel better about themselves. People who are insecure about themselves are dramatically more likely to try to criticize other people than people who are self-confident and feel good about themselves. Insecurity tends to lead to jealousy and blame.

Sometimes mean people are rewarded. Mean people are frequently promoted and paid more money because they are very capable of being mean to people.

Some people are mean because they are extremely self-absorbed. Most people spend most of their time thinking about what they want and need. Most people do not spend a lot of time thinking about what other people want and need. They simply care so much about themselves that they do not spend much time at all thinking about how to not offend other people.

Sometimes people are mean because they have a lack of awareness. For example, someone might cut-in-front of you in a line simply because they were paying attention to their phone or something else and they did not even notice you were there.

Sometimes people are mean because they grew-up in a culture that is very different from yours and some of the behaviors that are normal in their culture are strange in your culture. For example. Some people from some cultures hug each other frequently. Some people feel very uncomfortable with being hugged

Some people appear to be rude simply because they do not get their feelings hurt easily; consequently, they are completely unaware that the behaviors they consider to be normal are offensive to some others.

Some people are mean because they lack social skills. Some people were not taught to have manners and proper behavior. Some people lack having decent interactions with other human beings and they simply do not know how to behave without offending other people.

Some people do not use the proper tone of voice when they are communicating with other people. They may even use sarcasm that other people do not realize is sarcasm. They are not good at understanding that some of their behaviors are offensive.

Miscommunications and misunderstandings can also cause people to appear to be mean. Some people are completely unaware that some of the things they say and do are offensive. They may have no idea, for example, that people are offended when they tell them they should eat a certain food and slap that food on the persons plate even after that person announced they did not want that food. The offender thinks feeding people is a kind gesture. The person who had already announced they did not want to eat the food was already feeling uncomfortable because they had over-eaten. Even though the person who slapped the extra food on that person's plate was being rude and offensive. That person did not realize they were being rude and offensive.

Some people are perceived as being mean because they are very direct. They say exactly what is on their mind and do not sugar-coat anything. Their direct conversations can be hard to hear. For example. Someone who is very direct may tell someone, "I am not interested in dating you, no thanks. The information they convey to you may sting but you will not spend all kinds of time wondering what they were thinking either.

Some people are mean because they are indirect, and they are so afraid of hurting someone else's feelings that they refuse to communicate things that should be said. For example: This person might agree to go on a date with someone, then, never show-up for the date. This communication style is indirect meanness.

Some people are mean because they lack social anxiety. They just treat people the way they would like to be treated and do not worry about whether anyone will be offended. They do not ever wonder; might I offend someone if I speak to them this way.

Sometimes people are mean when they are overly helpful or overly analyzing everything you do. Some people are offensive because they love to give advice or tell people about all the things that could go wrong in their lives. They are really announcing to you that they do not trust that you will make wise decisions. Without intending to. They insult you.

Some people believe they must treat people harshly to get them to behave differently. These people are frequently incorrect and would be much more likely to get people to behave differently if they used less harsh methods. People who treat people too harshly are likely to have people rebel against them. These people intend to be mean to other people.

Some people are mean because they are too honest. They feel the need to announce everything they are thinking and do not adjust how they deliver the news to avoid hurting the subject's feelings. They may say, for example, "Those pants make your butt look big." If they were going to attempt to not hurt the subjects' feelings; they could have said, "I think these pants are more flattering on you than those." These people are not intending to hurt other people's feelings, but they do.

Self-protection is a huge cause of lots of mean behavior. Sometimes this type of mean behavior is malicious. Sometimes it is sub-conscious. Sometimes it is deliberate. This type of behavior usually occurs when the perpetrator is unable to take responsibility for their problems and solve their own problems. Within this group of people there are some who are healthier, and they do try to repair damaged relationships once they realize they have hurt someone. Some of the people within this category, however, never try to improve their relationships with other people. Some of these perpetrators continue to be mean to their victims and never admit that they did anything wrong. There are lots of different reasons why some people are mean because they are attempting to protect themselves. Among those reasons is:

PROJECTION:

These perpetrators do not want to admit they are flawed. If they are a liar; they try to act like everyone else is a liar. If they are lazy; they will want to convince other people that they are lazy.

SUPERIORITY COMPLEX:

These people try to act like they are better than everyone else. Even if they are someone who never cleans anything; they may try to tell someone who cleans everything regularly, how to clean. Of course, the person who is good at cleaning will be offended and annoyed. That does not stop the person who does not clean from acting like they are an expert on the topic of cleaning.

PASSIVE-AGGRESSIVE ESCALATION:

This type of person wants to make the victim be inconvenienced, screwed over, or look like they are a bad guy. They will find lots of different ways to make their victim look bad; without letting anyone know they did the evil deed. For example, someone who is passive-aggressive might take all her sister's bras out of her bedroom and replace them with giant bras that will not even come close to fitting her sister.

JEALOUSY:

These people tend to criticize the people who seem to have more than they do. They try to find reasons to explain why that person is acquiring stuff that the subject does not have. They might say, "I bet the only reason she is driving that nice car is because I think her husband is having an affair and he is just trying to keep her happy with that car; so, he can keep doing what he is doing."

RATIONALIZATION:

This type of person tries to find excuses to explain why bad things have happened. They might say, "The reason that Company I used to work for asked 4 of us to leave was not because we were doing anything wrong; they just wanted to hire younger people instead of us because they know they can pay them less."

Some people are mean because they were born with aggressive personality types. They tend to want to be in control. They want to be the decision makers. They want an excuse to oversee other people. Having power over other people is more important to them than other people's feelings. Among these personality types, I am going to place them in different categories.

ANXIOUS:

This type of person may be so fearful when she is alone that she constantly tries to control the people who are within her close social circle. She may try to convince them they must be with her all the time. Even though those people do not want to spend that much time with her. Her main goal is to avoid the things that give her lots of anxiety.

NEED TO BE RIGHT:

Some of these people desperately want to prove to everyone in the World that they are perfect, intelligent, or good looking or rich or all the above and more. Because they have this deep desire to appear to be special; they want to make sure the people around them appear to be less special than they are. They constantly try to silence others and do not want other people to offer their opinions because they do not want anyone to prove they are wrong.

VALIDATION:

The people who feel miserable all the time frequently want to find other people who agree with their opinion of things. They try to convince everyone that their viewpoint is correct. Even if your opinions oppose theirs; they will try to convince you your opinions are incorrect, and you should think the same way they do.

Some people have had some horrible experiences during their lifetime, and they are so afraid of having those same types of experiences again, that they have major trust issues. The behaviors they have developed because of their bad experiences tend to be:

WITHDRAWAL:

This type of person may avoid hanging out with people. They may turn-down invitations to get together with people. This person may be quiet. Some people will be likely to perceive this person as being mean or unfriendly. The real reason this person is not bonding with other people is because they are trying to avoid having more bad experiences. They might even be afraid that they will be in trouble with someone else if they start forming new relationships with other people.

IDENTIFYING WITH THE ABUSER:

This type of person believes they must act the same way their abuser did to feel like they are powerful. They may also think they will be able to avoid being bullied or abused again; if they act like their abuser acted. Protecting themselves has become more important to them than how they make other people feel.

VULNERABILITY:

These people do not want to appear to be weak to others. They develop a tough image to avoid having people look down on them.

Emotionally reacting to people is a common cause of meanness. This type of person reacts to people without contemplating how their action will impact other people. These people tend to be hot-tempered, impulsive and impatient. These people can be quite malicious. They think reacting to people dramatically will preserve the things they want and do not want. I am going to list 2 categories that fall into the Emotional Reactors Category.

FRUSTRATION:

An example of this might be, a woman gets upset because she just tried on a pair of pants that suddenly do not fit her anymore. Instead of wanting to accept the fact that she has gained weight, she announces that her pants do not fit anymore because her husband set the dryer at the high setting instead of the medium setting when he dried her pants. This type of person does not like to accept blame for anything that goes wrong in their life. Instead, they always try to blame someone else.

DENIAL:

An example of this might be a woman who has such a spending problem that she even tells her mail carrier to hide all the packages he delivers to their home, behind their bushes, so her husband will not be able to see them. Not long after she tells her mail carrier that their home is suddenly in foreclosure because she was no longer able to pay her bills and she did not tell her husband she had stopped paying the bills.

Some people feel like they are Superior to everyone else. They think they are entitled to have more of their share of everything. They think they should be treated dramatically more specially than everyone else. They think their wants and needs should come before everyone else's wants and needs. Within this category. I am going to list 3 categories.

SUPERIOR BY BIRTH:

These people tend to think they should treat other people with a lack of understanding or compassion. They automatically think they should treat others with disdain. They really do believe they are more important than other people.

SUPERIOR BY ACHIEVMENT:

Some of the people who do achieve success early in their life may get treated like they are important because they achieved success at an early age. Over time they get used to being treated like they are important, and they start believing it. Once they feel like they really are more important than other people, they may start treating other people cruelly.

MORAL SUPERIORITY:

Some people believe that their religious beliefs or their set of values is better than everyone else's religious beliefs or set of values. Because they think that, they automatically insult other people when they try to convince them their beliefs are inferior.

Some people are mean because they have a mental illness. Some of these people can be extremely malicious. I am going to list 2 categories here.

MENTAL ILLNESS:

Someone who has extreme OCD tendencies can hurt other people. They may be so demanding regarding how everything in their yard or home must be done; that the other people living in their home may feel very uncomfortable. For example, a husband who is so obsessed with how their lawn should be mowed, that if his wife mows the lawn, not at an angle, and does not collect the grass clippings, the husband might fly into a rage when he discovers what she did.

PSYCHOPATHY:

Psychopathy is the worst type of meanness that is related to mental illness. These people typically intend to be mean. These people are frequently malicious. This type of person gets pleasure from hurting other people.

This type of person tends to be the most dangerous because they can frequently be charming. Sometimes people do not realize they are dealing with a psychopath until it is too late. Psychopaths do not have a conscience. Sometimes psychopaths become salespeople and they take advantage of people through their job. Sometimes psychopaths become Politicians and they find lots of ways to take advantage of people through their career choice.

My final category of mean people is the Pleasure Seekers. These people are extremely self-centered and have a complete disregard for other people's feelings. These people are intentionally mean. They can do a great deal of damage to other people. I am listing 4 categories of Mean Pleasure Seekers.

ATTENTION:

Some people crave being noticed so much that they do not care what they must do to get noticed. They would rather have negative attention than no attention. They tend to do obnoxious things all the time. It is hard for the people who are in their presence to get a turn to talk or ever be the center of attention. Every time anyone, who is near someone who craves being in the spotlight all the time, they never get a turn. They never get to finish a sentence. The Attention Seekers disrupt everything other people do. They demand that everyone else stays in their background and never gets to be in the foreground.

RESPECT:

Some people think they must be mean to people to gain their respect. Sometimes Employers think their employees will not respect them unless they are mean and demanding. Sometimes parents think their children will not respect them unless they are mean and demanding. These people are mean intentionally. These people are controlling and manipulative. They think they should oversee everyone and everything all the time.

POWER:

Quite simply, these people want to feel like they are more powerful than other people. They feel a deep need to insult other people aggressively or passive-aggressively just to help them feel like they have power over other people. An example of this would be a lady was invited to your home for a

Christmas dinner. She brought her own tablecloth, removed your tablecloth without asking you if she could, and replaced it with hers; then, she announced to everyone her tablecloth is better than yours.

MONEY:

If you think about how this is done in the business world; you might think about how some people, try to find lots of ways to make their competitor look bad so they can have more sales. Some people believe they will get promoted and be able to earn more money if they are mean to the employees. Some people try to find ways to cheat customers by selling them things they do not want or need. One time my credit card started getting billed monthly by a company. I had no idea I had agreed to pay for whatever they were selling. I had been on their website and thought I had made a one-time payment for a product. They tricked me into paying monthly after that without my even realizing it until after it had happened. Lots of companies try to do that. There are a lot of people these days who try to steal people's identity, credit card information, checking account information, cash, goods, etc. All these people are concerned with gaining things themselves and they do not care about how much they will hurt other people.

SUMMARY:

Most people who are mean, do it because of a flaw or several flaws they have within themselves. Their flaws have caused them to have a distorted way of thinking. Most of the time; their actions are not about you. Mean people tend to look for minor flaws in other people to attack.

When someone is mean to you; try to understand that if you respond to them, they will strangely be rewarded and most of the time, you will be better-off if you can just respond to them very little.

Try to not worry about what other people's opinions of you are. Try to not feel bad about yourself when someone is mean to you. Tell yourself, 'That person is flawed, that is why they are acting that way.'

HER DAD WAS A PEDOPHILE, SHE AND HER SISTER BOTH MARRIED MEN WHO HAD MULTIPLE AFFAIRS, ONE OF HER DAUGHTERS HAS BEEN TRYING TO RISE ABOVE IT ALL.

I will be referring to this Mom as VICTIM # 2 and her daughter as VICTIM # 3. This Mom is a girl who went to the same High School I went to. She was 1 year behind me in school. We both grew-up in Indiana. Soon after she graduated from High School. She moved to Texas. At the age of 18; she met a guy via the internet. She told me; "If I knew then, what I know now; I never would have formed a relationship with this person." She told me, "I was young and fickle." She had a 25-year relationship with this man. She was married to him for 19 years. She had 2 daughters with him. She said she was naïve and too trusting when their relationship was new. She also told me she eventually learned he was a womanizer. He had many affairs while they were together. She was supporting the family. She worked while he got on planes, did not work and had romantic relationships with other women.

She told me; "When our 2 daughters were young, my older daughter N1 was a Momma's girl, and our younger daughter S. was a Daddies girl. She said she spent lots more time with N1, than S. because N1 had ADHD. N1 demanded a lot of attention. She had to take N1 to lots of meetings regarding ADHD. She told me she did not form a close relationship with S. until she divorced S.'s father. S. was in her teens at that time. Once S. entered college; Victim # 2 and S. became dramatically closer to each other.

She told me her 2 daughters acted nothing like each other. Her oldest daughter, N1, is currently 22 years old. She eventually became a partier who became addicted to orthoclone pills. That addiction led to her becoming addicted to other drugs. N1 has been on and off drugs. Once she became addicted to drugs, she started creating fake accounts on the internet. She has created more than 100 fake accounts on the internet. She has told some vicious lies to her mother. At one point, she told her mother that her younger sister had died. She announced to people that her mother had been in jail for child abuse. That accusation was false. S. currently does not want to have anything to do with her older sister. She will not allow N1 to become her Facebook friend.

Victim # 2 never knows when she will hear from N1 again. Currently N1 is supposed to call her Mom once per week; but as of the date I interviewed Victim # 2 on the phone; Victim # 2 had not heard from that daughter for about 3 weeks. When Victim # 2 tries to call N1, she only gets to leave a message on her daughter's voice mail. She knows her daughter has been clean and sober for a while but suspects her daughter has been using illegal substances again, because she has not communicated with this daughter for about 3 weeks. This daughter had been living in Kansas and had been working as a waitress. She had told her mother she was going to be moving to Virginia and was going to be living close to her family soon. I am not sure whether she did make that move.

Recently, I sent an e-mail to each of the people I interviewed. I asked them to take the Myers-Briggs Personality Test and let me know what their test results are. When I sent that e-mail to Victim # 2, I asked her to take the Myers-Briggs personality test and I asked her to have both of her daughters take that test. She responded to my e-mail with an e-mail that let me know her older daughter has been missing since March. Right now, it is June 26th. I asked her if she had contacted the Police. She told me, she had. She also told me the Police told her they could not help her find her daughter unless she gave them the physical address of where her daughter is living. I asked her if there had been any activity on her daughter's Facebook page since March. She responded, "My daughter blocked me on Facebook, so, I do not know." She also told me her oldest daughter has not spoken to her cousin B. since March.

Victim # 2 and her husband eventually lived in Oklahoma. After their divorce, Victim # 2 found a decent guy who she has been dating for almost 20 years. Victim # 2 told me both of her daughters do not want to have any type of a relationship with their birthfather.

Victim # 2's younger daughter, S. is currently 19. She is about to finish her Freshman year at a College in Virginia. Victim # 3 has always been a child who has been well-behaved. She has blond hair, blue eyes, a very nice figure and she is an Honor Student. She is kind, respectful, laid-back, mild-mannered and a very good judge of character. She is very careful regarding who she chooses to associate with. Her mother told me, about 75% of her daughter's friends are people she has met at church. She also told me she has very rarely needed to discipline this daughter for any bad behavior.

Victim # 2 told me she parented both of her daughters very much the same. They both grew-up in the same environment. Victim # 2 stated, she saw me go through a lot with her older sister. She has been through a lot during her lifetime. We have had a lot of money and we have been homeless. She has been through the divorce I had with her Dad. She then told me; I should have divorced him a lot sooner; but I did not want to break-up our family. I was really trying to keep our family together. I thought keeping our family together was going to be the best thing for us. Next, she told me, S.

was very close with her Aunt P. When S. was 12 years old, her Aunt P. committed suicide.

I knew her Aunt P. I went to school with her Aunt P. She was in my grade in High School.

Now, I am going to start calling S., Victim # 3.

Victim # 3's Aunt P. was a very Artistic person. She loved photography. She loved to photograph flowers, hummingbirds, nature, wildlife and her 2 children. I went to her daughter's High School Graduation Party. She had stayed-up late the night before getting ready for her daughter's party. She had not gotten much sleep the night before. She had created a slide presentation that had lots of pictures of her kids. She was a very nice person. She and I had e-mailed each other quite-a-bit. She and I shared a love for gardening and photography. She had told me about the lung disease she had called Histio-cytosis. She had told me she had limited lung capacity and she could not do a lot of the things she used to do.

When I was talking to Victim # 2; she told me, her sister P. was supposed to be wearing an oxygen mask 24 hours a day; but had not been doing that.

P. had told me she had married her husband, they got a divorce, then later, they re-married. She never told me the details of the relationship she had with her husband.

I saw P. at our class reunion during July 2011. She had lost quite-a-bit of weight since I had seen her at her daughter's Graduation Party. She was looking fantastic. She looked like she was ready to do some modeling. I told her she looked fantastic. I wondered why she had lost weight. I wondered if there was something going-on in her life that made her do that; but I did not ask.

When I was talking to Victim # 2; she told me her sister P. had a very volatile relationship with her husband G. She told me he was a womanizer too and he had lots of affairs while he was married to her sister. She told me she had begged her sister to not re-marry him, but P. did re-marry him. P. believed in standing-by her vows. She did not want a divorce.

Victim # 2 told me she did not know her sister P. and her husband G. owned a gun. She told me; "I did not know my sister knew how to shoot a gun."

She told me, on the night of March 16th, 2013, G. asked his son, "Where's your Mom?." Sometimes P. did go to a girlfriend's home on weekend nights and did not return home until around midnight.

Next, she told me her sister had been on the phone with G. during the middle of the night. They had been arguing on the phone from about 1:00 a.m. until 2:00 a.m. Once that phone call ended; he went to bed. She called him back at 3:00 a.m. That phone call ended at 3:25 a.m. on 3-17-2013. She also told me the time of her sister's death on the Police report was 3:27 a.m. on 3-17-2013.

Victim # 2 told me P. had told her husband; 'By the way, thanks for the cigarettes out of your truck.' She also told me G. had a gun in the cab of that truck right next to the pack of cigarettes.

Victim # 2 told me G. rolled over and fell asleep as soon as he got off the phone with his wife at 3:25 a.m. that morning.

Soon after that event; Victim # 2 was on the phone with G. He told her he wanted to have P. cremated. Victim # 2 was in Oklahoma at the time and could not travel to Michigan immediately. She wanted him to not cremate her until she at least was able to arrive in Michigan. G. told her, postponing the cremation would incur an expense. Victim # 2 told him she would pay that expense. G. had P.'s remains cremated before Victim # 2 was able to arrive in the State of Michigan anyway.

Victim # 2 majored in criminal law when she was in college.

This Michigan Police Department told Victim # 2; "We are not allowed to release the suicide note to anyone, including the deceased person's husband." P. left a 15-page suicide note that Victim # 2, P.'s husband and everyone else who might request it, will never be allowed to see.

This Police Department, did, however, send Victim # 2, everything else. They sent her pictures of the crime scene. They sent her the autopsy report and a detailed report.

I told Victim # 2; I would not want to see the pictures from the crime scene. I would; however, want to read the 15-page suicide note.

P. was on a beach that was about 40 minutes from where her husband was lying in their bed, in their home, when she ended her life.

Soon after the Memorial Service, G. was openly dating a new woman. He sold their home. He offered some of their possessions to their 2 children but never offered anything to anyone else in the family. Victim # 2 told me some of their Grandparents heirlooms are now long gone.

Victim # 2 will never be able to recover from that event. She was typing lots of long and detailed documents about how she was feeling and posting them on Facebook after this happened. I read all those documents. I told her to keep typing her thoughts because that is what I tend to do when something is upsetting me. For me, typing things-out, helps me heal from whatever is bothering me. I know Victim # 2 was extremely traumatized when this happened. I have never met Victim # 3. But I am sure she was dramatically traumatized too. When I first heard, P. had committed suicide; I thought, one of the main reasons she did that was because of the lung disease she had been living with and she knew that disease was going to be shortening her life anyway. I am a perceptive person, and I did not even think, 'Oh, I bet there was a lot of things going on in her life that caused her to do this', when I heard about this news. As soon as Victim #2 started telling me the events that lead-up to her sister's death; it was obvious to me that there had been lots of warning signs that preceded this event. I was thinking lots of things could have been done to prevent this from happening. I thought, 'What a shame that she remarried G. even though she knew what kind of a man he was. She knew he was a person who did not treat her respectfully and he did not make her feel good.

About 6 months before Victim # 2's sister committed suicide; her long-time boyfriend's Dad passed away. At that time, his Mom needed to have one of her children live close to her and help take care of her and their property. Victim # 2's boyfriend, W. was the most logical choice. W., Victim # 2 and their 2 daughters moved from Oklahoma to Virginia around that time.

Now, Victim # 2 travels to Washington D.C. twice each year. She talks to the Senator from Virginia. Sometimes she talks to some of the Congress Representatives. She travels there to try to get new laws enacted. Some of the new laws she is trying to get enacted involve Suicide Prevention. She is very involved with an organization called, 'American Foundation for Suicide Prevention.' She tries to help other people walk through the grief they endure after someone they were close to committed suicide. She stated, 'The grief never goes away completely.' You must learn how to live with it.

Some of the other laws she has been trying to get enacted involve laws that are necessary for people who do not have insurance. She has also been trying to get laws enacted that force Insurance Companies to cover all mental health disorders. She told me she has Borderline Personality Disorder, and she has not been able to get her insurance company to cover any help for treating her mental health disorder. She told me Borderline Personality Disorder is as real as heart disease. It is there, I have it, but my Insurance Company refuses to let me get any help for it.

One of the main reasons some people commit suicide is because those people have been bullied.

After someone has committed suicide. No one knows exactly what was going through that person's mind. I do, however, know of someone who committed suicide. That person's parents constantly compared him to his older sibling. His parents repeatedly told him over the course of his life that his older sibling was better than he was. They constantly let him know he was not good enough. His parents constantly put pressure on him to be someone he was not. Every person has talents and weaknesses. His parents wanted him to be good at the same things his older sibling was good at because the traits his older sibling had were the traits those parents valued. Some people are naturally good at academics. Some people are naturally good at athletics. Some people are naturally musically inclined. Some people are naturally good at being organized. No one is good at everything. Everyone's brain is different. Everyone's experiences are different. Even identical twins think and act differently. No parent should try to force any of their children to be exactly like someone else.

One example I am thinking of is: If someone is naturally a disorganized person. No parent on the face of this earth will ever be able to force that person to be an organized person. There are parents, however, who think if they keep poking and prodding that person and they repeatedly try to force that person to be an organized person; one day, that person will miraculously become an organized person. People who do that to another person are bullies. I do not understand why anyone would ever repeatedly try to force someone to become someone they are not; but I have seen lots of people do it.

I know of a mother who was parenting her son on her own. Her son committed suicide. He left her a suicide note that said something like. "Now you will never worry that I am not good enough, anymore." This woman is extremely unpopular in the community she lives in.

A simple definition of a Bully is: 'When someone intentionally hurts another person repeatedly.'

Do you think a spouse who has repeated affairs is a bully?

The person who is having multiple affairs understands they are hurting their spouse and they do that act repeatedly.

Yes, someone who is sleeping around on their spouse repeatedly is a bully.

That person blatantly does not care about how they are making their spouse feel, repeatedly over time.

Some people really do not care about how they make other people feel. They only care about themselves. People who have a lot of compassion and empathy for other people usually do not comprehend that some other people really do not care about other people. They automatically assume everyone has compassion and empathy.

Relationships are not just about love. Relationships are also about people trying to get their own needs met. Some people are incredibly needy. They want to have a spouse so they can have their spouse do lots of things for them all the time. They may even insist that their spouse is and always will be physically attractive; because that makes them feel better about themselves.

Unfortunately, some spouses really do not care about what they do for their mate. They only care about what their mate can do for them. Sometimes people assume their spouse really cares about their well-fare even when their spouse is too self-centered to care about anyone other than themselves. Anytime someone is repeatedly having affairs while they are married; that person is only concerned about their own wants and needs, and they are not concerned about whether or not they are hurting their mate.

Many people might try to make excuses for that offender. They might try to label that person someone who cannot control themselves. They might try to reason that person just has a strong sex-drive.

People who have a strong sex-drive are young and/or people who do a lot of exercise.

Not, all people who sleep around on their spouse are young and not all people who sleep around on their spouse are people who do a lot of exercise.

Sometimes the people who sleep around on their spouse are people who have a deep need to control and manipulate other people.

My phone call with Victim # 2 lasted for about 2 ½ hours. At the beginning of our phone call, she was only talking about how her younger daughter has been bullied. During the first ½ hour of our phone call; she was not giving me very much information. I knew she had stories. I knew that her sister had committed suicide. People do not just commit suicide because they had 1 bad thing happen to them. People do not have one bad day; then, decide to commit suicide the next day. When someone commits suicide, the likelihood that that person has had bad experiences repeatedly over time is extremely high. I knew Victim # 2 had lots of stories to tell; but I could tell she was not comfortable with telling me about the things that were hurting her the most. After about the first ½ hour of telling me things her younger daughter had been through, she started to open. She started to tell me lots of different stories where she had endured unpleasant events during her life.

She eventually told me she had struggled with an eating disorder. She said she had been in recovery for 10 years. Once her sister committed suicide; she started having lots of severe headaches. At that time, a Doctor prescribed a medicine for her to take for her headaches. Once she was on that medicine; she started losing weight. She had been up to 136 pounds after spending 10 years trying to get her weight up. After she had been on this medicine for 3 weeks; she had lost 7 pounds. Her weight kept dropping. By the time October rolled around, she was down to 100 pounds. She knew she was in crisis. She told me she felt like she was losing it. She was having thoughts regarding how she could lose another 2-3 pounds. She knew she should not be having those kinds of thoughts; but she was. She had also been down to 85 pounds at one point during her adult lifetime. She was afraid her weight would drop that low again. She told one of her Doctors she was losing weight and she had had major problems with her eating disorder in the past. She told this Doctor she was concerned she was going to end-up in that same place again. She told me an eating disorder is something you never completely recover from. She told me this Doctor responded, 'Some medicines cause people to lose weight, I wouldn't worry about it.' Next, she told me she told a different Doctor the same story she had told the other Doctor. This Doctor responded pretty much the same way. Victim # 2 told him, "I need to get involved with an eating disorder treatment program again.' This Doctor responded, there are not any Eating Disorder Treatment plans for people who are older than 45 years old. Victim # 3 is currently 55 years old. She has been trying to figure-out how to manage this disorder on her own. Her weight is currently way too low. She has been screaming out for help. These Doctors are telling her she is not allowed to attend an eating disorder treatment center. This is one more example of a person trying to announce, "I need help. I am trying to manage things on my own and I am failing; can someone please help me." The person who is screaming out for help is getting rejected and ignored. She needs help right now and no one is agreeing to help her.

She sent me an e-mail through Facebook and told me she wanted me to interview her and have her story posted in my book. I was kind of surprised she sent me that message because the message I posted on Facebook said, 'I am writing my 2nd book about Bullying. My first book about Bullying, 'Make the Bullies Pay', is fiction. It has humor in it. It is intended to be entertaining. This second book about bullying is non-fiction. I am interested in interviewing people who have been bullied, especially if the person who has been bullied is disabled." I had just interviewed a girl I went to High School with. She has a daughter who has Cerebral Palsy. She and her daughter have both been getting bullied. I have been told that books should be very specific. I thought if my book concentrated on interviewing disabled people who have been bullied; I would be able to find a specific audience who would be interested in the book I am writing.

Even though Victim # 2 and Victim # 3 are not disabled. In fact, they are both very intelligent people. They are both suffering because they both have endured lots of hardships they should not have had to endure.

A person I know told me a few months ago, "I was a bit of a bully when I was younger; but I do not think that is all bad, I think it builds character."

I completely disagree with what he told me. Since I have a non-cancerous brain tumor in my left thalamus. I am extra-sensitive when I am around mean people. I get my feelings hurt easily and I cry easily. When people are mean to me; I do not feel like my character is getting built-up. I feel like that person is damaging me.

She also told me that during 2014; she was diagnosed with Lupus, Fibromyalgia and Rheumatoid Arthritis. She also mentioned, during 2015 and 2016; she had 5 surgeries. She said she is currently taking 25 different medications.

Yesterday afternoon, I started typing this story. I am not a nosy person. I do not like to make people feel uncomfortable. I had questions I wanted to ask Victim # 2; but I did not because I wanted her to just tell me what she felt comfortable with telling me. One of the questions I had just kept eating away at me. I kept wondering what kind of a relationship Victim # 2 and her sister had with their father. A long time ago, I read a book called, 'Women who love too much'. This book was written by Robin Norwood. One of the things I learned when I read that book was the type of relationship a girl has with her father has a lot to do with the type of man she will be attracted to. One of the examples in that book was of a girl whose father was an alcoholic. When that girl met a guy in high school who drank a lot; his heavy drinking did not seem alarming to her because she was so used to her father drinking so much that drinking just did not seem like it was important to her. Eventually that girl's relationship with the boy who drank a lot became a horrible relationship because of his drinking problem. She allowed herself to get involved with him because she did not realize his drinking habits were as bad as they were.

I sent Victim # 2 an e-mail and I asked her if her father was someone who cheated on her mother or was he a man who flirted heavily with women. I told her I was wondering that since she and her sister both married men who had lots of affairs during their marriage.

She responded, "He was not a womanizer, he was a Pedophile."

I responded,

"EEEEEEEEEEEEEWWWWWWWWWWWWWWWW!!!!!!!!!!!!"

Suddenly, I thought. Look at all the damage that man did. He did so much damage that all his offspring are unable to be attracted to healthy people. The damage he did to his children has created a domino effect that has been causing bad things to happen to both generations that have followed him. At least 2 of his 3 daughters feel attracted to and comfortable around men who disrespect them. If I learned a man was having multiple affairs; I would be creeped out immediately and I would try to stay away from him any time I encountered him. My Dad is a very decent person who never would have done anything like that.

I do not know at all what type of a relationship Victim # 2's daughters had with their father; but the fact that both do not want to have any type of a relationship with him tells me there are stories there. I do not need to know what those stories are. His daughters are obviously repulsed by him and that speaks volumes. I can tell that both girls are really hurting. They are each dealing with their pain in different ways.

Victim # 3 has been trying to be a decent and well-behaved person. She has been trying to do all the right things. During her entire lifetime she has almost never gotten into trouble. When Victim # 2 was describing this daughter. I felt like she was kind of describing me. My entire life: I have been trying to avoid conflict. I have discovered, however, that it does not matter what you do or how well you behave; people will be mean to you. Some people are mean. Some people are mean to everyone they meet. No matter how you live your life. Eventually, you will encounter mean people. You cannot avoid them completely.

I have also learned that mean people and bullies are more likely to bully certain types of people. People who are likely to be targeted by a bully are people who: are nice, are not likely to fight back or report the bully, are interesting, try to improve things, out-shine the bully, make the bully feel like they are inferior, even if they do that without trying to do that, have different religious beliefs, are a different race, are from another culture or have a different sexual preference.

Since Victim # 3 is physically attractive, intellectually gifted, kind, mild-mannered and has great morals. I can see why she would be a threat to a bully. I can see why a bully would feel intimidated by her. Since she appears to be a laid-back person. I can see why some people would think they would be able to get away with pushing her around.

Lots of people have thought they would be able to push me around. The older, I have become; however, I have become gutsier, and I have developed an intolerance for mean people. I have decided I am not going to put-up with their garbage anymore. I used to be someone who did not fight back. I just got mad and stayed mad. I have an excellent emotional memory. Anytime I encounter someone who has been mean to me in the past; my instinct tells me to get away from that person immediately. I have even explained to the meanest person I have ever had to deal with how she has made me feel. That person just got meaner and tried to bully me some more. That person was mean to me repeatedly over the course of about 18 years. One day she demanded I apologize to her.

I am a person who probably only screamed 5 times during my lifetime before our daughter was born. Since we adopted our daughter, I have had to learn how to do some screaming. Our daughter has an unbelievable set of lungs on her.

Anyway, when this person, who had been trying to bully me for about 18 years, told me she was demanding an apology from me. I suddenly did some screaming I did not know I was capable of. I gave her a tongue lashing that would make Donald Trump seem like he is mild-mannered. I instantly collected my husband and daughter. We got into our vehicle and drove away. Ever since that day, this person has been trying to be nice to me. She has slipped-up here and there, however. She is an extremely Narcissistic person who is completely self-centered. She really does only care about how people make her feel. Being nice to people is a skill she has never learned. When she does try to be nice, she acts more like she is a machine, than a person. I appreciate the fact that she has been trying to be nice to me. I am never going to be spending much time with her, however. I know how she makes me feel and that is exactly what I am always trying to avoid. I'd like to never be around people who make me feel the way she has made me feel. Being around people who make me feel that way is at the bottom of my list of things I want to do. Even when she is behaving the best way, she is capable of behaving; she is still controlling and manipulative. She still thinks she should oversee everyone else. She thinks she should be running everyone else's life. She thinks she should criticize everyone repeatedly all the time. She thinks everyone should act and think the same way she does. The only time a

Narcissistic person cries is when someone has made them feel bad. They never cry at funerals. They never cry because they are upset about something that has happened to someone other than themselves. They only care about themselves.

One time my husband and I saw a Counselor for a while so we could learn how to deal with her. The Counselor told us. She was born with an extreme personality. She handed us a piece of paper that had 16 different personality types listed on the page. These personality types were described inside 16 squares. The squares were arranged on the page so there were 4 horizontal rows that intersected with 4 vertical rows. She told us the personality types that are in the middle of this grid describe the people who easily get along with other people. The 4 personality types that are described in the 4 corners of this grid describe the people who have the most trouble with getting along with other people. She told us, "The person you have been describing to me has the personality type that is in the bottom right corner of this grid." We read that description and it did describe this person very well. One of the things this description said was, 'poor problem-solving abilities. When my husband read that, he responded, "She can solve problems." After that day, however, he thought of lots of examples where this person had made lots of bad decisions. The more he thought about this person's ability to solve problems, the more he realized, this person really does not have good problems solving abilities. He realized that this person could not do a lot of the things she wanted to achieve; so, she had learned how to be a delegator. She was someone who thought she could sit in a chair and order other people around. She expected other people to not have any goals or dreams of their own. Instead, she expected other people to spend all their time doing things for her.

When Victim # 2 started telling me about how one of her younger daughter's dorm-mates at College had been trying to bully her. I could relate to this story extremely well. I used to be a very quiet person. Some people have assumed I am someone who would never fight back. I used to be someone who did not fight back. As I have become older; I have learned lots of different ways to fight back. I am so tired of having to deal with mean people that I am just not willing to put-up with being dumped-on and taken advantage of anymore. Writing this book is one of the ways I am fighting back.

Victim # 2 told me her daughter learned who her suite mates were going to be during July 2018. She was excited about going to College. She called each of her suite mates and started to develop relationships with them ahead of time.

Initially, everyone seemed to be getting along with each other. During August, Victim # 3 moved into this college suite with 3 girls who were named, J. K. and G. Among these 4 girls, 3 of them were honor students. K. was the only girl who was not an honor student. J. was so intelligent that she took a lot of college courses at a junior college while she was still in high school. She tested-out of so many classes that when she started college, she was already considered to be a sophomore. Because academics were so easy for J.; one might assume J. was self-confident. Unfortunately, J. was not self-confident. She frequently complained that she had thick thighs, and she was not attractive enough. Eventually, it appeared that she was jealous that Victim # 3 had blond hair, blue eyes and a very nice figure.

People who are self-confident and feel great about who they are do not feel the need to bully other people. The people who are bullies frequently feel the need to push other people down; so, they can feel better about themselves. If someone feels insecure about their intelligence level, they will be likely to try to find someone who is less intelligent than they are and make sure they let that person know they are less intelligent than they are. If someone is insecure about their physical appearance; they might try to find someone who is more attractive than they are and try to tell that person about all their physical flaws to feel more attractive themselves.

When I was listening to Victim # 2 talk, I could tell that J. could not stand it that Victim # 3 appeared to be superior to her in many ways. Deep down, J. wanted to make Victim # 3 feel bad about herself; but she was so sneaky and subtle with the way she was doing it that it was not obvious in the beginning that J. was bullying Victim # 3.

When the school year started, the suite mate named K. was breaking lots of rules. She was bringing alcohol into the suite even though that was against the college rules. These girls are only 19 years old and legally were not supposed to be consuming any alcohol. K. was sneaking her boyfriend into the suite and keeping him there during times he was not supposed to be there. He was not even a college student. He lived 3 hours away. K. was so noisy inside the suite lots of times. The other girls in the suite could not study or sleep when they needed to because of K.'s inconsiderate behaviors.

A girl I am going to call N2 started hanging out in this suite. She and Victim # 3 were both majoring in biology. They had lots of classes together. They frequently ate lunch together. For a while, Victim # 3, J. and N2 were just trying to stay away from K. Victim # 3 and J. had both been losing a lot or sleep because of K.

The beginning of this school year was not pleasant for Victim # 3 because of all the commotion that was going on in their suite from K. Victim

3 asked J. to report K. to the R.A. named C. J. refused to do that. J. and N2 both said they did not want to report K. because they both did not like confrontation. Also, J. and K. had been friends for a long time. G. was a nursing student who had a different group of friends. She was frequently not involved in all the stuff that was going on inside this Suite because she was spending time with her other friends at different locations.

Victim # 3 was at college because she wanted to learn. She wanted to get good grades. She wanted to study. She wanted to graduate from college with honors. She did not want to be surrounded by noise and partiers.

The obnoxious events that were happening inside the suite continued to get worse leading up to Christmas.

When all the girls returned to this Suite after Christmas Break. That is when everything came to a head. There was a night when J. was screaming on the phone. K. was screaming, 'Get off the phone', so loud that Victim # 3 was sure the R.A. must have heard all the commotion.

Victim # 3 stated, "This is ridiculous, I am going to report all this to the R.A. right now." She stormed-off. Once she was talking to the R.A. named C. she asked her, 'Did not you hear noise coming from our Suite?' C. responded, "I thought I heard something, but I did not know what it was." Victim # 3 strongly announced her complaints about all the nonsense that had been occurring inside their suite. That was about the time that Victim # 3 learned that J. and C. are buddy, buddy. Once Victim # 3 learned that; she felt like there was nothing she could do to get the suite she was living in to be a decent place to live.

Soon after that, however, K. started moving some of her stuff out of her room. When the girls asked her why she was doing that, she responded, "I just need to take some stuff home."

Not too long after that, K.'s Mom and Grandmother arrived and started moving K. out of this suite and into another location on the campus. Apparently, K.'s Mom had thrown a fit.

Once K. had moved out, Victim # 3 arranged to have N2 move in. N2 filled-out the necessary paperwork to be able to move-in.

Victim # 3, J. and N2 were hanging out together. Then, J. N2 and G. all decided they wanted to rush a certain Sorority. Victim # 3 did some research on this Sorority. She learned this Sorority had been under investigation because of hazing. There was a chance this Sorority was going to be shut down. Victim # 3 told the other girls she was not interested in rushing this Sorority. She told them she was only interested in joining a Sorority that would allow her to do some volunteer stuff. She told them she was not interested in joining a Sorority that was overly focused on having parties.

The numerous hours of volunteering this Sorority would require also made Victim # 3 uninterested in joining this Sorority.

This is the time when J. N2 and G. all turned-against Victim # 3. This is when J. started to become very vocal. Inappropriate things kept popping out of J.'s mouth.

At this point, Victim # 3's friends had abandoned her. Soon after that, Victim # 3 met a guy online through a Christian chatroom. Victim # 2 told me she has met this guy. He seems to be a very nice, respectful and well-mannered person. Victim # 2 thinks he is a great guy for her daughter to be dating. She told me J. started tracking Victim # 3's location when she was on a date with this guy. J. was acting like he was going to be a hardened criminal. This guy was not a threat. He was a decent guy.

J. created a ridiculous rule, however. According to J. none of those girls were allowed to have a boyfriend unless the rest of the girls had a boyfriend. Since the rest of the girls did not have a boyfriend, J. told Victim # 3 she had to dump her boyfriend.

Victim # 3 did not dump her boyfriend. J. increasingly made more negative comments to Victim # 3. She started trying to criticize everything she did. For example, J. would say to Victim # 3, "What is that smell." Victim # 3 would respond, "That is my retainer soaking in vinegar water." J. would then tell, Victim # 3, "You need to do something with it right now."

J. had started to become so mean to Victim # 3 that Victim # 3 started leaving the college campus every weekend just so she could get away from her.

Victim # 3 was the only suitemate who had brought any cleaning products into this suite. J. asked Victim # 3 when she would be leaving the college campus at the end of the school year. Since Victim # 3 was going to be leaving the campus earlier than the other girls, J. was trying to figure-out who was going to be cleaning the bathroom at the end of the year.

Victim # 2 and Victim # 3 both decided to tell her, "You can either buy your own cleaning products, or you can purchase ours for $100.00.

Victim # 2 and I both agreed when we were talking to each other on the phone. Everyone in the world must endure lots of difficult events during their lifetime. Some people really go through some very difficult times. Victim # 3 had already had to deal with lots more garbage than she ever should have had to deal with, partially because of the type of person her father was. She was trying to do all the right things to create a much better life for herself. Why would anyone go out of their way to make her feel miserable.

Unfortunately, there are a lot of people in this world who enjoy hurting other people. Some people feel better when they are making other people feel bad. They do that intentionally.

While Victim # 3 was trying to figure-out how she could create a better life for herself; she was going to need to learn that she should not allow other people to treat her badly. She was going to need to learn how to report people who behave badly immediately and try to get their harmful behaviors stopped. She was going to must learn that whatever bad things her father did to her were inappropriate and never should have happened. She was going to need to convince herself that she deserves to have a much better life than the one she had been living. She was going to need to learn to surround herself with people who are positive.

Victim # 3's older sister also needed to understand she should be living a much better life. She needed to understand that the hurtful things that happened to her because of the relationship she had with her father were not her fault. She needed to learn how to respect herself and expect much better behavior from herself and from other people.

Both girl's mother is suffering from lots of things. I am certainly not a Doctor, but I do believe stress causes lots of physical ailments when stress is endured repeatedly over time. She should try to get as much stress out of her life as she can. I have heard before, that for a person to be truly happy, they need to spend about 1/3 of each day doing things they enjoy doing.

The older I become, the more interested I am in doing the types of things that put me in a good mood. When I must deal with the kind of people who think it is a great idea to be mean to me and put me in a bad mood, I have learned to submerge myself in activities that get my mood to rise-up again. Some of those activities include, watching old sitcoms like, Seinfeld, Scrubs and/or King of Queens. Those kinds of shows make me laugh and put me in a great mood. I also like to photograph lots of flowers and landscapes. I love to garden. I've attended the Tulip Festival in Holland, MI about 7 times. Going there and looking at the fields of tulips blooming puts me in a good mood. I also love to listen to great music. I love to dance. All the stuff I just mentioned are activities that take me to my happy place. I think we should all learn what our happy places are, and we should spend more time doing our happy place activities.

THE SPECIAL NEEDS TEACHER AT THIS SCHOOL SENT DCFS TO MY FRIENDS HOME EVEN THOUGH THERE HAS BEEN ABSOLUTELY NO ABUSE OR NEGLECT GOING ON IN THIS HOME

I will be referring to this Mom as VICTIM # 4. I will be referring to her daughter as VICTIM #5. This Mom is a girl I went to high school with. She and I ran on the Track and Cross-Country teams together. I have known her for about 40 years, and I always appreciated her because she has always been very nice to me. I have always liked nice people.

She wanted me to interview her and place her story in my book. She told me about lots of different times she has been bullied and she has told me about many times that her disabled daughter has been bullied. I will be referring to my friend as Victim #4 and her daughter as Victim #5.

Victim # 4 took the Myers-Briggs Personality Test very quickly after I asked her to. Her daughter did not take the personality test.

Victim # 4's Personality is that of the ISFJ.

The ISFJ is known to be, 'The Caretaker.'

People who have this personality type tend to be very loyal to traditions and organizations. They are practical and compassionate. They are very caring and very motivated to provide for others and they deeply want to protect others from the perils of life. They have a deep sense of responsibility toward others. They want others to know they are reliable. They are conscientious. They tend to persist until a job is done. They typically work hard and really want to get along with others. They value relationships with other people highly. They want their relationships to have stability and longevity. They feel the most connected with the people they know they can rely on over the long term. Sometimes these people are referred to as Historians. They want people to respect established customs. These people tend to be humble and unassuming. They usually do not call attention to themselves. They like to work behind the scenes. They usually do not want to be in the spotlight. These people are compassionate listeners and tend to remember details about other people.

Common hobbies and interests for ISFJ's are cooking, gardening, painting crafts, picnics, nature walks and watching movies.

Victim # 4 married a man and had 2 sons with him. Her first husband died from cancer at the age of 37. When he passed away, she was 30. She eventually remarried and had another son and a daughter with her 2nd husband. Her second husband died from an asthma attack when he was 44. When he passed away, she was 43.

Suddenly Victim # 4 was not only grieving the loss of her 2nd husband. She also had to figure-out how she was going to take care of herself, her 3 sons and her disabled daughter.

As soon as I started interviewing her; she told me about the home she grew-up in. She described it as not being a pleasant place to live. Between the kids the father figure in their home had before he met her Mom and the kids her Mom had before she met the father figure in their home and the kids both parental figures had together; Victim # 4 had 13 siblings. She told me her Mom physically beat her and sometimes she grabbed chunks of her hair and pulled her hair out. She told me one time her Mom whacked her in the ear with a phone so hard that she still has trouble with being able to hear out of that ear. She told me her Mom sometimes told her she would never be able to make her shine; like some of her siblings would be able to make her shine.

At one point, Victim # 4's Dad took Victim # 4's Mom to court to try to prove she was an abusive mother. Her Mom, to prove to the court, she was not an abusive mother, tried to prove her daughter was mentally disabled and hard to handle. She produced her daughter's report card to the court. The accusations her Mother was making were false. The Victim is a very gentle and kind person. She is not mentally disabled. She is not hard to handle. I was on the track and cross-country team with her for 4 consecutive years. She is a cooperative person. She laughs at my jokes. She is easy to be around.

I learned a long time ago and this is great information. Parents are not supposed to dump their problems on their children. Parents are supposed to find friends to tell their problems to. Friends can listen to another friend's problems and not let all those problems they just heard; weigh them down and be a huge burden on them. Friends can forget about your problems and get on with their lives. When parents try to dump all their problems on their children. Their children will be affected tremendously. Their children will feel burdened and unable to forget about their parent's problems.

Victim # 4 told me she was active in extra-curricular activities at school, because she never wanted to go home at the end of the school day. Victim # 4 got involved with the track team, the cross-country team, swim team, the student council, the booster club and the girls varsity club. She was also a gym assistant and a matt maid. She strategically figured-out ways to be at school instead of at home.

She also told me that on many occasions she was alone in the locker room with another girl who said to her: "Why did you even join our track and cross-country teams, you are not any good at these sports. Why do not you just quit?"

Victim # 4 told me she liked being on our team because I and about 3 of the other girls on our team made her feel good. We were the ones who helped motivate her positively. We were not even aware of how much she was needing our companionship.

She also told me that during high school, she moved out of her mother's home and moved in with her Dad. Her Dad lived in the next town away from our community. She did not tell the school she had moved. Her Dad's significant other was driving Victim # 4 to and from school every day.

When she and I were in high school; I spent a lot of time with her. She did not ever tell me she was getting physically abused at home. She never told me she moved out of her Mom's home and into her Dad's home to avoid the physical abuse. If she had told me or some of the other girls on our team; we might have been able to do things to help her. Even if we could only have been someone she could talk to about those situations that would have helped her feel better. We did not even know all that was going on in her life.

Next, she told me the names of a few of the girls we went to school with who were treating her cruelly. She told me some of them told her they wanted to beat the doo doo out of her. Again, when I was in High School, I did not know some of the girls at school were saying things like that to her.

Since I know this person well. I know she would not have done anything to provoke any of the people who were being mean to her. I am sure these people did not have any good reason to bully her. I could tell these people hurt her deeply. The way she described these situations; it was as if the incidents had happened recently.

Victim # 4 is a Caucasian female who is heterosexual. I do not know what her religion is. I personally do not care what her religion is. She is dyslexic. She had some trouble academically because of her dyslexia but she is a very nice person who was friendly with lots of people. I am guessing some people bullied her and were very rude to her because she appeared to be someone who would not be likely to fight back.

Her life became significantly more complicated after she gave birth to her daughter. Initially, her daughter appeared to be a normal and healthy baby. After a while, it appeared that her daughter had some type of a disability. As her daughter became a little bit older, she learned her daughter had Cerebral Palsy.

Children who have Cerebral Palsy endured some type of brain injury before, during or soon after birth. Cerebral Palsy frequently includes a damaged basal ganglia. The basal ganglia analyze all possible actions. It analyzes physical actions and mental actions. People who have Cerebral Palsy have trouble with controlling their physical movements, muscle coordination, motor skills and overall body movement. Cerebral Palsy also affects mental movements. If someone has C.P. and they are overwhelmed with having too many stimuli around them, too many people around them, too many things to choose from all at once or if they are forced to do something they do not want to do; they might react with an unbelievable amount of anxiety. They may have terrifying rages that are way beyond a typical temper tantrum.

During my research about Cerebral Palsy, one person who has C.P. stated she had lots of full-blown panic attacks until she was about 12 years old. She said her hysterical behavior not only frightened the people around her; it also frightened her. She said she could feel the fits coming on and she did not know how to stop or control them. She knew that her rages were frequently set-off by something that was trivial, but she desperately wanted routine and predictability. She said after she was 12 years old, she gradually taught herself that when she had lots of decisions to make all at once, she should choose the best choice between 2 of the options and once she decided what her best option was between those 2 choices, she was able to compare that best choice to one more option.

Victim # 4 has had some unique challenges while she has been parenting her daughter. She told me her daughter automatically sees kindness and innocence in people. She told me her daughter is very friendly. Her daughter likes everyone until someone gives her a reason to not like them. Once her daughter does not like someone, she has major anxiety attacks every time she sees that person again or must visit a place where she has had a bad experience. Her daughter's anxiety attacks are so dramatic that no one can give her any medicine while she is freaking out. If they tried, Victim # 5 would bite their fingers.

She also has fears regarding separation anxiety, because her father died when he was 44 years old. She was 8 years old when her father passed away. She frequently worries her Mom will disappear and never return. Sometimes when her Mom needs to leave her for a while, she asks her, "Are you coming back, are you coming back, are you coming back, are you coming back............?"

Victim # 5 also has a hard time with hearing lots of noise. She overreacts when there is too much going on around her. She really prefers a quiet environment.

When Victim # 5 started High School; she loved it. She became a cheerleader. She joined the basketball team. She innately has a loving and forgiving nature.

I spoke with Victim # 5 on the phone. I asked her to tell me stories about times people have been mean to her. She speaks very clearly. She is easy to understand.

The 1st story she told me was about how 1 of her friends asked her to go put her swimsuit on and go swimming with her. As soon as she arrived at the pool, she was told, "We did not invite you to play with us or go swimming with us, go home."

Next, she told me some of the girls at school were ganging-up on her. They were telling her they were gonna tell the teacher on her. They were telling her they were gonna call the Police on her. The girls knew saying those things would cause Victim # 5 to become extremely angry. They kept doing it with the intention of making her angry.

Typically, when this sort of thing happens to her, she starts screaming, "I want my Mommy, I want my Mommy, I want my Mommy." That is what she did this time.

Next, she told me about a time when she went into the bathroom that is across from the gym. That is when a girl asked her, "Why are not you are using your own special bathroom, retard?"

After that, Victim # 5 did not want to go to gym class anymore.

The next story she told me was about how one of the girls at this school formed a group of about 6 girls and tried to make sure they were all against Victim # 5. One of the things this girl did was go on Victim # 5's Facebook page, become friends with some of her friends; then she convinced those girls to do mean things to Victim # 5.

Victim # 4 and Victim # 5 were both on the speaker phone. This is when Victim

4 told me, the girl who formed this hate group against her daughter was a girl who wanted to take Victim # 5's boyfriend away from her. She also explained that when some of these disabled children's hormones become active; those kid's mental ability is not developed enough for them to be able to handle their new desires and emotions well. Some of them dramatically over-react to lots of situations suddenly.

Even after these initial incidents happened with the girl who formed a hate group against Victim # 5; time passed, then this girl, who instigated lots of hate toward Victim # 5 started to be nice to Victim # 5 again and acted like she wanted to be friends with her again. Victim # 4 had to explain to Victim # 5 that she should not become friends with this girl again. Victim # 5 was too trusting and let herself become exposed to people who were harmful. She was unable to predict that their behavior could become bad again.

At one point, Victim # 5 had to change seats in the lunchroom because this same girl was causing trouble again. Victim # 5 felt like the girl who was causing the trouble, should have been forced to change seats, instead of her. She did not like it that on the bus and in the lunchroom she was being forced to sit away from her true friends.

Sometimes the girl who formed the hate group would tell Victim # 5, "I do not know who you are." She also started inviting some of Victim # 5's friends to spend the night at her home.

Victim # 5 had been taught that when she starts to feel anxiety, she should do things that can help her get calmed down. One of those things is to write down what she is frustrated about. One time, when an incident happened in her classroom, there was no paper available for her to write on. She started writing her frustrations on the chalk board. One of the things she was frustrated about was that she was getting in trouble over an incident and the girl who formed the hate group was not getting in trouble for the same incident.

Victim # 5 understands that when she starts to get upset, she should walk away, and it may take her 20 minutes or more to get calmed down.

Victim # 4 also told me about how this same girl who formed a hate group against Victim # 5, created a video about how she hated a teacher at the school.

A Behaviorist at the school told Victim # 4 that some of the incidents her daughter had been dealing with were reportable.

Victim # 5 also told me her bus driver was picking on her. She told me she was forced to sit at the front of the bus instead of sitting with her friend. The bus driver also told her she was not allowed to brush her hair on the bus. Eventually, a girl who had been causing trouble on the bus was not allowed to ride the bus anymore. After that, Victim # 5 still was not allowed to sit with her friend on the bus.

Victim # 5 also told me her teacher was picking on her. She told me she was having many students write in a journal specific things Victim # 5 had been doing.

Victim # 4 eventually told me she paid $2,000.00 to hire an Advocate to help her figure-out what she should do. She was very concerned that her daughter's anxiety was becoming increasingly worse. She knew she had to do something to get her daughter's anxiety attacks to stop. She told me the Advocate helped her get a copy of her daughters file from the school. She believed the school meant to take some paperwork out of her daughter's file before they gave it to her; but they forgot to remove some important information. Inside that file, Victim # 4 found about 8 pages of documentation that was in lots of different handwriting. She believes the various handwriting styles were from students who had been following her daughter in the classroom and writing things down about her.

In this instance, the school was dramatically violating Victim # 5's privacy.

Eventually, Victim # 5's positive attitude changed, as she had some negative experiences at school. Eventually, she had some anxiety attacks at school and would return home from school in such fits-of-rage that she even yanked her closet door completely off one day. She was raging when she was getting off the school bus, regularly.

After having lots of bad experiences at school, Victim # 5 did not want to participate in cheerleading or basketball anymore. She had also been on the track team and had participated in Special Olympics for a while. She suddenly did not want to participate in that either.

Victim # 4 told me she spoke with the Principal of the school about some of her concerns. She told him children should never be involved with a dispute at the school.

At this point, Victim # 5's Doctor told Victim # 4, she really should not send her daughter to this school anymore. He suggested she home school her. Victim # 4 and the Doctor both knew that anxiety is one of Victim # 5's biggest challenges in life. They both knew that if she kept being exposed to people or places where she had negative experiences, her anxiety would keep returning. Victim # 4 told me there are times when her daughter is at home and a negative memory pops into her head and all a sudden, she will start to have a lot of anxiety. She also told me that her daughter's anxiety attacks were becoming increasingly more frequent, and she was taking increased medicine for the anxiety. Victim # 4 did not like it that her daughter was needing to take so much medicine.

One of the teachers at this school was supposed to call-on Victim # 5 when she raised her hand. This teacher was frequently ignoring Victim # 5 and did not call-on her when she raised her hand. She told her, instead of raising your hand, just set a cube on your desk, when you have a question. Why would anyone believe the teacher would respond to a cube on her desk if she were not responding to her hand in the air. The cube, of course, would be less noticeable than a hand in the air, so this made no sense. This teacher also stated she had 10 students, and she did not have time to give this student any special attention and she said she cannot police every student. This teacher said she did not must follow Doctor's orders. That also made no sense. The rest of the world seems to understand that a Doctor's orders should be followed.

Victim # 4 told me her daughter had attended a different school when she was younger. At that school, there was a calming desk, there was a motion cushion that rocked back and forth. There was a bean bag that was helpful for children who have seizures. She told me this other school also had a calming room students could go to when they needed to get calmed down. She told me she asked this teacher if this school could get these same items, because those items helped her daughter get calmed down at the other school. This teacher responded. We do not have the funding for those types of things.

Victim # 5 also had to be a student for a Coach who was very competitive and mean. He caused her anxiety to return.

The Female Behaviorist, at this school, has a Husband whose Occupation deals with working with physical abuse cases. He stated some of the things that were happening to Victim # 5 were inappropriate and the Police should be notified.

Even though Victim # 4. Lives in a very nice school district. This school was ignoring basic privacy policies. They were following Victim # 5 with a camera while she was at school. They were writing in her log every 10 minutes. Some of the students at this school were writing comments in Victim # 5's journal. The school called Child Protective Services on Victim # 4.

When Child Protective Services did inspect Victim # 5's home; they made sure Victim # 5 had enough clothes to wear. They made sure there was food inside the refrigerator, they walked around, then told Victim # 4. There is no abuse here. My trip here was a ridiculous waste of time. The representative proceeded to tell Victim # 4; you would not believe what I have seen. I have had to remove children from the homes they are living in.

I have been inside of Victim # 4's home. It was blaringly obvious to me that this Mom takes very good care of her daughter.

Victim # 4 felt like the school sent Child Protective Services to her home just because she had been asking to have improvements made at the school that would help her daughter not have so much anxiety.

At one point, Victim # 5 had a horrible earache. Victim # 4 took Victim # 5 to see her Doctor. She photographed the Doctor draining fluid from her daughter's ear. With those pictures and the Doctor's notes, she was trying to prove the earache was not happening because her daughter had been physically abused.

Victim # 4 told me the Director of Special Education is supposed to help protect the children's rights, but this Director did not try to protect her daughters rights at all. This Director also has a child who is disabled. Victim # 4 does not understand why she could not be more understanding, cooperative and try to find solutions to problems instead of just trying to find fault with people and blame them.

Victim # 4 told me the Teachers at this school are supposed to give the parents a Quarterly Report. Victim # 4 told me she did not receive hers. After requesting a copy of this report, she received it late. Teachers are not ever supposed to hand these out late. She said there were positive and negative comments in the report about her daughter that did not make sense. Some of the comments were about her daughters behavior on a particular day and the descriptions conflicted with each other. Since there was different handwriting in the report, it seemed like some people were writing positive comments in the report and other people were writing negative comments in the report. She suspected that some of the handwriting was from other students.

Victim # 4 told me there were Parents of other children at this school who were telling her stories that were like her own story.

Teachers are supposed to follow IEP (Individual Education Plan). Victim # 4 told me they do not always follow the IEP. She said they have sent her documents after they have changed the wording in the documents and have asked her to sign this paperwork. She told me a lot of the other parents at this school do not read the IEP and do not have any idea what their rights are. Victim # 4 told me she did read the IEP. She knew what her rights were, and she felt like this school was targeting her because she was trying to make sure her daughter was being treated fairly. She felt like she had an obligation to try to make sure her daughter was being treated decently at school; especially since her daughter has some special needs. She told me this school tries to intimidate lots of the parents.

Victim # 4 also told me there were students who lived in other communities in the area who were receiving free vouchers to attend this school because the schools in their communities had been closed.

This school requested that Victim # 4 attend a meeting at a Library. She could not afford to hire an Attorney to represent her. She said the school had brought Advocates, Attorneys and Psychologists to this meeting. At this meeting, it was decided that Victim # 5 should be forced-out of this school.

Victim # 5 stopped attending this school during 2016. Her Mom home schooled her until she was able to earn her High School Degree. After Victim # 5 stopped being a student at this school, this school did have some Seminars that were about bullying and how to talk to your friends in a positive way.

Victim # 4 told me she thinks teachers and the Disability Board should not be allowed to look at your Facebook page and try to use the information you have posted there against you.

If you do a search online for, 'bullying and disabled children and video;' then, watch some of those videos, I think you will be completely shocked by how much children who have disabilities get tormented by their peers. I watched some of those videos. I was completely appalled. Once again, I have always been very disappointed with how badly lots of people treat each other.

I know Victim # 4 well enough to know she was not doing anything to try to cause her daughter to have terrible anxiety attacks. I also have common sense. My common sense tells me: If Victim # 5 was excited about this school when she first started going to this school and she became a cheerleader, joined the basketball team, and joined the track team, then, suddenly started having lots of violent outbursts every day when she got off of the school bus and did not want to be a cheerleader and did not want to be on the basketball team and did not want to be on the track team anymore; then, it seems pretty obvious to me that things were happening at school that were upsetting her. Instead of trying to figure out what the problem was or how to find a solution to the problem; the school decided to attack the parent and act like she was the problem.

Victim # 4 lives in a gated community. She has called the police who are supposed to serve and protect. She has asked them to try to get certain neighbor girls to stop bullying her daughter. Their response to her has been: "Just keep your daughter indoors." Victim # 4 pays association dues just like everyone else who lives in this community and the Police in this community have decided they are not even going to try to get any of the neighborhood kids to stop bullying this disabled child. I told Victim # 4 to go above those Police Officer's heads and call the Police in the city the next time this happens instead of calling the Police within this gated community. I also told her if the Police in the City do not try to help get the neighborhood kids to stop bullying her daughter, I can write an effective letter and find some people to send it to who might be able to get the Police Officers in your community to do the job they are supposed to do.

In my opinion this is just one more example of how bullying happens and lots of people do nothing to try to stop the bullying.

I asked Victim # 4. Do you have ideas regarding how you think the school your daughter attended could be improved? She responded, "There should be a parent panel for disabled families." She strongly feels the parents should have the opportunity to be heard. She also told me sound deafeners in the schools would be helpful.

She told me the school has a Best Buddy Program where regular students are paired with disabled kids; but some of the regular kids tell the disabled kids they are going to be best buddies forever while people are watching them interact; but as soon as no one is looking, they ignore the disabled children. The disabled children typically never hear from the regular students again.

She also stated she thinks the schools should learn what each disabled child's issues are. For example, Victim # 4 has some specific sensory issues. She cannot tolerate anyone touching her head or combing her hair. She dramatically over-reacts to too much noise or too many people. She gets her feelings hurt easily. Then the school should try to make sure those children are not exposed to the things that dramatically irritate them.

In my opinion, the disabled children have very little control over how they respond to negative experiences. It makes sense to me that the school should try to remove the negative experiences, not the students.

I personally, have photographed lots of children who have autism and other disabilities. I know that they all act differently. I have seen some of them violently refuse to be photographed. I know that you cannot force a disabled child to be photographed if that child does not want to be photographed. I have seen lots of people try to force disabled children be photographed even though they did not want to cooperate. I have never seen a disabled child suddenly change their mind and decide to start cooperating after someone has bullied them into being photographed. I have, however, seen people get a disabled child to cooperate and take a great picture by playing the kind of music that child likes, singing to that child, by setting a stuffed animal on top of the photographers head, by throwing a soft toy at the photographer, by laughing, by making funny noises, by having the child's teacher do a somersault or fall suddenly on purpose or by acting silly. In other words, find something that will put the child in a good mood if you want them to pose for a picture. It is that simple. Bullying a disabled child does not produce any positive results ever and people should stop trying to bully disabled children. Bullying healthy children who do not have disabilities does not produce any positive results either.

One year in the fall, I was working 2 jobs. My 2nd job was as a school photographer. One day I was sent to a school that had only disabled children. As soon as I arrived, one of the administrators told me they were very disappointed with the photographer who showed-up to photograph these students the year before. She told me that if it had been her decision to make, she never would have re-hired this company to photograph their students again. I had no idea what the photographer from the year before had done. I just photographed the students the way I do it. I tend to be playful and a lot more patient than a lot of the other photographers. Some of the other photographers I have worked with are kind of military-like and try to photograph everyone as fast as they can so they can go home earlier. Of course, our Photography Employer liked it that those photographers could photograph everyone very quickly. I personally, cannot photograph people that way. I want the pictures to turn-out great. I want the parents of the students to get really excited about how the photos turned-out. Some of those students were not in the mood to cooperate and pose for a photographer. Their teacher and I agreed that they could leave and do something else for a while and they could come back later and try again. I let the teachers place stuffed animals on top of my head while I was photographing these kids. I let the teachers play the child's favorite music. I acted like I was going to fall over some of the time. I did not try to rush these kids. I tried to make sure I got the best pictures of them; I could possibly get. By the end of the day. The lady who told me she never would have re-hired this company to photograph their students again told me she was going to request that I am the only photographer they send to their school to photograph their students again. The next fall, she did request me again and I did get sent to that same school again. The fall after that; I was no longer working for that photography company.

Because I have photographed a lot of disabled kids; I know that trying to force them to do things they do not want to do is close to 100% in-effective but learning how to get that child to be in a good mood is pretty gosh darn effective. These kids do not suddenly become in a good mood 100% of the time, when you try to get them in a good mood, but positive reinforcement is a heck-of-a lot more effective than negative reinforcement is. That is a fact.

When my friend was telling me about the trials and tribulations she has had with dealing with the people who work with the disabled children at the school; I was kind of shocked that those people have not figured-out that positive reinforcement is dramatically more effective, when working with these kids, than negative reinforcement is. I was really surprised that the school was quick to accuse the child's parent of wrongdoing when this child was happy and in a great mood when she first started attending this school.

Countless times, I have been shocked and disappointed when I have seen people treat other people badly. I do not understand how lots of people are capable of being mean. Lots of people think they can treat me horribly. Even though I have earned 2 College Degrees and I paid for my College

Degrees on my own. Even though I am an honest person. I am reliable and punctual. I am a hard worker. I am well-behaved. Every place I have ever worked. Eventually, someone will treat me horribly and I will be ready to find a different job. I would rather keep changing jobs and not earn much money than must deal with difficult people; but everywhere I have ever worked, I have had at least one difficult person to deal with.

It has been my experience that it does not matter what I do, or how I behave, I will deal with difficult people. There are a lot of them in this world and I cannot avoid all of them completely.

Now you have some insight regarding where my point-of-view is coming from. I can relate to these disabled children, because, I have a disability too. No one knows I have a disability unless I explain it to them. I do not get picked-on nearly as much as disabled children do because my disability is not obvious. I am extra-sensitive to being picked-on, however. When people treat me horribly, I am not interested in dealing with those people ever again. Unlike this girl, who has Cerebral Palsy, I can anticipate that certain people are likely to be mean again.

Victim # 4 told me lots of other examples regarding ways people have tried to bully her. Those incidents include things such as:

- ✓ Telling her she should not post certain pictures of herself on Facebook. This happened right after she was feeling good about herself because she had lost 25 pounds.
- ✓ Telling her she is not allowed to post pictures of some of her Grandchildren on Facebook; even though some other people in the family are posting pictures of those same kids on Facebook.

✓ Criticizing her spending habits even though she usually shops at the Goodwill and other Thrift Stores.

✓ Telling her she should not let her daughter interact with ponies even though that is one of the things her daughter absolutely loves to do.

✓ Telling her she should not let her daughter have a prom dress.

✓ She feels like some of her siblings have shunned her.

✓ She feels like she does not have much communication with one of her 4 children anymore.

Victim # 4 told me her daughter gets bullied so much, that her daughter, who is now 21 years old, is afraid to try anything new or go anywhere new.

Victim # 4 told me her entire life has become taking care of her daughter. She said she has even been criticized when she has said, "I need to take a break from my daughter." It is normal for parents to need to take some breaks from their kids even when their kids are not disabled. People should not be criticizing her for admitting that she needs to take some breaks.

Victim # 4 told me she and her daughter have endured so many hurtful acts over time from lots of different sources that they both feel like not interacting with people much. All the painful experiences they have endured over time have accumulated. As of now, Victim # 4 feels like she only has one person in this world who she feels like communicating with regularly.

Victim # 4 also told me that she has tried to help her daughter learn how to count money and figure out what the change will be when she is buying something at a grocery store and someone in line behind her said: "Isn't there another place you can teach her that?"

When I have done research on negative reinforcement versus positive reinforcement, I have learned that childcare experts agree that children should receive a ratio of about 4/1 positive reinforcement versus negative reinforcement. Childcare experts agree that children should receive lots more positive reinforcement than negative reinforcement, but some negative reinforcement is necessary.

I have witnessed lots of authority figures, employers, parents and adults in general be extremely negative and hardly ever use any positive reinforcement. I know that when people are nice to me, I feel like doing nice things for them and when people are mean to me, I do not feel like doing anything for them.

I have learned that there are some personalities that need to be forced to do the things they are supposed to do. Using negative reinforcement on those people might produce good results.

Using negative reinforcement on some people can backfire, however. Some people, like myself, are responsible and automatically do the things they are supposed to do. People like me become extremely annoyed when people try to boss them around, talk down to them, insult them and talk to them like they do not know anything.

In my opinion, negative reinforcement should be carefully doled out.

My opinion of Victim # 4 and Victim # 5's situation with dealing with this school is that there have been way too many negative accusations, way too many people hurting other people's feelings, way too much of people trying to get someone else in trouble and way too little understanding, way too little quality communication and way too little of the Authorities-figures trying to find solutions to problems.

It seems to me that adults who work with disabled children should at least understand that bullying the disabled children, allowing other kids to bully the disabled children and bullying the disabled children's parents is completely ineffective and very harmful.

These are excellent examples of when people witness bullying and do nothing to stop it.

I wonder if this sort of thing happens because the bullies love to fight and argue, and the nice people hate fighting and arguing.

I do know that some bullies love to make other people feel miserable. That is their goal.

The nice people in this world need to start doing a lot more to stop the mean people from emotionally damaging other people.

THIS SKINNY GUY WAS SO SICK OF GETTING PICKED ON, HE LOST IT ONE DAY AND GAVE THE OTHER GUY A BLOODY FACE

I will be referring to this guy as VICTIM # 6. This story is about a guy who I have known for about 40 years. He dated, then, eventually married one of my friends. I was a bridesmaid at their wedding.

He was born in Louisiana. His biological mother left him with his father, then, disappeared. His biological father did not think it would be a good idea for him to try to parent his son by himself. Consequently, his Mom, who lived in Indiana decided to parent this child. When Victim # 6 was about 1 ½ years old, his Grandma (caretaker) passed away. She had been enduring terrible headaches because of something that was mal functioning in the veins and arteries in the back of her neck. She passed away on Mother's Day, 1965. At that point, Victim # 6's Uncle and Aunt began to parent him.

His Aunt had a very strict personality. She was extremely concerned about appearances and what other people thought. When it came to housework and yardwork; this family was on a very rigid schedule. Everyone in this household had to make their beds every day. Every Tuesday, they washed, dried, folded and put-away all their dirty laundry. Every Friday, they had a definite list of chores they had to do, etc. The inside of their home needed to be clean, neat and orderly all the time. This family had a large back yard. They were not allowed to leave leaves, twigs or lawn-clippings on their lawn. If there was a storm that knocked twigs out of their trees. As soon as the storm passed; they, all had to run out into their yard and collect all the debris on their lawn. While he was telling me this story, I was reminded of some of the extreme cleaning I had to do when I was a child. I fully-know that when you live this way, there, is not much time left-over to relax or have any fun. When I told my husband part of this story; he reminded me that when he was a kid; he had a neighbor who could not stand to let any debris lie on her lawn or driveway. This lady had a gigantic and beautiful magnolia tree near her driveway. When her magnolia flower petals fell; she ran out to her driveway frequently, swept those flower petals, and discarded them immediately.

Victim # 6's Aunt also forced him to take 9 ½ years of piano lessons against his will.

I know that when you spend most of your time when you are a child doing yardwork and housework; you, are not spending much time learning socialization skills.

Yes, kids who do chores learn lots of great things; but I do not think, a young child should be so busy tasking all the time, that, they never get to be a kid. I think learning how to have fun and learning how to relax and not be worried all the time are important too.

Also, Victim # 6 was an extremely skinny kid. He told me that when a brand-new mall opened near where he lived; he could remember going there to look for pants that would fit him. He said, no dress pants fit him. He said he had to find jeans that had a 26" waist and even those were hanging on him.

I wonder if the way he was parented taught him how to be a victim. I do not know whether it did or not; but I have a feeling he was more obedient and disciplined than a lot of his peers were because of how he was parented.

He told me when he was in the 4th and 5th grades he was always bullied. He told me he went to 3 different Elementary Schools.

The first Elementary School he attended was eventually shutdown.

When the community he lived in built a new High School. The existing High School became the Junior High. The existing Junior High became a consolidated Elementary school. One of the existing Elementary Schools became a Senior Center. The other existing Elementary School became a building that was used as a Boys and Girls Club in their community.

This communities School System was ranked very high. Victim # 6 said he did receive a very good education.

When he was in the 5th grade, however, he did get the Doo Doo beat out of him.

When he was in the 6th grade, he was getting bullied then too. He told me anytime the boys got lined-up to go to the boys room, he started getting hit and kicked. He said he had to cover his private area every time he entered a bathroom at school. He said boys frequently tried to kick him in an area that should never be kicked. He, then, transferred to another school that was within the same community.

After he finished the 6th grade, he attended the Junior High School. His Mom worked at that school. Since his Mom was extremely strict; having his Mom there all the time presented its own set of challenges. Also, his Mom had her own set of friends who also worked there. He was surrounded by adults who were watching everything he did when he attended this school. Apparently, though, even though many of the adults in this building were supposed to be trying to help protect him; they did not get the bullying stopped. While he attended this school; he was being bullied by a girl. He said she used to wear white boots and she frequently kicked him in the shins and ankles. He said he believes this caused him to have some problems with varicose veins later in life. He medically had that problem relieved.

When he was in the 8th grade, the boy whose locker was right next to his was harassing him all the time. Over time, Victim # 6 became so tired of being harassed, that one day he lost it. He punched the boy whose locker was next to his 3 times in the face and gave him a bloody nose. He said he almost got kicked out of school because of this incident.

His Uncle, who had been parenting him suggested he just ignore the bullies and walk away? He told Victim # 6; "I never got bullied when I was a kid." Victim # 6 responded; "How can you ignore someone who is physically hitting you?"

He said, while he attended the Junior High, he earned good grades.

Victim # 6 was born with a heart that was not functioning properly. He has needed to have 2 heart surgeries during his lifetime. He had is 1st heart surgery when he was 4 years old. He had his 2nd heart surgery when he was 47 years old. When he was 14 years old, during July of 1977, he was at a Children's Hospital. He was having a stress test and some other tests done. While he was there; his chart was near him at one point. He opened it and started looking through it. He noticed a copy of his birth certificate was in this file. His birth certificate listed his biological father and his biological mother. For the first time ever, he knew what his biological mother's name was. He had never even seen pictures of her before.

He asked his biological father about his biological mother. He told him. She married someone else before you were even born. Victim # 6 eventually found his biological mother during December of 2010. He then learned she had in fact; married someone else before she even gave birth to him. Many years later, he finally met his biological mother and many of his other relatives. His biological father died from lung cancer at the age of 60.

His Uncle and Aunt, who parented him, have both passed-away. It sure is a good thing that he found the name of his biological mother written on his birth certificate when he was 14 years old.

Once he was in High School, he was getting picked on by the same people.

Once he was a Senior in High School, though, he had grown to be taller than 6'. He said, once, he was a much larger man in Stature. No one picked on him anymore.

Victims of bullies frequently report that while they were being bullied; there was an audience and they were very frustrated that no peers, siblings, parents or teachers even tried to help get the bullying stopped.

It seems like most people do not want to get involved; they stand-by and do nothing. Some people are afraid of retaliation. Some people always try to avoid conflict and confrontations. Some people just do not care.

Bullying is frequently the reason people who commit suicide do it. It is strange that so many people can watch other people get treated horribly repeatedly over time and they do nothing to try to stop the bad behavior.

Now that cyber-bullying is very common; bullying has increasingly become a much bigger issue than it was in the past.

Bullies frequently choose targets who will not have the means to be able to defend themselves. They tend to harass the weakest and easiest prey. Bullies typically are people who do not like to fight. If they did like to fight; they would find people who were their size to bully. When a bully targets someone who is much smaller than they are; they are likely trying to bully someone who will not be capable of having a long and drawn-out physical fight.

Male bullies usually bully other boys physically. Female bullies usually bully other females mentally. Female bullying is much more difficult to spot because females tend to play mind games. They tend to use shame, criticism and ridicule. Bullies, in general, have different reasons why they bully. Not all bullies are looking for the same type of target. Some of the traits bullies look for are:

Individuals who are weaker than they are, emotionally.

Individuals who are weaker than they are, physically.

Individuals who are weaker than they are, socially.

Individuals who are weaker than they are, emotionally, socially and/or

physically.

Individuals who are different than they are, religiously, racially or sexually.

Individuals who are alone, or usually not with a group of friends.

Individuals who are nice and not likely to fight back.

Individuals who are interesting.

Individuals who try to improve things.

Individuals who make them feel inferior and they are jealous of.

Individuals who will be entertaining to bully.

Individuals who are annoying.

Individuals who are too needy.

Most bullies want to taunt people who will not fight back or will not be capable of fighting back. A small percentage of bullies really do want to fight.

In general, humans, much like animals in the wild, tend to expel the weakest individuals in the pack / heard / group. They usually do not attack the ones who are in the middle of the heard. The members of the group who are not, 'fitting in', are likely to get targeted.

Bullies crave power. Bullies want to be thought of as the one who oversees everything and everyone. Having power is incredibly important to them. Bullies tend to be people who do not care at all about other people's wants and needs. They are extremely self-centered, selfish and greedy. Frequently, bullies do not have good problem-solving skills. They usually are people who like to make lots of decisions. They like to act like they have the best ideas. They want everyone to think their ideas are better than everyone else's ideas. These people tend to get promoted because they desperately want to oversee other people. Sadly though, these people frequently are not capable of making good decisions. They make so many bad decisions that they cause problems everywhere they go.

Within the working world, the reason most people leave their employer and find another job is because they could not stand how their Superior was treating them.

Bullies are frequently people who have not been victim's themselves. Not all bullies are cowards. Even though lots of people believe these people are acting badly because someone has treated them badly; that is not always the case.

Are bullies the way they are because of nature or nurture? There are lots of conflicting opinions on that topic. Someone must be born with a domineering personality type to be able to act that way. I, personally, could never act that way no matter what type of environment I grew-up in. I think if you care about how you make other people feel; then, you are not capable of bullying people.

I have had to learn how to defend myself. I have taught myself how to put a bully in their place. I would not treat an innocent person that way, however.

True bullies are not likely to ever acquire a happy and healthy life. Since they constantly try to prove to everyone else in the world that they are better than and more important than everyone else; people get tired of dealing with them. They will be likely to have lots of people leave them and / or retaliate against them. Some people bully others when they are young; but as they age, they learn to treat others more decently. Some bullies, however, become worse as they age, and they never learn from their mistakes. They truly have trouble with being able to solve problems. They tend to be loaded down with lots of problems their entire lives. They will be likely to have trouble with being able to find anyone to take care of them when they become elderly and need lots of help.

WHEN A NOTE THAT WAS FILLED WITH PROFANITIES WAS PLACED UNDER ONE OF THE WINDSHIELD WIPERS OF HER VEHICLE, THE POLICE DID NOTHING.

I will be referring to this girl as VICTIM # 7. She is someone I have known since she was born. I know the people who adopted her. When Victim # 7 was born; she appeared to be normal and healthy. I interacted with her frequently when she was a baby. It was always easy to get her to laugh. She has a very jolly laugh. It was obvious that she gets excited about people who are nice to her. She gets very attached to people.

Once, Victim # 7 was in school; she was not learning all the material her teachers were teaching her as fast as some of the other students were. Her parents provided lots of tutoring for her.

Victim # 7 told me that once she was in the 2nd grade; 1 boy started teasing her relentlessly. He said the following things to her in addition to other things: You are fat, you are overweight, you are not like the other girls. He made fun of her because she was adopted. He made fun of her because she had trouble with learning. She said people also started rumors about her that were not true. She said she lost one of her close friends who she had been friends with for 2 years; because of a nasty rumor that was started about her, and the rumor was false. She heard people were telling her friend that she was saying bad things about her. She had not said anything bad about her friend at all. The bullies had successfully convinced her friend to no longer associate with her.

Victim # 7 is not fat. She has never been a skinny girl, but she has never been a fat girl either. She is a little bit overweight; but not enough for that to even be an issue. I was surprised when she told me people were criticizing her for her weight.

She told me the bullying became worse as she became older. Over time, more people bullied her. Some of the bullies were boys. Some of the bullies were girls.

She said the bullying became worse during High School. She told me when she was in High School, there was a lot of name calling, a lot of drama, a lot of untrue rumors getting spread. People were telling her, "You are not pretty", "You're a fat friend", people kept making up lies about her and spreading rumors about her.

She also told me there are Special Needs kids at her school. Some of the Special Needs kids are kept separate from the general population of students; but some of the Special Needs kids do interact with the other Students at this school. There are regular High School Students who get paired with the Special Needs kids to tutor them. Victim # 7 is not in the Special Needs program at this school; it just takes her longer to learn a lot of the material that is presented to her at school then it does for many of the other Students. She told me the Special Needs kids at this school get treated horribly. A lot of the students call them stupid, dumb, retarded and ugly. She told me these kids get told, "You will never amount to anything." She even told me there is a girl in the Special Needs program at her school that is good at swimming and at running. She is on the track team, and she has won a lot of awards; yet people still bully her and treat her horribly.

She told me; one day she drove her parent's Ford Expedition to school. She told me she parked in the back row where most of the people who drive trucks park. She told me someone left a note under her windshield that said, "F.U. Cunt, do not F'n park here." She told me she reported this incident to her School's Police Department. She said the Police did nothing about it.

She also told me, one time she tried to defend one of her friends who was being made fun of at school. When she did report this incident to the Dean at this school. The Dean not only did nothing to help; she told Victim # 7, "If I ever see you in this office again, I will expel you from school."

Next, she explained to me that anytime; she has ever tried to report anything to the administrators at this school. It was always obvious to her that this school sided with whichever student appeared to be the successful one. It was obvious to her that this school would much rather help the students who get good grades or who were doing well on the Sports Teams and were likely to succeed. Since Victim # 7 was not a student who was helping bring this school's GPA up; they were not interested in helping her. She also stated; the Teachers have their favorites.

She told me there were a lot of physical fights inside this school. The students who got into physical fights at this school; typically got suspended. She also said there are a lot of petty girl fights at this school. This school is in a very good school district. This school is well-funded.

She told me she has an ex-boyfriend who was being very rude to her and calling her rude names. She told me she used to try to say things back to the people who were mean to her; but she eventually realized that made everything get worse. She said, she decided she was just going to ignore the rude people.

She said she had quite-a-few friends who were getting bullied.

Victim # 7 told me there is a Teacher of Record at this school who was assigned to her to help make sure she got her homework done and was managing her life at school well. Victim # 7 liked this lady, and she told me she has known this lady most of her life. She did tell her about things that were going-on with her at school. This Teacher did try to help her. She did call the offending students down to her office and spoke with them. She did try to help; but there was only so much she could do.

This girl will be graduating from High School on June 6th, 2019. She has a job working with young children between the ages of 3 – 5 years old. Some of these children have special needs. Some of these children have been traumatized. She said she loves her job. She said there is a boy who sits on her lap for a long time and does not want her to ever leave him.

She is signed-up to attend a local college this fall. She is planning to major in elementary education. After that, she is planning to attend a different college and major in special needs there.

She also told me her adoptive parents have been sending her biological mother letters to the Organization they adopted her from; every year at Christmas time, ever since she was born. They want to make sure she will be able to contact their daughter if she ever chooses to. So far, this girl's biological mother has never tried to contact her.

Victim # 7 told me she is not allowed to try to contact her biological mother until she is 21 years old. She told me she wonders if she is still alive. I asked her if she is planning to try to find her once she is 21. She responded; I am not sure. She said, "I love my parents, I do not know whether I will or not."

She also said, "When I was a little younger, I tried to hang around with people in our town; but there are too many mean people and people who get into trouble hanging around in our town. She said sometimes the Police get called because of the things the people who hang-out in the town do. This town has a very low crime rate. I try to just hang around with my family, 2 of my girlfriends and my boyfriend. I do not even try to interact with anyone else who lives in our neighborhood. I try to stay busy; so, I will not be thinking about the people who have tried to hurt me.

She also told me there is a lady who she calls every day because that person always makes her feel better. That lady is someone who spent a lot of time babysitting her when she was young. She said she tries to not bottle-up her emotions. She describes herself as being someone who has a big heart and tends to be more emotional than most other people. She said she gets overly attached to people and she is super-close to her family.

Unfortunately, many people do not have a good moral compass. A moral compass is what tells us which choices we should make when we are trying to decide if we should do the right thing or the wrong thing. Some people have great character and make great decisions most of the time; but make bad choices in 1, 2, or a few areas of their life. For example, Martin Luther King had an excellent character. He made lots of great decisions. He was committed to non-violence and the pursuit of social justice. He also had multiple affairs on his wife. We should not discount all the positive things he did because he was weak and very human when it came to infidelity. No one is good at everything they do. We are all flawed. We all have areas of our lives that could be improved. We should all try to not harm other people. Even though some people bully. Those people may mature and learn how to not continue to act that way. Some people never learn how to stop acting that way. Your concern should be how to protect yourself. Not how to attack the bully. I think everyone should ask themselves, 'Is this world a better place because I have lived here?'

The responsibility of a Dean at a school is to:

Interact well with the staff and the students.

Focus on the overall delivery of education to the students.

Help develop plans and curriculum.

Work with the teaching staff, other staff members and the school district

when creating the curriculum design and educational plans.

Handles discipline

Orders textbooks and other supplies.

Obtains supplementary resources.

Trains staff to maximize student success.

Ensures students have adequate resources at the school.

They may also be responsible for helping students with financial aid,

housing, tutoring and health services.

Enforcing academic probation, grade disputes, expulsion and disciplinary

referrals from instructors and professors.

The bullying laws in this State require that each school reports the number of bullying incidents involving a student annually. These laws also state the Department in this state may audit the schools in this state at any time to make sure the # of bullying incidents are being reported accurately.

Schools will naturally want to report a low # of bullying incidents involving a student to make their school look good.

What kind of things can someone does when they are being bullied at school and the Administration and the Police at the school refuse to help them?

1.	The child should have an adult they can safely talk to about what has been going on.

2.	The child should be encouraged to express themselves.

3.	The child should understand they should never fight back physically.

4.	The child should know ahead of time, which adults at their school they will be able to reach out to. They may feel comfortable with communicating with a Teacher, The Principal, a School Counselor or The Bus Driver.

5.	They should use the buddy system. They should try to always be with one buddy or a group of friends instead of being alone, when they are in public.

6.	They should learn how to walk away from a bully calmly and not let the

bully see them react.

7.	They should understand that ignoring a bully doesn't stop the bullying; bullies should be reported and dealt with.

8.	Understand that reporting bullying will help the child feel empowered instead of feeling like a victim.

9.	Understand that enduring on-going bullying can be detrimental to your self-esteem.

10. Understand that supporting a child's interests, hobbies, thoughts and

 ideas are very important.

11. If your child is lonely, you should help them find an extra-curricular activity or a community activity they can become involved in to help them build a social group.

12. If a crime has been committed or someone is in immediate danger.

9-1-1 should be called.

13. If bullying happens during school hours; the proper authorities inside your school should be informed immediately.

14. If the authorities at your school do not respond properly. You should report the incident to that school's authorities. For example, the District Superintendent. If the District Superintendent does not respond the way he should; you should report the incident to someone at the State Level.

15. If the bullying occurs while you are on a school bus and you do not get cooperation when you report the incident to the bus driver; you should report the incident to the District Transportation Officials.

16. The Department of Education is another place you can report bullying if the staff at your school is not handling the bullying properly.

17. You can contact the State's Department of Education to learn what the bullying laws are in your state.

THIS GUY SPEAKS-UP AND PROTECTS HIMSELF IMMEDIATELY, ANY TIME   HE FEELS LIKE SOMEONE IS TREATING HIM BADLY

The 8th person I interviewed is a NON-VICTIM. I have become friends with him because we both worked near each other for quite-a-while. I sent him an e-mail and asked him if he has ever been bullied or treated poorly because of race. He is bi-racial. He is Black and German. He responded, "No, but my older brother has. I will call him and ask him if he would be interested in doing a phone interview with you." Soon, he sent me an e-mail and told me his brother is not interested in doing a phone interview with me. He then said, "My younger sister has; but she is at school right now. Give me a minute and I will let you know." A little while later, he sent me an e-mail and told me his younger sister is not interested in doing a phone interview with me.

I told him, "I could interview you if you know specific stories about people who have been bullied or treated badly because of their race." He responded, "OK."

He took the Myers-Briggs Personality Test soon after I asked him to.

He has the ENFP Personality Type.

The ENFP is known as, 'The Champion'

People who have this personality type are warm and enthusiastic. They tend to be very bright and full of potential. They are constantly thinking about the future and possibilities regarding things that could happen. They can become very passionate and excited about things. They tend to have the ability to inspire and motivate other people. They tend to be very good at doing things when they are interested in what they are doing. They tend to be charming risk takers. They tend to be sensitive, and people oriented. Their capabilities range across a broad spectrum. They tend to trust their gut instincts. These people are ruled by their hearts, not by their heads. They tend to hate doing boring, mundane and routine tasks.

Common traits among people who are ENFP's tend to be: warm and genuinely interested in people, they enjoy being around people, they easily relate to other people, they resist being controlled and directed by others, they can usually grasp difficult concepts and theories with ease, and they prefer to focus on long-term goals instead of focusing on short-term goals.

My phone interview with him started-off with him telling me lots of reasons why he thinks he has not been bullied or treated badly because of race. He told me he is very quick to speak-up and defend himself if he thinks someone is about to start treating him badly. He said I tell people right away, "I do not appreciate bad behavior; or I do not appreciate the way you are talking to me; or I do not play games." He said, "If I am speaking to an adult, I expect that person to act like they are an adult." He said, "I do not care if the person is someone who is supposed to be my boss; if they start acting like they are a child, I will call them on it." He said, "Bullies prey on the mild-mannered and the weak. They go after the people who appear to be people who will not defend themselves." He said, "I always let people know right away; I will not put-up with bad-behavior." He said, "If someone does me wrong; I will correct them." He also said, "I respect my elders but if someone is my elder, and they are talking down to me, I will call them on it. I will tell them I do not tolerate wrongdoing."

I was surprised when he rattled-off: "Bullies prey on the mild-mannered and the weak." That is something I recently learned when I have been doing research on bullying. Because I have been interviewing people who have been bullied; I have learned that people who have disabilities really get treated horribly. How they get treated is way worse than I thought it was. I wondered, "How did he know this, and it took me such a long time to learn this." I have recently learned that it is common for people who have disabilities to be overly trusting of people. Am I overly trusting and that is one of the reasons I become so disappointed when I learn someone is mean or cruel, I wondered?

I responded, "Some people are willing to fight much harder and longer than anyone else in the room. Some people fight to win. They will fight until the end. That is one of the reasons, I avoid fights. I always think letting someone know you disagree with them might change the disagreement into a much larger battle than you started-out with."

He told me a story about how he had been working somewhere where the people who worked there always tried to be the one to get to use the yellow pallet jack. He told me there is a guy who works in the freezer there who is difficult to get along with. One day he walked into the freezer and tried to borrow the yellow pallet jack that was in there. All-of-a-sudden; he and the guy who was difficult to get along with had a fight over who was going to get to use the yellow pallet jack.

After he told me that; I thought, I am the kind of person who would not even attempt to use the yellow pallet jack because I am always trying to avoid conflict. Even if there were no people around and the yellow pallet jack was right in front of me and was not being used; I would still probably not use it because I would not want anyone to appear out of nowhere and try to challenge me about why I am using the yellow pallet jack.

He also mentioned that he knows when people are bullying other people there is something going on in their life that is making them miserable, and they are taking their frustrations out on you. He said there is no other good explanation for bad behavior. He believes if people are happy and well-adjusted, they will not intentionally hurt other people. He told me he was working at a warehouse a while ago and one of the Bosses there tried to treat him badly. He mentioned, "He called him on it right away and let him know he did not appreciate that kind of behavior." That Boss backed-off and did not hassle him again. He also mentioned that Boss had been cheating on his wife and he did get a divorce, eventually. When he learned that; he assumed that guy had been dumping his frustrations on him and other people.

He also mentioned that a long time ago; he had been working at his Mom's business. He parked in a parking lot and had not noticed a sign that was posted that said something like, "Do not park here; this parking lot is about to be paved."

He said a Boss who worked there was a very grumpy guy. That guy was furious immediately when he noticed there was a car parked in this parking lot. Right away he confronted him and yelled: "Why did you park there?" Once he responded, "I did not see the sign." The Grumpy Boss told him, "Whatever, just move it." He said that time, he let it slide because he was a new employee there.

He also talked about how when he was in high school; kids had groups and clichés. He said some of the groups were kids who were all rebelling. Some of them were groups of kids who were all acting out in some way. Some of the groups were the jocks. Some of the groups were the nerds. Then he mentioned, once he got out of school and was working among adults; he noticed the adults were acting pretty much the same way as the kids in school were acting. He noticed; some people never seem to mature. They just keep acting like they are insecure kids.

He also said the lady who he is with now; came to the United States from another Country. He said when she first arrived here; she was staying with her Uncle. He said her Auntie would not feed her all day. Her Auntie was calling her a whore. He also said her Auntie's behaviors were all signs of immaturity. He said one day she may have an epiphany, look back at this, and laugh.

Then he stated, "anger comes from unhappiness." He also mentioned that if something bad happened to you when you were very young; it may still be affecting you somewhat when you are older; but unless the wrongdoing was something that happened over-and-over again or was still happening; he does not understand why people would let that event that happened a long time ago keep troubling them.

He then started talking about how he was a happy kid, but he grew-up in a bad neighborhood. He said he did have issues with feeling accepted. I told him, I have never been someone who tries to fit-in or do what everyone else is doing; so, I really do not understand that way-of-thinking. He said he did not have high self-esteem when he was in grade school or in Junior High. He said there were gangs near where he grew-up. He said the rules at the school he was attending were not that strict. He said this school had a lot of bad teachers who did not encourage the students. One of the Teachers, he mentioned, gave all the students the answers to the test right before they took the test. He said, it was common for students at that school to ditch class and sneak out into the hall during class.

He told me he grew-up in a Christian Home. How he and his family behaved inside their home was very different from how a lot of the people he interacted with when he was outside of their home acted. A lot of the kids who lived near them did not grow-up in a Christian home. He is now 30 years old, and he and his family are still very active at church. He said he and his brother, who is 4 years older than he is, were both quiet kids.

He mentioned that when he lived in this neighborhood; he was wanting to own flashy shoes that cost $60.00 per pair. He spoke of having deep desires to get new stuff all the time; but eventually he realized that after he did own the new item(s) he had been desperately wanting; he would lose interest in those items right away. He also realized that getting those new items was not really fulfilling his desires. He also said, he and his family later moved to a community that was mostly populated with white people. He said once he started attending this new school; he was surprised that most of the kids at this school wore the same boring shoes every day. He said lots of those kids wore adidas shoes. He said at the school he had been attending before this one; it was a thing to wear different shoes frequently. He said the cool kids at his old school wore dickies or dockers. The docker shoes were more expensive.

Later, during our conversation, he mentioned that his sister, who is 11 years younger than he is did not have the same appetite he did for owning expensive and flashy stuff. She has never been into wearing brand-name stuff. They both must tally different styles. When he was about to become a Junior in High School; his family moved to a white community. His younger sister was about 5 years old when they moved there. They both have the same parents. She has a beautiful singing voice. I heard her sing on You Tube. Her brother says she is too shy to show-off her voice and she still has not broken out of her shell.

When he was talking about desperately wanting to own flashy and expensive shoes; I started thinking about our daughter; who we adopted. We were at the hospital when she was born. She too is bi-racial. She is Black and German. She very desires to have fancy hairdos and fancy finger nails all the time. My husband and I are both thrifty and careful with managing money. Our daughter could not possibly have learned from us that having fancy hairdos and nails is important. Our daughter is 12 years old and not careful at all about managing money. Any time she receives money for her Birthday, a Holiday or for any other reason. She spends it all right away. She has friends who have a lot of money saved-up. Our daughter has never saved any money.

He also talked about how there are more white kids now who are into what the Black kids are into. He thinks this must be because of the type of music they are listening to. He said lots of the white kids are now wearing the same kind of stuff the Black kids are wearing.

When he was in the band at the school he had been attending originally; he was learning how to play the drums. He said he had been losing interest in being in the band because the school he was attending before he was a Junior in High School had a music department that did not have enough instruments. The instruments they did have were mis-matched. He said the music teacher was not teaching him anything new and he was getting bored. Even though he had a strong desire to be a part of the band he had been losing interest in going to band practice. He said the band at this school only had about 150 members.

Once he and his family moved to a community where mostly white people reside. He started attending a school that was ranked very high. The band department at this school had about 600 – 700 members. This band had nice instruments and the instruments matched. This school was well-funded. All-of-a-sudden, he wanted to be a part of the band all over again. He said being a part of the band at this school was fun. He said he liked to hang-out at this school after the classes had ended. He said, he hung out there and talked to the girls. He said he was now hanging out with the popular kids, and it seemed like they were trying to learn from him, how to be cool. He said, it seemed like some of the kids wanted to hang-out with him because he was black. When he had been at the school in the bad neighborhood; he was not hanging out with the popular kids. At this new school he was hanging out with a set of twins. He felt like he was living in their shadows. He frequently did not get home until 8:00 at night during the week. He also said, if a student tried to sneak out into the hallway during class at this school; they would get written-up. The rules were vastly stricter at this school. He stated these teachers were not afraid to tell your parents you were not doing well in school. He also mentioned he had the attitude that he did not need to care about how he did academically because he was planning to be a musician. He said, since he only attended the school in the white neighborhood for 2 years, he did not have enough time to grow there. He said his grades were a little bit better at the new school than at the old school.

Because he and I have spent quite-a-bit of time working near each other; we have had some conversations with each other. I remember talking to him about how it is frequently hard for artists (or musicians) to be able to earn enough money by just being an artist (or a musician). He told me he had been trying to be a successful drummer; but eventually he realized, he would need to do other types of jobs in addition to pursuing his dreams to be able to earn enough money.

Since I have an artistic personality too. I realize that doing the same repetitious job day-in and day-out can seem like torture. If you have an artistic personality, you are the happiest when you are being artistic. Some people are completely content with doing the same job and working with the same people repeatedly for 40 years or more. Not all of us are wired that way, however. Some of us must listen to music and try new things and try new flavors and travel to new places because living a repetitious life is just not fulfilling enough. Many of the people who are content with living a repetitious and boring life do not understand that some of us really need to be doing more with our lives. Anyway, when I started to get to know him; I recognized right away that he is someone who needs to be doing more than a repetitious job with his life. I also understand that when you are trying to make-it as an artist, one of your challenges is learning how to become, 'popular'. People who are already Celebrities can sell anything they try to sell, easily. Whether you are a writer or a musician; you still have the challenge of trying to connect with a large group of people who are interested in what you are doing.

I asked him if he liked living in the white community or did not like living in the white community. He said he did like it.

He told me he was a little bit overweight when he was in High School. Once he graduated from High School, he was bored and did not know what he should be doing. That was when he started to gain weight. He felt like once he graduated from High School; he did not have a purpose anymore. Suddenly, he had nothing to occupy his time. He said, he knew of some people who were still hanging out at the high school 3 years after they graduated from there. He mentioned he only returned there once after he graduated. Once he was out in the real world; he did not know how to be social outside of school. Since he was gaining weight he was not happy with who he was. He said he wanted to go out on dates and had girl's phone #'s; but he did not call any of them. He wanted to go out; but he did not want to go out because he was not happy with how he looked. This phase of his life lasted for about 7 years. He mentioned he was angry, unhappy and depressed all the time. Someone told him he was mean all the time. He said he did not like who he was. He told me he needed to feel, 'OK', with the way he was before he could lose the weight. He said, we all feel the same emotions, regardless of our skin color. We all feel sad sometimes. He said his Mom asked him, "Why are you grouchy all the time?" He said he was fighting and arguing with his Dad all the time.

When he was about 25 years old; he decided to start walking. He started helping around the house. He had been attending a church and he was friends with one of the girls at this church. After he had dropped about 20 pounds from the exercise he had started to do; he started to gain confidence and his self-esteem was rising. During that time, his relationship with this girl at the Church switched from being just friends to becoming much more. He said his relationship with her helped him be motivated to lose more weight and helped him improve his attitude. He said she told him, "I've never dated a big man before."

He said, once he was motivated to do a lot of walking; the weight started flying off.

He is still with this same girl now.

When I met him; he was a normal size. He told me; now, that he has lost the weight; he is talking to everyone. He is very friendly and sociable. He showed me a picture of himself when he was heavier. He did not seem like someone who used to be bigger. He has usually been, 'full of energy,' when I have been around him. He also told me that a long time ago; he did not talk much. He said he used to think no one was interested in anything he had to say. He eventually realized it takes 2 people to have a conversation and if you want to have a relationship with other people; you must relate to them somehow.

He and I have both had to work some 12-hour days. That was the reason we started talking to each other. One day last summer, I saw him working at one location at about 6:30 in the morning; then around 6:00 that night; I saw him working at a different location. I asked him, "When did you start working this morning?" He responded, "6:00." After that we started talking to each other a little bit. Eventually, I told him, "The job I am doing right now is just getting the bills paid. I am the happiest when I am being artistic." I told him I had been writing a book about bullying. I told him I would really like to earn a living from being a writer. He told me he had gone to school for film making and he had done some writing too.

I told him, "I have never intentionally been mean to anyone. I have never gone out of my way to dump on other people."

He said, "He has." That is why he understands that when people are dumping on other people; those people have plenty of frustration in their life. He said he did that when he was overweight. His weight loss has helped him have a much better attitude.

Once our phone interview was over with; I started wondering, 'Why did he gain weight after he graduated from High School. Why did it take him

7 years before he started to get his situation turned around?' I started thinking about something my husband told me a long time ago. He told me he had heard a report on the news that was about when are men the happiest during their lifetime and when are women the happiest during their lifetime. The report revealed that men are usually the happiest once they reach a point in their life when they feel confident that all their financial responsibilities will be taken care of. Once they feel like they have accumulated enough money to be able to feel they will be able to retire comfortably is when they are able to start to relax and feel happier. This news report stated that men usually do not reach that point at least until they are in their late 50's. I wondered if the fact that all those kind of responsibilities were ahead of him; yet, he did not have a solid plan in place yet; regarding how he was going to get to that point, was part of the reason he had been feeling very sad.

This same news report stated that women tend to feel the happiest around the ages of 18 to 21 because at that point in their life, a large majority of them are physically attractive and they have lots of guys chasing them. This report stated that once a girl's physical appearance starts to fade and the guys stop chasing them; their level of happiness begins to decline.

This morning I did some more searches on the internet regarding at what age are men the happiest and at what age are women the happiest. I read a few different articles. The articles did not all agree with each other. One of the articles said men tend to be the happiest around the ages of 23 and 69. This article claimed that at the age of 23, most men are overly optimistic regarding how their life is going to go. Most of them do not anticipate all the things that will go wrong during their lives. They tend to think they are going to be successful during their career. Another article I read said people tend to be the happiest around the age of 37 because by that age; most Men will have developed self-confidence and earned some respect from authorities and have a sense of achievement. This article stated Men are the happiest when they are married, have started a family and after they have climbed a career ladder. According to this report, they are the happiest when they have a close circle of friends.

According to this same report, Women tend to be the happiest after they have all the care-taking responsibilities behind them. After their children have become adults and have moved out of the house; all-of-a-sudden, the woman can find a lot more time to do the things she really likes to do. This article also stated women who never get married and never have children tend to be the happiest. The author believed this had a lot to do with the fact that this person will not spend so much time taking care of other people and will be able to spend more time taking care of herself.

Another article I read stated some things that make Men happy. That list included:

1.	Becoming a parent

2.	Getting Married

3.	Seeing their favorite sports team win.

4.	Buying a house.

5.	Buying a car.

6.	Proposing to their partner.

7.	Graduating from a University.

8.	Romantic men tend to be happy when they are spending time with their partner.

According to the same report. Some of the things that can make a Man unhappy are:

1.	Having to plan for retirement.

2.	Paying for their children's college education.

3.	Having to take care of aging parents.

This report stated that married couples are happier than everyone else. It also stated married men take fewer risks, earn more money from their careers and live a little longer than non-married men.

I told him I have done a lot of research on bullying; but there is still stuff about it I do not understand. I asked him, "When someone is mean to someone else, what is the reward; what benefit does someone get from being mean to someone else?"

Next, he started to explain to me that he understands that when people are feeling down about how things are going in their life; they tend to take their frustrations out on other people. He said when he was gaining weight and was not figuring-out what he should be doing with his life; he was taking his frustrations out on other people. He told me when he was feeling down; he was feeling a bit sadistic. He said, if you are in pain; you want to hurt others. He said some people always must get even or get people back. The people who treat other people badly want to hurt them. He said anger comes from unhappiness. He said, there is a dramatic difference in his personality when he is in a good mood compared to when he is in a bad mood.

When he said that, I started thinking about how our daughter acts. Our daughter is extremely hot-tempered. My husband and I are both even keeled. We do not really understand why our daughter has done so much screaming during her lifetime. She has had a pretty good life. She has never been traumatized. I have done a lot of research regarding temperament; just so I could understand why her personality is so volatile. She does have ADHD, OCD, ANXIETY and some OPPOSITIONAL DEFIANCE issues. She is very impulsive. For lots of reasons, I am sure the front part of her brain is under-developed. One of the things I have learned from my research is that some people tend to act before they think. Our daughter is like that. She calms down quickly after she gets upset about things. She completely heals from whatever was bothering her. She can be in a perfectly good mood just moments after she has exploded over something that is trivial. Once she has snapped out of her fit-of-rage; she acts like she does not care about the damage she just did to the people who were surrounding her. My husband and I look at each other and wonder, 'What the heck just happened.' Some of her behaviors seem outrageous to us. Fortunately, for her, she can make new friends easily. She has lots of friends. She can be lots of fun and a joy to be around when she is in a good mood. When she is in a bad mood, however, LOOK OUT!!!!!!!!! She will disrupt anything that is going on in your life if she is upset about something. If she is upset about anything; she will act like everyone around her has to stop doing what they are doing right now and tend to all her needs.

When I have done research regarding how much of our behavior is from our environment and how much is from our genetics; the conclusion tends to be, about 75% of our behaviors come from our environment and about 25% comes from our genetics.

I did see a program on TV one time about a girl who was locked in a bedroom during most of her childhood. Her mother did not interact with her much and she did not let her daughter interact with anyone besides her. The mother placed food in her bedroom often enough to keep her alive. Once this girl was a teenager; she was removed from this home and an adoptive family moved her into their home. This girl was suddenly surrounded by people. She had never learned how to talk. She had never learned how to do much of anything because she had never had much interaction with other people. Her new adoptive family was teaching her how to do lots of things. That program I saw on TV was proof to me that people need lots of interaction with other human beings. I also thought, when I watched that show, that it is sometimes hard to find positive people to interact with. There are lots of people in this world who love to scold people, shake their fingers at them and point-out all the things they are doing wrong. It is hard to find people who compliment others and appreciate them. I wondered how much different this world would be if everyone in it complimented and appreciated everyone else regularly.

This morning, I did more research regarding, "Why are some people mean?" One of the articles I read stated:

Most people are basically good. Most of us feel distressed if we see a living thing in harm's way. There is a small percentage of our population that does not feel that way. Within that group of people, there are some people who will do anything to get ahead. Some of the people in that group can be mean even when they have nothing to gain personally from behaving that way. Some of us who are kind and generous people can have moments when we act cruelly and suddenly burst into a violent rage.

This article stated that most of the time, when people are mean, they are being mean because they have negative personal issues going on in their lives.

PERSONAL ISSUES:

Most of the time, when people are mean; they are acting that way because they are unhappy with themselves. Their unhappiness can spread like a virus that causes them to be mean. Also, they are trying to convince other people they have it all together. They frequently try to create the illusion that they are better-off than they are. They may exaggerate or tell lies to convince people their life is more together than it really is. If that person's bad emotions are chronic; they will constantly treat other people poorly.

LOW SELF-ESTEEM:

When people are not confident with themselves; they may degrade others. Criticizing others helps them feel better about themselves. For example, if someone has a lot of trouble with managing their money and knows they spend too much; but cannot seem to improve their spending habits; they will be likely to despise anyone who is thrifty and good at managing their money. The big spender will be likely to try to find fault with the careful spender and prove they are better than the careful spender in lots of other areas of their life. Even if the careful spender has done absolutely nothing to try to hurt or show-up the big spender. The big spender might deeply despise the careful spender and do things to try to hurt that person.

ANGER:

Sometimes anger takes over a person, then all-of-a-sudden, they are incapable of using logic, common sense and other basic brain-functions that involve planning. In other words, that person is suddenly unable to consider what the consequences of their actions will be. Sometimes angry people do damage to other people before they can realize how this will affect the person on the receiving end.

STRESS:

Stress tends to cause people to act with a fight-or-flight response. When people are stressed-out; they become more likely to snap, get angry, cry and/or not care about how their actions will make other people feel.

THOUGHT PROCESSES:

Personal issues, low self-esteem, anger and stress are emotional reasons people sometimes become mean.

Thought processes are another reason people can sometimes become mean.

It has been proven that the best way to succeed in the business world is by developing good relationships with lots of people, promoting good will and learning how to get other people to want to work with you and do business with you.

Unfortunately, lots of people never learn how to get ahead by treating other people well. Lots of people think they need to push other people aside and step on other people to get ahead. Some people's thought processes tell them to keep their eye on the profits. They constantly try to make themselves look better than their colleagues. Some people think being rude and threatening other people will cause those people to produce positive results. Some people truly believe this is the only way to act if you want to get ahead and succeed. These people do not worry about how much damage they are doing to the people around them. They do not care that all their negative behaviors toward other people will accumulate and may eventually cause the recipients of their bad behavior to seek revenge. They just continue to act like they know more than everyone else. They are condescending when they try to interact with other people. They feel a deep need to act like they are better than everyone else.

BRAIN CHEMISTRY AND COMPOSITION

Some people are not born with the ability to have compassion for others. These people have a personality disorder referred to as psychopaths. These people are likely to commit serious crimes. Studies have shown that many people who are categorized as high achievers and hold positions of power also meet the clinical criteria for being psychopaths.

I know a man who is a Police Officer. He once told me that the criminals are typically easy to deal with. He said, most of the time, they are people who know they were doing something they were not supposed to be doing and they are aware that, they just got caught. He said the people who are difficult to deal with are the people who think the laws do not pertain to them. He said some people really think they are above the laws, and they should be allowed to do anything they choose to do. They think Police Officers should not be trying to force them to obey the laws.

In all the examples above, whether the perpetrator is acting because of emotional reasons or acting because of the way they think, they are acting badly because there is something wrong with them.

I also found an article that was about how MISERY LOVES COMPANY.

The basic premise of this article was that fellow sufferers make unhappiness easier to endure.

Unhappy people try to bring other people down with them. Miserable people do not want to see that there are people who appear to be much happier than they are. Miserable people tend to be miserable because they are jealous of other people, and they resent other people. Miserable people are likely to attract each other.

An example of someone trying to bring someone else down would be: If I told someone I am writing a book and they responded with, 'That will never work; you are wasting your time.'

Frequently, it is close friends or relatives who try to launch attacks against you, when you try to succeed. Sometimes, these people get jealous of you or resent you immediately; if they think you are about to grow, and they do not even have a plan in place for how they can improve their lives. Some people really want you to be at the same level as they are; or below them. Some people would rather undermine you; then try to elevate their own status.

Some people look for other people who are as miserable or unhappy as they are. They are hoping to find other people who have a worse situation than they have; so, they will be able to feel like their situation is not that bad after all.

HIGHLY SENSITIVE PEOPLE THINK VERY DIFFERENTLY THAN INSENSITIVE PEOPLE

When I was a child; I had absolutely no idea why I would get upset easily and my 2 brothers did not. Now, I understand that the personality types they have cause them to make most of their decisions based on logic. I make most of my decisions according to my emotions.

I have always been a physically active person. I was an athlete. I have never been someone who just sits around. I appear to be strong. Physically, I am strong.

Emotionally, I am not strong. When I was 43 years old, I learned that I have a non-cancerous brain tumor in my left thalamus. One of the things the left thalamus controls is emotions. I have spent my entire life being completely confused about why people treat each other so roughly. Even though I have done a lot of research on the topic of bullying, I still really do not understand why so many people are mean and intentionally do things to harm other people.

When I was young; I thought it was strange that there were jails. I wondered, "Why can't people just teach those people to behave properly." If everyone in this world thought the way I think. We would not have any wars; we would not have any jails and we wouldn't have any Police Officers.

Now, that I am older, I understand that wars, jails and Police Officers are necessary because a lot of people really will not do what they are supposed to do.

I do understand that there are a lot of people in this world who are insensitive. They really do not care about how they make other people feel. They constantly try to prove they are more important than everyone else and they constantly try to have power and control over other people. They are bossy, negative, degrading and rude. These people have Aggressive Personality Types. These people do not have any clue that they should not be condescending and treat everyone roughly. They do not understand that they do a lot of emotional damage to people. These people frequently act like they already know everything, and they are not interested in learning anything new. Some of these people are so insensitive that they harm people emotionally repeatedly over time and they do not stop damaging people until someone forces them to stop. These people do not comprehend and do not care that there are a lot of sensitive people in this world who cannot handle being treated harshly day after day.

The sensitive people in this world are constantly trying to figure-out how they can avoid having to deal with these obnoxious people. The sensitive people must find ways to escape having to interact with the perpetrators who are always trying to dump on them. The sensitive people are frequently people who are not good at standing-up for themselves. They tend to be people who are always trying to make sure they do not hurt anyone else's feelings because they understand how cruel that is. Unfortunately, though, they are trying to deal with people who do not care at all about how much emotional damage they do to others.

Since technology has advanced, bullies now have more ways they can emotionally torture their victims. Even though social networking is great for a lot of things, it also has a dark side. There are Internet Predators and Internet Bullies. These online bullies cause a lot of psychological damage to their victims and sometimes things that appear on the internet never go away completely.

Since bullying now happens online as well as in person, online bullying seems to be the reason the # of suicides have been increasing dramatically during the past 16 years.

According to USA Today, about 1 in 33 American adults seriously thought about suicide during 2016. Suicide is thought about way more frequently than it is discussed.

Some of the survivors of suicide have admitted they did not have a desire to die. They had a desire to escape pain. People who do attempt or commit suicide tend to get to the point in their life when they start to think, 'I can't live like this anymore.'

Therapy for individuals who are considering suicide includes having social connections with positive people. One of the problems with this is that some of the people who are considering suicide do not have any friends. Therapists must find warm and accepting people for these people to interact with. Sometimes these people who are considering suicide have gotten to this point because the type of people they must interact with in their daily lives are the opposite of warm and accepting. Also, once someone does not successfully commit suicide or gets talked out of jumping off of a ledge, they must return to living the same life that they can't stand living. They must return to the same life that forces them to interact with people they cannot stand interacting with. A lot of people think that when people are considering suicide, there must be something mentally wrong with that person. That is not necessarily the case. Sometimes those people are just people who have more than a normal amount of emotions and they must interact with people who regularly harm them emotionally.

As I was doing some searches online to learn more about how cyberbullying has affected our suicide rate. I found some articles that stated cyber-bullying seems to have a direct effect on how many people have been committing suicide since the use of cell phones and social media has dramatically increased. The articles I read seemed to believe that when someone uses technology more than 2 hours each day, they are dramatically more likely to be adversely affected from using the technology.

A 16-year-old girl from Sherman Oaks, CA, named Natalie Hampton created an online App called, 'sit with us'. Her App makes it easy for high school students to find a group of people to sit with during their lunch period. Natalie had eaten alone during her entire 7th grade year, and she had become a target for bullies. She learned that bullies are more likely to target someone who is alone. Because of her app. She has been helping lots of other students avoid being bullied.

I think all schools should have an app like this available to all their students.

Time after time, during my lifetime, I have been completely flabbergasted by how many people have been mean to me. I have also been flabbergasted by how many times I have witnessed people being mean to other people. I think being mean is a very destructive behavior that should only be used sparingly. Some people act like being mean is their favorite hobby.

I have been a very good and decent person my entire life. I have never done anything intentionally to hurt another person who has done absolutely nothing to deserve being treated harshly. I think a lot of people do not have a conscience and never feel guilty.

One of the personality traits that was described in my Myers-Briggs results was that someone who has this personality type can be a force to be reckoned with. I feel like that is where I am at right now. I feel like one too many people have been mean to me and I AM READY TO START FIGHTING BACK IN A VERY BIG WAY. That is one of the reasons I have been writing this book. I am ready to start helping other people in this world who have been getting treated horribly and cannot defend themselves. I used to be someone who just stayed mad for a very long time when people were mean to me. Over time, however, I have learned that I need to start standing-up for myself. There are way too many people who behave inappropriately, and I am completely DONE with putting-up with the garbage these people like to dump on me.

All of us good people need to do more to help the defenseless people who are getting treated horribly every day.

I have read the book called, 'Strong-Willed Child or Dreamer', written by: Dr. Ron L. Braund and Dr. Dana Scott Spears. When I read this book; I learned a lot about myself. I am a Dreamer. The authors of this book described me throughout much of this book every time they were describing a 'Dreamer.' These authors understand me better than my parents do, and I have never met them. These authors describe a dreamer as someone who likes to learn new things. For dreamers, the learning process is the reward. They also said, the Strong-Willed People are not interested in doing anything new unless they are rewarded for their efforts. The Dreamers are always trying to find great experiences. The Strong-Willed People are always trying to find great rewards. This book helped me realize that even though Dreamers are a minority among our population, they are the ones who make big improvements in the World. This book helped me realize what some of my strengths are.

I was working as a vendor in a grocery store during March 2019. There was a Store Manager there who was mean to me every time he spoke to me. He had never even said, "Hello" to me. One day, he walked up to me quickly. He scolded me and acted like I was committing some huge crime. I was not even doing anything I was not supposed to be doing. He is just a control freak who loves to criticize people. Very quickly, I started crying in public. I could not stop crying. I soon realized that I was not even capable of staying there and doing the job I was there to do. I walked out to the parking lot and sat in my car. I called my boss. My immediate boss is one of the people in this world who cares about how he makes other people feel. This guy can make very good decisions. He told me to go to a different store and work there. He told me he would show-up at this store and finish the job I had started.

I had never told him that I have a brain tumor but a couple of days after that incident, I had to explain it to him. I told him, I will be just fine if people will just leave me alone. I cannot handle being criticized all the time. I told him I am not interested in working at that store anymore. He has only sent me back to that store a few times since then and he has spoken to both Store Managers there. He has told them they must be nice to me. Since that day, the mean Store Manager has said, "Hello" to me once. That is all he has said. At least it seems like he has tried to stop being mean to me.

I told my immediate Manager I had started looking for a different job since that Store Manager has treated me so badly. He told me he does not want me to look for another job. He told me, "You do everything you are supposed to do, I do not even need to give you any instructions, you are an excellent employee." He begged me to keep working for him.

I have never understood why it is so hard for people to appreciate other people. I have never understood why so many people try to tear other people down instead of building them up. I am someone who does a lot for other people and works very hard for people when they are nice to me. When people are not nice to me; I do not feel like doing anything for them.

At this point in my life, I had already written a book about bullying that is fiction. It is called, 'Make the Bullies Pay'. Once this Store Manager treated me so horribly, I suddenly felt like he had just lit a fire in me. Very soon after he made me cry in public, I decided to write a non-fiction book about bullying. I decided to interview some people who have been bullied. I posted a notice on my Facebook page announcing I was interested in interviewing people who have been bullied. I did not have much trouble finding people to interview. It seemed like all the people I interviewed were happy to participate.

As I interviewed people, I did some searches on the internet to learn about different things. I did searches for Cerebral Palsy and Tourette's Syndrome because I interviewed someone who has Cerebral Palsy and I interviewed someone whose daughter has Tourette's Syndrome. I stumbled across some videos of kids who have special needs getting bullied at school. I was so appalled and disgusted when I saw those videos. I could not believe how badly those kids get treated at school.

When I interviewed these people who are very involved with the Special Needs Programs at the schools, I was once again appalled and disgusted with how poorly some of the schools treat the parents of the kids who have special needs.

From what I was hearing, it seemed to me like there was not enough problem-solving going on at the schools when there was a situation that needed to be dealt with. It seemed to me like it was common for people to just blame people and try to punish people any time there was a problem.

I know that I must not get upset when people are mean to me. I have even explained that to some mean people. Some of the mean people just keep being mean to me anyway. When they do that, they, completely ruin any opportunity they ever had of having a decent relationship with me. I will never be the helpful person toward them I would have been if they had been nice to me.

As I have become older; I have started to realize artistic people tend to be more emotional than non-artistic people. I have learned ways to get myself out of a bad mood. I have learned that sometimes, just watching an old movie or an old sitcom that I really like puts me in a good mood very quickly.

When I was in grade school, My Dad, Mom, 2 brothers and I all took a personality test. According to the results from that test, all 5 of us have analytical personality types. After that, I noticed I do analyze things. I also realized the people who are on my Mom's side of the family tend to be people who want to fix everything. They cannot stand to have things be messed-up or broken.

I have noticed that everything affects my mood. If I am around people who are whining and complaining; my mood drops. If I am around bad news or fighting and arguing; my mood drops immediately. If I am around nature, flowers, great music or fun people, my mood rises immediately. I do not watch the news. I do not like to watch anything on TV that involves politics. All that kind of stuff is too much bad news for me to be able to watch and listen to without having my mood drop. My husband loves to watch the news and know everything that is going on in politics. He says he feels like he can make better decisions if he is informed. He tries to tell me about all the news and Political stories he hears about even though I have explained to him lots of times, 'I am not interested in hearing about all that kind of stuff.'

I have learned that a lot of different personality types base most of their decisions on logic. Some of the personality types base most of their decisions on emotion. I am in the emotional category. I am a logical person, yet I am more emotional than I am logical. People who are logical and unemotional cannot seem to comprehend what I am explaining when I explain to them that lots of things negatively affect my moods, so, I would prefer to just stay away from those things.

When I was young, I had no idea that most of the other people in this world do not have moods that fluctuate quickly like mine do.

After I earned and paid for, almost completely on my own, 2 college degrees, I took a test at the 2nd University I attended that was supposed to help me figure out what type of a career I should pursue. The results from that test told me my biggest strengths are that I am organized, and I am creative. A few of the recommended careers for me were, architect, landscape architect and chef. This test also explained that most of the people in this world, who are organized, are not creative and artistic people are frequently not organized people. So, once again, I was learning that my personality type is very unusual.

I have always been cautious about starting-up relationships with other people. That included males and females. I have always tried to avoid the people who are mean. I got my first kiss after I graduated from high school. That was a kiss I did not even want. I was at our home. We were having my high school graduation open house. My older brother had invited some of his friends to my party. One of his friends asked me, "Would you like to go for a motorcycle ride?" I responded, "Sure." He drove me down a country road. As soon as we had complete privacy. He turned the motorcycle off, got off the bike, he grabbed me and started kissing me. I was grossed out. I did not have any idea he was going to do that. I never talked to him again after that day.

When I was 32 years old. I met my husband. I am 7 days older than he is. When we were both 34 years old. We got married. We have now been married for 21 and a half years.

My husband likes to talk to me all the time. He is not talkative when we are in other settings. He is a much more talkative person than I am. He and our daughter want me to pay attention to them frequently and they both like to interrupt me so much that I must be home alone or sometimes I must lock myself in a room for me to be able to do the things I want to do. I like to be a productive person. I like to be able to get a lot of things accomplished every day. I like to daydream. I do not think they both demand my attention all the time because they are trying to make me mad. They do that because I am a good listener and because they both have ADHD. They are both impatient. It is kind of weird that they both want so much attention. My parents did not talk to each other all the time. My Dad let my Mom be a productive person around the house every day.

I have learned that the thing that keeps marriages together the most is when both marriage partners have similar interests and life goals. Also, I have heard when couples have great communication, their relationship tends to be strong. I have also learned that people are typically compatible when they believe the other person will help them accomplish some of the things they want to accomplish during their lifetime. Even though Hollywood frequently advertises that opposites attract, research proves that is incorrect. My husband and I both love to garden and we have other life goals that are similar. Even though he is a good match for me. I have never been able to get him to understand some of my basic needs. For example, when I arrive home and I have a car full of groceries that I need to carry into the house, I am anxious to get those groceries carried-in and put away. I have explained to my husband and my daughter both, more than a hundred times. When I arrive home, I need to take care of my own personal matters before I can drop everything and pay attention to you. My daughter expects me to stop doing what I am doing and pay attention to her every single time I enter our home. My husband tries to wait until I have unloaded the car, but he usually cannot stand to wait that long. He almost always starts talking to me and asking me questions before I have finished unloading the car. It makes me mad every time they do that. I always think, they should be able to look at me and realize, I need help carrying the groceries into the house. Nope, they do not figure that out even when I ask them to help me carry the groceries into the house.

My husband and I decided to be married for a couple of years before we tried to get pregnant. Once we tried to conceive, we were failing. I went to a fertility clinic. I never got pregnant when I was going there. After I turned 40 years old, I became pregnant 3 times on my own. I lost all 3 of those babies. When he and I were both 43 years old, we adopted our daughter. We were at the hospital when she was born. She is bi-racial. She is ½ black and ½ German. My husband and I are both Caucasian. She will be 13 years old soon.

When our daughter was about 6 years old, I learned there is a procedure called neurofeedback that can help calm-down symptoms from ADHD. I heard this procedure can also help people who have trouble with sleep, get much better sleep. I decided to have our daughter try these neurofeedback procedures and I tried them too. Before we could receive any of these treatments, we both had to have an EEG done of our brains.

Her EEG test results revealed that many areas of her brain are extremely over-active. In fact, when the Doctor was explaining to me; the results from her EEG, he told me her brain is about 9 times more active than the typical female who is her age. Since our daughter has always been extremely over-active physically and verbally, I was not surprised when he told me those results.

The results from both of our EEG's were extremely accurate. Those test results told us exactly which areas of our brains were over-active. Those test results directly reflected which areas of our lives are out of the normal range. For me, 2 areas of my brain were over-active. The area that causes me to stay mad and hold grudges was way out of the normal range. Also, the area of my brain that dreams was way over-active.

After myself and our daughter had been receiving these neurofeedback treatments for a while, my husband decided to have an EEG done of his brain too. The results from his EEG revealed that he has a lot of OCD and some ADHD.

All-of-a-sudden. I understood why he is so particular about how everything is done in our yard. He is not particular about cleanliness and order inside of our home. I have learned that just because someone likes to live in a home that is neat and clean does not mean that person has OCD. Between the 3 of us, I am the only one who cares about whether the inside of our home is neat and clean, and I am the only one who does not have OCD.

Our daughter screamed a lot during the 1st year she was alive. I really had not been getting much sleep at all during the beginning of her life. When she was 4 ½ months old, my left eye started to hurt. After a series of events, I learned I have a non-cancerous brain tumor in my left thalamus, It cannot be removed, After I learned I had this tumor. I did research on what the left thalamus does. I learned the left thalamus controls emotions, most of the senses and the awake / asleep cycles. All a sudden, I understood why I am more emotional than almost everyone I meet. I understood why I am extra-ticklish. I understood why I jump when I hear noises or when people startle me. I also understood why I have so much trouble with sleep. At the age of 43, I finally had an excuse for being extra-emotional. That did not cause people to be any nicer to me, though. The mean people continued to keep being mean to me. I discovered that if you tell a Narcissist you cannot handle people being mean to you because you have a non-cancerous brain tumor in your left thalamus; the narcissist will immediately try to convince you that their life has been much more difficult than yours has. One day after I had brain surgery, I still did not have the results from my surgery yet. I did not know if I was going to be living or dying. I did not know if I had less than 6 months to live. A narcissist called me, and she told me she was calling me to find-out how my surgery went. Then she proceeded to tell me she had just had a worse day than I had. She told me she fell that day. She went on and on in detail about the horrible day she had just had, and she was completely sure that my day had been easier than hers. Narcissists really cannot stand for anyone, other than themselves, to be in the spotlight.

I had already done a lot of research on bullies and narcissists because I was so frustrated from how mean some people had been treating me. I had learned that narcissistic people really do think they are better than everyone else. They think they were put on this earth to boss other people around. They think everyone should be their servant. I was still not good at standing-up for myself, however. Extroverts seem to be a lot more capable of speaking-up and saying what is on their minds than introverts are.

Our daughter does not like to be alone at all. She is an extrovert. She seems to blurt-out everything she thinks. It seems to me that lots of extroverts do not understand that introverts need to have alone time.

Now, that I am 59 years old, I realize that I am the happiest when I am being artistic. I love gardening and photography. I love dancing. I love listening to great music. I cannot seem to sit still when great music is playing. I must move to the beat of the music. I love to watch old sitcoms and great movies. I always wish I had the time and money to be able to go to lots of concerts and plays. I have become more aware that I am in a great mood when I am doing the kinds of things I love to do. I have noticed that I have great concentration when I am alone, but I have bad concentration when people are interrupting me and upsetting me. When I was young and had more free time; I loved to cook and bake. Now, it seems like doing those tasks is too time-consuming and if I do a lot of that, I do not have enough time to do the other things I like to do.

I have also learned that when I am frustrated because someone has hurt my feelings again; if I sit at our computer and type about what I am frustrated about. That helps me feel better. I have done a lot of typing at our computer during the past couple of years. I have spent a lot of time trying to figure out why so many people have gone out of their way to make me feel miserable.

I have done lots of research about ADD, ADHD, Anxiety, Bullying, Controlling Personalities, Narcissism, Obsessive Compulsive Disorder, Oppositional Defiance Disorder and Perfectionism.

I have also done lots of research on the various difficult personality types. Those types include Ego-Centered Princesses, Gurus, Hard Core Bullies, Impulsive People, Negative Ned's or Nancy's, Passive-Aggressive People, The Attention Seekers, Socialized Psychopaths or Sociopaths. The Babies, The Non-Players and The Wannabe's.

There are other Difficult Personality Styles, but I tried to focus on the types of people who are not incarcerated and have not been diagnosed with a Personality Disorder or a Difficult Personality Type. There are a lot of people who we interact with every day who have extreme personalities and, unfortunately, we must learn how to deal with them.

Because of the research I have done, I have learned that a lot of the people who frequently behave badly, do so, because their brains have areas that are over-active and way out of the normal range.

My husband and I have had to find ways to earn money outside of our jobs. Neither one of us has ever had a job that we really wanted to keep. Neither one of us has ever felt like we were appreciated by our employers. He and I have found ways to earn money outside of our jobs. We are both anxious to never need to have an employer again.

PEOPLE GET INTERRUPTED, BULLIED AND DUMPED-ON MUCH MORE NOW, THAN EVER BEFORE

"At the beginning of the school year; you must be very mean in order to gain control of the class; you can always lighten-up as the year progresses," she said to me.

I was a new Religious Education Teacher. I was going to be teaching the 6th Grade Class. I am not a mean person. This Seasoned Religious Education Teacher was telling me, "You will must be mean." When she spoke to me she seemed like she was a machine who did not care about anyone, I thought. I did not believe in what she was telling me at all. In fact, I despised Teachers who acted the way she did. If I were a student in her class, I would have been mad any time I had to sit in her class. I would have been thinking, 'If I were your daughter, I'd be trying to move out of your house as fast as I could.' I would not be able to concentrate well while I was sitting in her class. Now, that I am older, I understand that there are other people who are capable of being treated the way she treated people and recover from it quickly. That lady spoke to me 30 some years ago and I can still remember that conversation well.

I was not about to be mean to every student because a few of the students were not well-behaved. As soon as she spoke those words to me; I was not interested in communicating with her anymore. I had been the student who got into a bad mood anytime someone was mean to me and that bad mood I got into always lingered. I am completely aware that mean teachers do permanent damage to the Sensitive Students in their classes. I have never understood why so many people have the attitude that everyone should be treated horribly because some people will not do what they are supposed to do unless you are mean to them.

Since that day, I have also had a 2nd job teaching an Engineering class after school. I discovered that it is much more difficult to get a classroom that is filled with kids to be quiet and listen to you at the end of the day; after they have been sitting in classrooms all day long and they know that most of the teachers have gone home for the day. I understood what that Seasoned Teacher had told me because there were a few kids in one of my after-school classes that were so noisy, no one in the classroom could even hear me speak. I still thought it was a horrible idea, however, to be mean to every kid in the class, to be able to get the 3 rowdy ones to be quiet. There were times when I asked the lady who was monitoring the halls to hang-out with the rowdy kids for a short while. When those kids were out of the classroom; teaching this class was easy.

Recently, I have been encountering a man frequently when I have been working. He is very sociable, and he likes to talk to lots of females. When he first started trying to interact with me, he was being nice to me, and he was complimentary. I noticed, however, that he makes negative and rude comments about other people and to other people. A couple of weeks ago, I saw him, and he made a very negative comment about me, in front of 3 other people. I knew that if he keeps making negative comments about me, I will not be able to handle that well. I saw him again about a week ago. When I saw him, I told him, "I only want to talk to you if you have positive things to say." He responded, "I'll be positively negative," then he chuckled. He acted like I was kidding around. I was not kidding. He thought he was being funny.

I was needing to let him know that I will not be handle it if he makes negative comments about me every time he sees me. If he continues to make negative comments about me, I will do something to get that behavior stopped. Perhaps the next time, I will need to have a more thorough conversation with him and hopefully he will then understand that I really cannot handle people treating me negatively. He wants to be friends with me, but he really does not have any idea what kind of communication he should have with me. If there was a BULLY BOX in the building where he works I would write a note about him and drop it in the BULLY BOX. That would be easier for me to do than to have a long conversation with him about how I have a sensitive personality, I get my feelings hurt easily and I cry easily. I really do not want to must explain that to him repeatedly. I think by the time people are adults they should automatically be nice to other people, but they are not always.

A couple of months ago, I received a friend request on Facebook from a guy who I did not know. I assumed he was an OK guy because Facebook told me he was Facebook friends with one of my guy friends on Facebook. I assumed that my guy friend, who I have known for more than 30 years, was only Facebook friends with decent people. That same day, I started getting some weird messages from this guy. I needed to leave the house for something. I just ignored his messages. The next morning, I received a message through Facebook from a girl, who I went to grade school with. She told me she had received a friend request from this same guy and some of her other female Facebook friends were receiving friend requests from this guy. She told me that ever since her husband passed away, a lot of creepy guys had hit on her, and she thought this guy seemed creepy.

I unfriended this guy right away, but I thought it was strange that Facebook did not give me any options to report this guy. Or else, Facebook does give options to report people like this, and I do not know how to do it. After that incident happened, I started thinking, 'When I get weird e-mails, I can highlight those e-mails, then click on 'spam.' I think all the social media sights should give us lots of different options of buttons to push when we suspect someone has bad intentions. I think I should have had a button to click-on that said something like, 'I suspect this person has bad intentions,' or 'This person is trying to become friends with all my female friends all-of-a-sudden,' or 'This person seems to be preying on older women,' or 'This person is from another country and doesn't have pictures or information on their site, yet, they are asking to be friends with me.'

Many times, I have gone to Doctor's offices for Doctor appointments and there was someone there who tried to bully me into paying for my services at once. I have excellent credit. I have always paid all my bills on time. No one in this entire world has any good reason to bully me about paying for services, yet, it has happened to me many times because other people cannot be trusted. Every time that happens to me, I change Doctors and I send an e-mail to the new Doctors office that clearly explains to them that if they try to bully me. I will never return to their office.

Yesterday morning, I had to go to a Doctor's Office as a new patient. As the Nurse was typing my information into the computer, he asked me if I have been physically abused or bullied at home. He told me if I have any information like that I need to share, I can talk to the people at this office about it. He told me they keep that kind of information confidential. I thought, that is a different approach about this topic than I have heard in the past. In the past I have heard people in Doctor's Offices say they are supposed to look for bruises and abnormal injuries on people and report that information to authorities. This guy told me yesterday that they would not report that kind of information to authorities. I thought someone must have realized that victims sometimes need to have someone to talk to about abuse. Perhaps people are finally figuring out that if you report violence to authorities, which can sometimes cause more violence.

Recently, I was listening to a radio station and one of those DJ's announced, Doctor's will be able to officially prescribe patients with work-related burnout starting on some date during 2021. Once this new law is enacted, Doctor's will legally be able to prescribe patients with things that will help them recover from being over-worked and overly stressed out. The same DJ reported that lots of people are getting burned-out because their employers are pestering them even when they are not at work. Many employees these days are expected to respond to phone calls, text messages and e-mails from their employers when they are not even on-the-clock.

I am thinking that in the future, there will be more laws that allow people to be able to safely talk about violence they have been enduring without reporting it. I think enabling victims to be able to talk about this sort of thing in a safe environment is a step in the right direction.

Almost every time I am leaving our local Walmart, someone, checks my receipt to make sure I am not trying to steal a gallon of milk, or some other item. Since I have been shopping at this same Walmart for more than 10 years, I think, these people, who check my receipts, should know by now, that I am not a thief. They all have security cameras pointing at them, however, and they could get into trouble if they treat me like I am decent person who is appreciated. Instead, they are supposed to treat me like I am probably a criminal.

Even though we are on the donotcall.gov list; almost every day, phone solicitors call us and try to sell us items in which we are not interested. I can log onto donotcall.gov and report the unwanted phone calls but I need to personally tell those people to not call us again before I can report them. Even though I do that, new phone solicitors call us all the time.

Frequently, I go to a school that is near where I live, so I can exercise on the track early in the morning. One time, when I was the only one on the track and my car was the only car in the parking lot, a police car pulled into the lot and parked there for a while. A few minutes later, that female Police Officer got out of her squad car and yelled at me, "Is this car yours?" I responded, "Yes." She responded, "OK, I am just checking." One week later, I was once again exercising on the same track and my car was the only car in the parking lot. The same Police Officer pulled into the parking lot and parked behind my car. A few minutes later, she drove away. There has been a couple more instances when I was exercising on this same track and my same car was parked in this same lot and that same Police Officer pulled into this parking lot and parked there for a while.

I keep thinking, "This is how my tax dollars are getting spent?" A Police Officer keeps trying to make sure I am not a low-life scumbag." She should recognize my car by now.

It seems like there are lots of instances these days when I must spend a lot of time and effort proving to people that I am not a bad person.

I also must spend a lot of time and effort trying to make sure the bad guys do not take advantage of me. A lot of those bad guys try to call our home and get us to give them access to our computer and they try to get us to give them our personal information over the phone. I have called the Police several times to report phone scammers. One of those Police Officers told me those people are very hard to catch because they use drop phones. As soon as they know a Police Officer is trying to find them; they just start using a different phone #.

A few days ago, I accidentally typed, 'eFacebook.com.' Immediately, I received warning signs on my computer that were blinking, and I heard sirens. The message on my screen said, "You have a virus on your computer. Do not shut your computer off. Call this phone # right now." I know this is a scam and the people who answer that phone # are criminals who want to gain access to my computer and steal my information. I am sure a lot of people do not know that, and they do call that phone #. How could I have reported that incident? Should I have called the police. I do not think our local police would handle that sort of a crime. Who does handle that sort of a crime? I do not even know who I should contact to try to get that scam stopped. Even if they were reported. They would probably be able to continue doing what they are doing by changing eFacebook.com to fFacebook.com or another similar web address, to cause people to receive their scam webpage. I think there will be more of these scams happening in the future unless we all learn effective ways to block these kinds of messages and people are able to identify the criminals and those criminals must pay consequences. Technology has also made it easy for the people who are trying to take advantage of other people to pester enormous #'s of people frequently. Once the bad guys build an extremely large list of potential victims, they can prey on enormous groups of people by typing some basic stuff on a keyboard, then clicking 'SEND.'

Another day recently, I was driving my car and I heard a DJ on one of the radio stations I listen to say, "According to a recent survey, about 84% of Americans report that they feel angry." That DJ also reported, "The results from this survey were compared with the results from a similar survey that was taken a generation ago." The people who conducted this survey stated people are angrier now than they used to be.

There has always been crime and bad guys but a generation ago, most people were not aware of most of the crime and the bad guys. People did not worry about that kind of stuff then, nearly as much as they do now. Also, a generation ago, the criminals did not have as many ways they could prey-on their victims. All the technology we must day has made it easier for bullies and criminals to take advantage of and try to penetrate their victims. Many bullies have learned it is easy to bully someone online and do it without their victim ever discovering who is mentally terrorizing them. Bullies have reported it is easier for them to bully online than in person.

In our home, our microwave beeps at us if we do not rush to get our food out of it as soon as it has stopped heating our food. My husband's insulin pump beeps at him frequently. Our phones beep at us. Our doorbell gets rung, our smoke detectors start beeping even if our home gets to be too hot inside. A lot more gadgets beep at us now, than ever before. All those interruptions are annoying.

One time, about a year ago, I was at the returns counter at a Walmart and there was an old lady at the counter in front of me. She wanted to wire some money to someone in Mexico. The lady behind the counter told her she could not let her do that because there has been an unbelievable # of instances where scam artists have convinced people to wire money to a great cause in Mexico, but the thieves are convincing these people to wire money to their personal accounts.

We are all getting pestered much more frequently now, than we ever did in the past. We get pestered when we are at home. We get pestered when we shop. We get pestered when we go to Doctor's offices. I have not even started talking about all the aggressive drivers on the road who like to get really close to your bumper, blow their horn at you and wave their hands in the air to let you know they are completely disgusted with you, even though you are driving the speed limit and following the rules of the road.

Another example of people not caring about how their actions impact others would be: Many times, when I have taken my car to a repair shop. When I picked my car up, it smelled like B.O. and cigarette smoke. My car stunk so bad, I had to keep the windows rolled down when I was driving home, and I had to spend a couple of hours scrubbing everything inside my car that is carpet or fabric with very soapy water. I also placed air fresheners inside my car. I do not know if this sort of behavior is worse now than it was in the past, but it is one more example of things that have happened to me that have really gotten on my nerves.

I have noticed that on a scale from $0 - 10$. Many of the people who go out of their way to make me angry would accomplish making me angry if they did all their rude antics at a level 2 or 3. Many of these evil doers think they need to crank-up all their rude behaviors to a level 10. Watching the bullies behave badly at level 10 is way more than I can handle. I must get away from the people who act that way.

I have also noticed that these people who try to behave rudely at a level 10 all the time; tend to be the people who do not have any close friends and they have a hard time with getting anyone to spend any time with them. They all seem to think they can order people around and everyone must do whatever they tell them to do. They never seem to figure-out, people would do a lot more for them if they were nice.

HOW COMMON IS BULLYING?

Even though bullying is against the law in most states; it has been becoming a

bigger problem over time.

Bullying should be reported to the Police. People need to start reporting it.

About 13 million people are bullied every year.

About 1 in 3 kids in school get bullied.

Bullying is a major public health problem. It causes people to have a lot of physical health issues, depression, anxiety and sometimes people commit suicide because they have been bullied relentlessly for a long time.

Bullying laws are posted at: stopbullying.gov

Online Counseling is available at www.betterhelp.com/start/. There are more than 2,000 licensed Counselors at that site. These Counselors are available 24 hours a day, 7 days a week. If you prefer to see a Counselor in person. This site can help you find a Counselor near you.

WHAT CAN BE DONE TO REDUCE BULLYING IN THE FUTURE?

Anti-bullying needs to be taught to all children at a very young age. Everyone is born with an individual personality type. Some people are born with a personality type that is much more likely to be domineering. The people who have a more domineering personality type need to be taught at a very young age; how much damage they do to people when they abuse them physically or verbally.

Every school needs to have programs that teach all the children not to bully and what types of effects bullying has on people.

Every school needs to help raise awareness about how much damage bullying does to our society.

Police Officers need to help the people who are being bullied. Unfortunately, sometimes, they do not want to spend their time doing this. Sometimes Police Officers do not get involved with helping people who are being bullied because there are not laws in place in their state that allows them to help the victims of bullies. New laws need to be created that will allow Police Officers to help victims of bullies everywhere.

Reports have shown that about 60% of bullies are people who were physically, mentally or sexually abused by someone within the homes they grew-up in. Obviously, things need to be done to minimize the amount of abuse that happens within homes.

Experts believe that if the natural aggression toddlers automatically have is not handled properly by the time they are 5 years old, those children will be more likely to become bullies. Perhaps communities should offer free programs to parents that can help them learn proper parenting skills.

Bullying is a major public health problem, and everyone needs to realize that it is.

About 13 million people are bullied every year. About 3 million kids are bullied at schools each year.

Everyone needs to help raise awareness about how common bullying is and how damaging it is.

Everyone needs to help reduce all the bullying that occurs within our society.

Everyone should be taught that bullying is a cowardly act.

Everyone should be taught that some people bully so much that they never form any close relationships with any other human beings.

Everyone should be taught that bullies will keep bullying until they are forced to stop. The more they get away with bullying; the more they feel empowered to bully. If no one tries to stop them they will most likely get worse. That is one of the reasons all the non-bullies need to learn how to stop the bullies.

Everyone needs to be aware that bullying is illegal in most States and bullying should be reported to the Police.

Everyone should be taught that everyone has their own crosses to bear. Everyone has challenges and hardships during their lives. No one has an easy life. You never know what kind of ordeals people may be enduring. It does not make any sense to try to dump on other people. You may be dumping on people who really cannot handle having any more hardships dumped on them.

SOME OF THE BAD THINGS BULLYING CAUSES ARE:

Lots of kids stay home from school

Lots of kids become withdrawn

Lots of kids tend to become aggressive toward their younger siblings or other relatives.

Lots of people suffer with health issues, severe anxiety, severe depression or sometimes even suicide.

SENSITIVE PEOPLE AND POSITIVE REINFORCEMENT COMPARED WITH NEGATIVE REINFORCEMENT

Childcare experts agree that children should be raised with dramatically more positive reinforcement than negative reinforcement. A common belief is that infants and young children should receive a ratio of about 4:1 positive reinforcement compared with negative reinforcement. These experts also agree that some negative reinforcement is necessary. If a child is raised with only positive reinforcement; they may develop unrealistic opinions of themselves. They may think they are more capable of accomplishing things than they really are. They may be unprepared to eventually live in the real world as a competent adult. When a child receives dramatically more negative reinforcement than positive reinforcement; however, they will likely become resentful and develop lots of negative feelings toward the person or people who are constantly sending negative reinforcement their way.

Not all children should be parented the same way. Each child has a different personality. Some children are difficult to parent; they dramatically resist their parent's requests. Some children are easy to parent. Those children cooperate with their parent's requests, without questioning them. Some children are easy to parent some of the time and not easy to parent other times.

Doctor Phil is a firm believer that parents should figure-out what each child's currency is and remove that currency any time that child is not cooperating. For example, one child's currency may be their play dates or their phone. The belief is that forcing that child to do without the privileges they love so much will encourage that child to suddenly do the behavior the parent wants that child to do.

Another child may suddenly be motivated to cooperate with their parents if their television watching privileges are suddenly removed.

Some experts say negative reinforcement tends to be only effective in the short-run and if too much negative reinforcement is used, it stops working completely and your subjects may turn against you. These same experts believe negative reinforcement is effective when you use it to initially get someone to change their behavior. You should follow-it-up by using lots of positive reinforcement to attempt to reinforce the new behaviors.

Some children will only cooperate with their parents for a short period of time, then, they will quickly return to their old behaviors once, no one is forcing them to behave.

Childcare experts say parents should not be overly strict. They should not expect their children to be perfect. They also say parents should not be helicopter parents who try to make sure their children never endure any challenges or hardships. Parents also should not be so lackadaisical about rules and enforcing rules that their children are allowed to do whatever they want. The consensus among childcare experts is that parents should try to be in the middle of being too strict and too lenient when they are parenting their children. They also say that if parents are too lenient or too strict, their children will likely rebel around the age they start to enter puberty.

The reason I am writing about this topic is because there are categories of children who do not fit the typical mold. Those children should be parented very differently from how typical children are parented. Lots of parents never figure-out that the emotional children need to be parented very differently from how typical children are parented. If you try to parent emotional children the same way you parent non-emotional children, you will fail, miserably.

Some people are born dramatically more emotional than other people. They are wired that way and they cannot be unemotional. Artistic people tend to be dramatically more emotional than non-artistic people. If you are more emotional than most of the people you meet; there is a strong likelihood that you are gifted artistically. If you are extremely artistic and you are introverted. You probably have lots of talents that most people do not even know you have. You may not even realize you are artistically gifted.

In Hollywood, most of the actors and actresses who play mean characters tend to be people who are nice in real life. Artistic people tend to have a wide range of emotions in their repertoire. They tend to have higher highs and lower lows than non-artistic people. Lots of non-artistic people have a very simple emotional make-up compared to artistic people. They may feel happy, sad, mad, tired, hungry, sleepy and that is about the full range of emotions they ever feel. The artistic people tend to experience a very large range of emotions that can change very quickly. These people tend to be very good actors and actresses. Jack Benny is a comedian who frequently did comedy routines that implied he was a very cheap and thrifty. In real life, he was a very generous man.

When people are emotionally wired. They do not handle negative reinforcement well at all. If they hear negative comments made about them on a regular basis; they may become furious. All their creative juices stop flowing and they are not interested in doing anything for the people who have been treating them badly. When artistic people are complimented and appreciated, suddenly, they feel elated, and they are extremely motivated to do things for the person who complimented them.

Unfortunately, our society in the United States tends to use dramatically more negative reinforcement, than positive reinforcement. Even though people are supposed to work so they can live; our society tries to force people to live so they can work. Studies have been done that have proven, people are much more productive and happier when they work 4, 8-hour days each week, then when they work 5, 8-hour days each week; yet most employers refuse to try anything like that. Many cultures realize that people need down-time. People need Siestas. They need to spend time doing the things they love to do to be happy people. The United States does not embrace that lifestyle.

Artistic people have a hard time dealing with this culture because everywhere they go, they have negative vibes dumped on them. Even when they knock-themselves-out for people; lots of people in our society never mention any of the 99 things that person did well. Instead, they try to find something that person did incorrectly, then, criticize them for the one thing they did not do perfectly. Artistic people tend to like to create and build things. The non-artistic people frequently do not appreciate the artistic people. The artistic people, then become, unmotivated to do anything for the unappreciative people.

Sometimes there are aggressive salespeople who stand inside of stores, and they try to bully me into talking to them. Anytime I see them; I do not walk near them. When I do accidentally get close to them; they, typically put me in a bad mood. Most of them do not say, "Oh, OK" after I tell them I am not interested in buying what they are selling. Most of them try to argue with me immediately and I hate that. Once I have said no, my answer is 'NO'." A lot of people have aggressive personalities and they do not hesitate to be aggressive with everyone they encounter. I am always surprised when I witness that because I do not understand why anyone would want to do anything for those kind of people. I always want to get away from those kind of people immediately. I am always pleased when I encounter nice people.

Lots of people believe that nice bosses get stepped-on, and an effective boss cannot be nice to their employees. I am astonished by how many bad bosses I have encountered during my lifetime. I understand that some people need to be treated more roughly than others to be motivated to do the things they are supposed to do. Lots of bosses, however, are mean to all their employees and treat everyone roughly. Lots of those bosses are dramatically resented by their employees and they never learn to behave any differently. Many of those bosses seem to think their management style is the best one and they have absolutely no desire to change their management style. Even when those bosses cause profits to take a dive and employee turnover to reach an all-time high; those bosses tend to be left in charge. I am always surprised by how frequently people do not change their behaviors when their behaviors are not giving them the results they want.

Anyway, during my lifetime, lots of people have hurt my feelings so badly that it has taken me weeks, months and sometimes years to recover from the damage they have done to me.

Lots of people get bullied every day. Most of the time, bullies bully when there is an audience around. I want to encourage people to help other people who are being bullied. Some of those victims are unable to protect themselves and they need your help. There are lots of phone #s you can call listed near the end of this book, which can help you figure-out who you should call to report bullies.

Bullies tend to be people who have a giant ego. They tend to be people who think they are entitled. They are selfish and greedy. They think they should have more than everyone else when it comes to everything. They enjoy hurting other people. They dramatically lack empathy and compassion. Since they really do not care about how they make other people feel; it is easy for them to hurt other people. They do not stop their bad behaviors until someone forces them to. We all need to try to help stop the bullying that goes on in this world.

I think this World would be a much nicer place if adults could start treating other people with a much closer ratio of 4:1 positive feedback versus negative feedback. Most people do not do that. Most people spew a lot more negative comments about other people than positive comments. Lots of people never compliment or encourage other people at all. We all encounter lots of different people during our lifetimes. If we could all start treating other people much more positively; we would dramatically improve this World.

WHAT GOES ON INSIDE THE BRAIN OF A BULLY?

Studies have been done that involved brain MRI's. People who bully others were tested and people who have been bullied were tested.

In all the brain MRI's done on the bullies, the testing proved that all the bullies truly enjoy harming others. Harming others made them feel good.

In all the brain MRI's done on the victims of bullies, the testing proved that the area of their brains that proves they have compassion and empathy was very active.

Lots of people believe bully's bully because they have been bullied, they have an inferiority complex, they did not grow-up in a decent home environment. Lots of people think that if those people had experienced different circumstances during their lifetimes, they would not have become aggressive people.

There are studies, however, that have proved, many of the people who bully, are people who have an inflated ego. They are people who think they are entitled. They are selfish and greedy. They think they are more important than other people. They think they should have more of everything than other people have. They are constantly bragging about themselves, trying to prove they are more important than other people and feed their egos. They never hesitate to hurt other people if hurting other people helps them get more of what they want. They tend to be people who have a lower-than-normal amount of compassion or empathy for other people if they have any at all. Brain MRI's done on bullies have proved this is true. Bullies brains are wired very differently than the brains of people who are not bullies.

When bullies hurt other people, they get an adrenaline rush. People who have compassion and empathy for other people feel bad if they realize they have hurt someone else.

SOMETIMES BOSSES BULLY THEIR EMPLOYEES

Some Bosses have a very arrogant attitude toward their employees. One that I am thinking of was in her mid-40's. She had no history of having any stable relationships with any man or woman ever. No one understood how she could be so self-confident. My research has taught me that quite often the people who act like they are self-confident are acting that way because they are trying to cover-up their feelings of inferiority.

The people who worked for her frequently thought, 'If she would be nice to her employees; they would be a lot more interested in doing things for her.' 'If she would complement us or appreciate us; we would all get along much better and we would all be in a much better mood'.

Unfortunately, the agenda of a bully is to make sure they make people feel miserable. She always thought her ideas regarding how everything should be done were right and everyone else's ideas were wrong; even though, she dramatically lacked common sense. It is common for the people who want to oversee other people, to be the people who do not want to must do any of the work. Frequently, these bosses have never even done the job they are supposed to be Supervising.

Unfortunately, many of the people who have a cold-hearted personality type tend to get promoted in the working world. The people who have this type of personality seem to love being in-charge of and in-control of other people. Even though they usually do not have a clue regarding how to motivate people positively.

Some people do not have any remorse when they make other people feel bad. They quite-simply, do not have a conscience and they tend to act like they are 2 years old their entire lives.

I have also learned that some people are born with an extreme personality type. Those people will always have trouble with having decent relationships with other people. Their brains do not allow them to be mentally flexible. They have rigid personalities.

Some people have so much OCD that they cannot adapt to other people's wants and needs.

The people who personalities are typically willing to fight other people significantly harder than other people are willing to fight them. Many people who have a difficult personality type are Narcissists. Narcissists fight to win.

The Boss I am thinking of has never been married and she has rarely had a second date. On-lookers always think, she should figure-out there is something wrong with her behaviors. Quite the contrary. She thinks her behaviors are perfect and all the guys do not know what they are missing out on.

If you must work for someone who makes you feel miserable all the time; is there anything you can do to create a more tolerable work environment for yourself?

Most of the time; finding a different job is not an option. If it is and you do change jobs, you might end-up having to work for someone else who also has a difficult personality.

If your best option is to keep working at the same place; there are a few things you can do to hopefully improve your situation.

Visit your State's Labor Laws and review them. Start secretly recording or documenting the things your Boss does incorrectly. It is very important that no one besides you knows you are doing this. Luckily, however, Toxic Bosses typically break a lot of rules. You may be able to find lots of examples when they forced an employee to work more consecutive days than is legally allowed in your state. Perhaps this Boss has been forcing employees to work too long without taking any breaks. Perhaps this Boss has been demanding the employees work 12 hours or more. Some of these Toxic Bosses expect their employees to work a regular daytime shift, then, keep working over-night too. Does this Boss follow all OSHA's laws? It will probably be easy for you to find things that this Boss is doing that they should not be doing.

Once you have accumulated a nice sized list of your Bosses illegal acts; find a place where you can type a letter explaining these offenses. Of course, do not sign this document. Go ahead and wear some gloves before you pull this document off the printer, collect some envelopes and stamps. Keep wearing these gloves until you have dumped these letters in a blue mailbox. You will be sending these letters to your States Department of Labor and OSHA. You may wish to also send a copy to your Bosses Boss. Perhaps your Bosses Boss has a Boss too. Go ahead and send one to that person too. After you do this, you should not tell anyone you did this.

You may be delightfully surprised when you discover your Boss is suddenly going to be transferring out, retiring early, or using some FMLA or a Doctor's note to take some time off. Even if your Boss does not make any of those sudden changes to her work schedule, she might start being a lot nicer all sudden.

Getting these people in trouble does tend to get their attention.

Good Luck!!!

WHEN PARENTS PRESSURE THEIR CHILDREN TO SUCCEED TOO MUCH:

When parents place too much pressure on their children to perform, those children will have negative developmental effects. Some of those adverse effects are:

Higher rates of mental illness

Self-esteem problems

Sleep deprivation

Higher risk of injuries

Increased likelihood of cheating

Refusing to participate

Depressive

Discouraging

Keeps children from having entertainment, fun and enjoyment

Affects their mental well-being

They are more likely to procrastinate or rebel

THINGS THAT HARM A CHILD'S MENTAL DEVELOPMENT ARE:

Too many rules

Over-the-top threats

The parents rules overstep parental boundaries

The parents love is conditional

The parents are not careful about the words they use

The parents do not put the time in

The parents constantly police, nag, monitor and remind their kids of things

Your child starts to leave you out and not communicate with you

Your child does not bring friends to your home

Your child is seen and not heard

Your child is all work and no play

You are the parent who restricts your child from lots more activities than other parents do

You forbid everything

You think your rules should not be questioned

Parents who use the Authoritarian Parenting Style, not the Authoritative Parenting Style

You are as cold as ice

A recent survey done in Bangladesh proved 20% of their children suffer from various mental disorders because their children have a lack of recreation.

When kids feel like they are valued according to the activities they participate in and their abilities; they will be likely to have trouble with developing their self-confidence.

If they are judged too much because of their accomplishments, their identity and ability to feel good about themselves may decline every time something they do does not go well.

Children who receive relentless pressure from their parents to succeed are about twice as likely to suffer from anxiety and depression than their less-pressured peers.

Kids need to feel like they are loved for who they uniquely are. They do not need to feel like they are only loved when they accomplish certain tasks.

WHEN PARENTS ARE TOO PERMISSIVE (PUSHOVER PARENTS)

Have no routines or limits

The parents always avoid conflict

The children use school activities and homework as an excuse to not must help-out around the home and they get away with it

When the parents try to be their kid's friend instead of their kid's parent

When parents reward their kids with technology

Studies show that kids who have parents who do not pay much attention to what they do are better-off than the kids who have helicopter parents who hover-over their children and constantly try to make sure nothing goes wrong in their kid's lives.

The kids who have lots of freedom because they have parents who do not pay much attention to what they are doing have lots of opportunities to interact with the real world and learn from those experiences. The kids who have very little experiences with the outside world because their parents protect them too much will suffer greatly because of their lack of experiences and their lack of interacting with lots of different kinds of people.

Adults do not behave perfectly, and they shouldn't expect their kids to behave perfectly.

SOMETIMES PARENTS BULLY THEIR CHILDREN

'My sister is more successful than I am, just ask my Mom.'
Unfortunately, I think a lot of people can relate to this statement.

Everyone is born with their own personality style. You cannot change someone's personality style.

Among these styles, there are introverts, extroverts, people who are not sociable, people who are sociable, people who are talkative, people who are not talkative, shy people, arrogant people, quiet people, loud people, artistic people, non-artistic people, coordinated people, un-coordinated people, people who are athletically inclined, people who are not athletically inclined, people who love to be in the spotlight, people who do not want to be in the spotlight, people who are musically inclined, people who are not musically inclined, people who tend to be conservative and cautious, people who tend to be adventurous and not cautious, people who are good at planning for the future, people who are not good at planning for the future, people who are organized, people who are not organized, people who like to be indoors, people who like to be outdoors, people who love animals, people who do not want to be around animals, people who need to be in a clean environment, people who do not care about whether or not they are in a clean environment, people who want to be very involved with Religion, people who do not want to be very involved with Religion, people who are good at cooking, people who are not good at cooking, people who insist on having a lot of leisure time in their lives, people who insist on working and being productive almost every moment they are awake, people who are healthy, people who are not healthy, people who are physically advantaged, people who are physically dis-advantaged, people who are lazy, people who are ambitious, people who have big imaginations, people who do not have an imagination at all, people who believe everyone should follow lots of rules, people who do not believe in living in a place where everyone must follow lots of rules.

Even though everyone is born a unique individual and everyone has strengths and weaknesses; it seems reasonable to me, that most people would understand that everyone in the World is supposed to be different. However, I have encountered many people who act like everyone must think and behave the same way. Those people tend to think if there are not lots of rules in place everywhere we go and if people are not forced to think and act the same, 'All heck will break loose'.

WORKPLACE BULLYING

Workplace bullying is a widespread problem that has been gaining momentum. Studies show that nearly half of all U.S. workers are affected by workplace bullying.

Also in 2017, the **Workplace Bullying Institute** found that:

• 19 percent of Americans are bullied…and another 19 percent witness it

• 61 percent of Americans are aware of abusive conduct in the workplace

• 60.4 million Americans are affected by it

• 70 percent of perpetrators are men; 60 percent of targets are women

• Hispanics are the most frequently bullied race

• 61 percent of bullies are bosses, the majority (63 percent) operate alone

• 40 percent of bullied targets are believed to suffer adverse health effects

• 29 percent of targets remain silent about their experiences

• 71 percent of employer reactions are harmful to targets

• 60 percent of coworker reactions are harmful to targets

• To stop it, 65 percent of targets lose their original jobs

• 77 percent of Americans support enacting new laws against bullying

• 46 percent report worsening of work relationships, post-Trump election

Lots of people will try to keep you from reaching your highest potential simply because they have a lack of ability to make it there themselves.

AGGRESSIVE PERSONALITIES

All the people who have aggressive personalities cause problems within their relationships with other people and with our society in general.

Most of the people who have aggressive personalities are Narcissists. There is a percentage of people, however, who act aggressively because they love behaving aggressively.

Aggressive people behave that way for many reasons. Some of those reasons are:

They seek the dominant position in any relationship or encounter.

They abhor submission. They never want anyone to act like they are in charge

of them. Even some young children are born with this mindset.

They are always ready to be at war with anyone who stands between them and

their desires.

They are ruthlessly self-advancing and do not care if they must harm others

who try to stop them.

They never hesitate to exploit, victimize or trample others when doing so helps

them get the things they want.

Satisfying their own desires is always more important to them, than the rights or needs of other people.

Aggressive people always want to maintain being in a position of advantage.

These people do not just disregard the truth, they are typically at war with the

truth.

They do not want other people to figure-out what they are doing, that would

upset the balance of power they are trying to have over you and other people.

They exercise very little control over their impulses. They lack internal brakes.

They think of life as being a combat. They think every situation they encounter

involves them winning and their opponent losing, them winning and their

opponent winning, them losing and their opponent winning or them losing

and their opponent losing. They are constantly striving to be the one who is…

winning and they love it when their opponent loses. That scenario always

helps them feel dominant. They completely detest situations where they lose

their opponent wins. That puts them in the inferior position and they never

want to be in that position.

If they sense they are about to lose at something, they will want to take opponent down with them.

CONTROLLING PERSONALITIES

These people have an extremely limited perspective. They cannot see things any differently than they do.

They think other people should never disagree with them.

They think when other people do disagree with them, the other people are wrong, stupid and/or evil.

They do not want anyone to question anything they do or say.

These are the people who are constantly trying to correct other people and run their lives.

These people are also the ones who are the least likely to do anything to improve their own behavior or lives.

They make-up universal rules and apply their rules to everyone.

Controlling people do not see themselves as controlling people.

These people are extremely set-in-their ways, and they need to have other people bend to accommodate their desires.

These people have extreme ideas about what Supervision means. They want to Supervise other people, but they do not want anyone to Supervise them.

Controlling people are likely to be very flashy and dote heavily on people when they first meet them. They try to impress people dramatically when they first meet them. They want people to need them. They want people to feel like they will never be able to leave them. Once the relationship is not new anymore, the controlling person will not dote or do much for the other person anymore, they will expect the other person to do things for them all the time.

Controlling people try to isolate other people.

They try to make sure you are not self-confident.

They get mad very quickly when you question their ideas or demands. They want you to just conform to the way they want you to behave, and they do not want you to question anything they say or do.

Controlling people are likely to be liars. They never want to admit they do not know something. They almost never respond to someone, "I do not know" to anything. They would rather tell lies and act like they do know the answer to everything. They try to act like they are an expert on every topic.

These people always want to be in a complete position of authority, power and control. They are always trying to get to the point where they can have power over other people.

They want people to idolize them.

They try to change other people. They are unable to appreciate that other people are different. They always want everyone to think and act the same way they do. They cannot comprehend that different people have vastly different likes and dislikes. They think everyone should like all the same things they like.

They love to criticize other people. They do this to try to prove they are more impressive.

The excessive criticism they do, usually stems from their extremely low self-esteem.

They do not take, 'No', for an answer. If someone tries to threaten or scare you every time you do not do something they want you to do; that is a sure sign that person has an extremely rigid and inflexible personality.

These people are extremely likely to be jealous people. They do not want the people who are in their lives to associate with other people.

They are likely to look through other people's personal information to see who else they have been communicating with.

DIFFICULT PERSONALITY TYPES

About 21 years ago, my husband and I were speaking with a Counselor. She told us some people are born with difficult personality types. She said some people have a lot of trouble with forming good relationships with other people their entire lives. Some people's personalities are so extreme that they are not capable of having normal people skills. She also said, you need to make sure you only have small doses of exposure to these types of people. You need to decide how much time you are willing to spend with them and do not spend more time with them than that. Some people will make you feel miserable any time you are in their midst. You can love someone and hate that same person at the same time. Sometimes, you must stay away from certain people for you to feel, OK.

Ever since she told us that; I have recognized many people who fit into that category and frequently those people are in positions of power. Sometimes they are people for whom you must work. How can you limit how much time you spend with those people; I have wondered? Sometimes you must spend a lot of time with those types of people. Frequently, those types of people are the ones who think they should not do anything, and other people should do lots of stuff for them all the time. They tend to be the types of people who like to boss other people around. They are full of advice; even when their personal lives are in complete shambles. They are likely to be people who have poor problem-solving skills.

ACCORDING TO DR. MARILYN MANNING, THERE ARE 7 DIFFICULT PERSONALITY TYPES.

HARD CORE BULLIES

They are hostile, abusive and intimidating. They charge like angry bulls anytime you cross them or challenge them. The people who have this personality type love to use threats and ultimatums.

An example of this personality type would be:

Bully: You will not be getting a pay increase ever again and you will not be able to

        leave this office until all your work is done. I do not care if it is midnight

        when you finally finish your work.

EGO-CENTERED PRINCESS

The people who have this personality type try to appear to know more than everyone else. They love to let everyone know they know lots of facts. They feel like they are superior to everyone else. They want everyone to think they are special. They want lots of attention all the time. They love to show-off.

An example of this personality type would be:

Bully: When I trained her; I was extremely thorough. I not only showed her what

to do, I gave her copies of the notes I have written down about this job over

the years. I trained her way better than anyone else in this building trains

anyone and she should have been able to do this job.

PASSIVE-AGGRESSIVE

People who have this personality type typically do not want to be on the center-stage. They want to be mischievous without people knowing they were the ones who did the misdeed. They like to be devious and use sarcasm. They tend to be indirect with their criticism.

An example of this personality type would be:

Bully: This person might let the air out of all 4 of the tires of someone's car

during the night when no one is watching. They might poor something

smelly into someone's locker when no one is around and there are no

security cameras in the locker room.

A BABY

The people who have this personality type like to whine, complain and act defeated. Their cup is always half empty. They often believe no one thinks they are important.

An example of this personality type would be:

Bully: "I shoveled the driveway the last time. I should not shovel it this

time. Those snowplows are just gonna dump the snow back on our

driveway anyway. It will melt in about 4 days; so, we can just drive over it for

now. I do not like to be out in the cold. I might slip and fall if I try to shovel

the driveway. You do not want that do you?"

NEGATIVE NED OR NANCY

The people who have this personality type are much worse than the people who have the baby personality type. These people love to disrupt the people who have power. These people think the way they do things is the only right way to do things. They do not adapt for anyone. People who have this personality type love to tell others, 'I told you so.' These people see what could go wrong with every issue.

An example of this personality type would be:

Bully: You must bag the lawn clippings. If you let the lawn clippings
lay on the lawn: the lawn will not look good, and the grass will not get
enough sunlight.
         You need to dump the lawn clippings on the edges of the
flower beds to
         keep the lawn from creeping into the flower beds. The lawn
clippings can
         make the grass die. You must cut the lawn at an angle;
otherwise, our
         yard will look like a bunch of retards live here. You should
always cut the
         front lawn before you cut the side yards or the back yard in
case something
         interrupts you while you are mowing. Then, hopefully you
will at least
         have the front lawn cut before you must stop mowing.

A PEOPLE PLEASER

The people who have this personality type are typically easy to like; but
can be difficult to work with because they have a lot of trouble with telling
people, 'NO.' Not only do they have trouble with telling people they cannot

do something; they may also be unable to tell people, their family, friends, co-workers or staff they cannot do something.

An example of this personality type would be:

Bully: We are going to clean this house from the top to the bottom, then we will

do some grocery shopping, then we are going to make some homemade blueberry pies, then we are going to wash the dishes, then, I will drop you off at your part time job. Next, I will pick you up and bring you home. Once

you get home, you will do your homework. Next, we will all take our baths,

get ready for bed, then say our prayers. Then we will be able to go to sleep

if we get everything done.

A NON-PLAYER

The people who have this personality type tend to be people who have hidden agendas. They do not tell other people what their true motives are. Their agenda may be very different from what everyone else in their group is trying to accomplish.

An example of this personality type would be:

Bully: For only $10.00; I will send a telegram to your loved ones and let them know where you are. This person collects $10.00 from lots of people; but never sends the telegrams. Fast talking salespeople tend to be in this category.

I read another article that places adult bullies into 4 categories. This article states that adult bullies tend to be people who have adult bodies; yet, still act like they are children. These people can become mean in an instant. These people tend to lose friends very quickly.

ATTENTION-SEEKER

The people who have this personality type tend to be people who are very narcissistic. They tend to be control freaks who are very manipulative. They are emotionally very immature. When they are challenged or held accountable, they can become violent.

These people are very careful when it comes to who they are willing to become friends with. If anyone exposes their weaknesses; they will instantly become very cold and aggressive. They are overly friendly with new targets (friends). These people tend to be overly dramatic. They tend to not solve problems in their own life and want everyone to feel sorry for them. They want to be the center of attention all the time. These people tend to make excuses for everything. They have lots of self-pity. These people can turn-on the charm when they are trying to deceive others or get other people to do things for them. These people are very demanding of others. They are easily provoked. They can claim they are the victim, and they are being bullied and harassed even when they are the ones who are doing the bullying and the harassing. These people can be very malicious. These people can and will do anything that places them in the spotlight. Their main goal is to be the center of attention all the time.

WANNABE

The people who have this personality type desperately crave respect for being a competent person even when they lack competence and professionalism. They can be very deceptive. These people are not nearly as malicious as the attention seekers.

These people tend to be chronic under-performers. They crave respect and attention even when they have not earned attention or respect. These people like to hang around with people who are accomplishing the things they wish they were accomplishing. These people are unwilling to do the work it takes to become skilled at things; yet, desperately want everyone to think they are skilled. Even though these people are not willing to place effort into learning new things; they are willing to put-forth a lot of effort into deceiving people, manipulating people and making false claims. These people are spiteful towards and despise anyone who is good at the very Profession they want to be good at; but are not competent enough or are not willing to put-forth the effort that is necessary toward becoming good at this same profession. They may be people who desire to have authority over the authorities in the Profession they wish they were a part-of and they try to criticize and condemn those authority figures because they want to get them out of their positions of power. The people who have this personality type tend to be attracted to doing jobs that allow them to condemn other people.

They are likely to become a police officer, a trade union official, an inspector, a politician or any other type of position that allows them to enforce rules and punish people. The people who have this personality type like to surround themselves with people who are brown-nosers, fellow wannabes, clones, drones and other types of butt-kissers. These people tend to object to improving things, reforming things, suggestions of change, progress or evolution even when they have no positive suggestions of their own. These people tend to oppose every suggestion, opinion, idea or contribution that comes from other people. These people are likely to steal other people's ideas and act like they were the ones who came-up with the idea. These people are emotionally immature, controlling and become easily provoked. They like to accuse people who hold them accountable as being bullies; then, they act like they are victims. These people like to make threats and demands. They may demand an apology from other people. These people like to spew empty threats. These people are easily controlled and manipulated by a superior bully, such as a sociopath.

Female wannabes are likely to surround themselves with drones of the opposite sex. These people are likely to discard their drones as soon at their drones are no longer useful to them. The people who have this personality type are likely to have affairs to gain a position of power or status.

GURU

The people who have this personality type tend to be focused on tasks. These people are confused. They are completely incapable of understanding how other people think or feel. If this person is just a Guru and does not have narcissistic or psychopath traits too, they are not likely to be malicious. They can be serial bullies, however.

The people who have this personality type can be very skilled in a narrow field of expertise. They are likely to be considered an expert. These people are likely to be able to bring lots of money or status to an organization; therefore, may be valued by employers. These people may be people who pursue agendas and do not think about how much their agendas will cost. Their desire to succeed is ruthless. These people tend to have no people skills. These people are control freaks. Most of the time, these people are males. These people strongly dislike people who are more competent than they are, people who have good people skills and anyone who starts to receive more attention than them.

Male gurus who are in a position of power may exhibit inappropriate conduct. These people tend to be aggressive and unpleasant; but not evil. These people do not always crave lots of attention; but they cannot stand it when someone starts to get more attention than they get. These people are likely to throw temper tantrums when things do not go their way. They are selfish, self-centered and thoughtless. These people are emotionally immature. They can be cold and frigid. These people tend to be intelligent people who lack common sense. Usually, these people do not hesitate to tell lies. They are likely to have rigid routines.

These people do not accept responsibility for their own behavior. They like to blame others for their inadequacies. They refuse to admit that they have any shortcomings. These people tend to be extremely neat and organized. These people tend to have stereotypical ideas regarding gender roles. These people are not likely to follow social rules. They are likely to have bad table manners. These people are typically unwilling to engage in small talk. Anytime people hold them accountable; they act like they are very confused, and they act like they have no idea why their behavior is inappropriate. These people tend to reject responsibilities that are typically part of human relationships. These people are incapable of meeting the emotional needs of others. These people tend to place work and their duties on top of everything else. These people tend to be know-it-alls and they tend to be secretive. These people are likely to be possessive of objects and sometimes they are possessive of people. They are likely to view people as objects. These people do think they are superior, and they are above laws, rules and regulations. These people are likely to use denial as a defense mechanism.

THE SOCIALIZED PSYCHOPATH OR SOCIOPATH

The people who have this personality type; desperately crave power, personal gain, gratification and survival. They are extremely manipulative, deceptive and evil. These people can be extremely malicious.

These people can be incredibly charming. It is easy for them to deceive people. These people like to distort people's perceptions and emotions. They love to use guilt and anger. They tend to outwit other people any time there is a verbal conflict. They love to become authority figures of organizations. They love to have information flow through them. These people love to deny people of things. They like to offer weak and inadequate people positions of power; so, they will be able to control and manipulate the people who are working for them. They want these people to be permanent manipulates and pawns in their game. They are also eager to get rid of people who suddenly refuse to be manipulated. Sociopaths are likely to be surrounded by people who have been controlled, manipulated and punished by the sociopath. The people who surround the sociopath tend to appear to be dysfunctional, sullen, aggressive, defensive, hostile, counter-productive and cult-like. These people tend to cause lots of personal stress among their followers, unexplained suicides, destroyed families and communities, dysfunctional organizations, destroyed businesses and ruined careers.

Sometimes it takes many years for the sociopath to be recognized as a sociopath. These people are skilled at undermining, discrediting and destroying anyone who exposes the sociopath as a wrong doer. These people are always ready to restrict the actions and rights of others. These people will negatively pursue relentlessly, anyone who tries to hold the sociopath accountable. These people love to create their own rules and laws to punish and control other people. They often recruit the Wannabee types to work as minor bullies under them. These people feel gratified when they successfully convince other people to perform negative acts for them. These people enjoy exploiting other human beings. These people tend to attack their accusers with the same thing the accusers are blaming them for. These people have no limits when it comes to how vindictive they are willing to be. Their need to control, manipulate and punish people becomes an obsession or an addiction with them. These people can say what people want to hear. They are very capable of winning people over just before they betray them, deceive them or rip-them-off. These people are pushy and extremely persuasive. These people tend to be sexually inadequate and sexually abusive. They are likely to defend anyone who is accused of inappropriate sexual activity. These people are incapable of having emotions or understanding other people's emotions. These people are incapable of understanding, initiating or sustaining intimacy.

Male sociopaths are likely to have many women thinking they are in love with him all at the same time. These people are likely to start projects but quickly lose interest in these projects. These people frequently take unnecessary and uncalculated risks, and they accept no accountability for consequences. These people are reckless and untrustworthy with money. These people are likely to steal money. These people are unreliable and untrustworthy when it comes to everything they do. They are likely to be criminals or participate in near criminal-like activity. These people tend to disrespect all rules, laws and regulations. These people are arrogant, over-confident and egotistical. These people tend to have bad eye contact. These people are callous, cold, calculating, devious, clever, cunning, ruthless and extreme. They have zero empathy. They have no conscience, remorse or guilt.

EMPATHS

Empaths are people who feel too much empathy for other people. Their moods drop down very quickly when people upset them. Their moods can also rise very quickly when someone makes them feel good. There are different types of empaths. Various types of empaths can dramatically react to certain stimuli.

EMOTIONAL EMPATHS:

This type of empath deeply feels what other people are feeling emotionally. This type of empath can easily become emotionally drained; then, need time to recover from the dramatic mood drop.

PHYSICAL EMPATHS:

This type of empath can develop physical symptoms when they spend too much time with someone who is experiencing physical ailments. They can develop fibromyalgia. They can become physically drained when they spend too much time with people who are physically sick.

ENVIRONMENTAL EMPATHS:

This type of empath can feel very uncomfortable or very elated in certain environments or situations. These people can become very attached to certain places in our natural world and may grieve dramatically if any of the places they are attached to become damaged. They can become horrified if they see trees get cut down or landscapes get destroyed. The people who are environmental empaths are likely to feel re-energized when they spend some time in nature. They are likely to be people who need to be in an indoor environment that is decorated in such a way that their surroundings lift their spirits. They will be likely to feel better if they surround themselves with pleasant scents and houseplants.

PLANT EMPATHS:

This type of empath tends to intuitively know what plants need. These people will be likely to be people who take excellent care of plants. These people will be likely to choose careers that allow them to work with plants or landscapes. These people truly enjoy spending a lot of time with trees and plants.

ANIMAL EMPATHS:

This type of empath naturally spends a lot of time with animals. They tend to be able to sense what animals need. They instinctively know how to take care of animals. They may feel they are able to telepathically communicate with animals.

INTUITIVE EMPATHS:

This type of empath can glance at a person and very quickly understand a lot about that person. These people easily know when people are lying to them. They can read the energy of other people instantly.

These type of people may need to try to spend most of their time with people who they feel comfortable around. Spending time around people who frustrate them can cause them to feel completely drained very quickly.

Being an empath is difficult. Other people can make you feel like you are completely wiped-out. Your empathic gifts and abilities, however, can help you figure-out how you can help yourself and other people.

Empaths should be very careful to not spend too much time with Narcissists. Narcissists are always trying to find people who will wait on them and cater to all their wants and needs non-stop every day, all day long. Narcissists notice when people show too much empathy or kindness toward them. When a Narcissist decides they want to lure a kind and decent person into their chaotic and un-balanced life; they may do dramatic things to try to entice that person to be a part of their life. The Narcissist will put an unbelievable amount of effort into trying to recruit someone into their world. The Narcissist will never keep-up that charm and flattery they initially used. Once they have successfully gotten their innocent victim to be trapped in their deceitful world; all or most of the charm they initially used will be gone.

Sometimes Empaths do hook-up with a Narcissists because Empaths constantly crave being appreciated. They always want people to notice that they are kind and decent people. Since Narcissists put so much effort into impressing their victims when a relationship is new; sometimes, the empaths really do feel like the Narcissist really notices their good deeds and appreciates them.

Empaths are frequently loyal people who are so used to being decent and reliable people that they find it hard to end a relationship with a Narcissist.

Empaths have a huge conscience, and they may assume everyone does. That is incorrect. Narcissists do not have much of a conscience. They do not feel guilty after they do bad things like most people do. Narcissists genuinely do not care about how they make people feel. Many Narcissists will not stop behaving badly until someone forces them to stop.

SOME OF THE THINGS EMPATHS ARE LIKELY TO DO, KNOW OR EXPERIENCE:

They do not need to have everything explained to them. There are a lot of things they 'KNOW,' without having to be trained.

Being in crowded places can overwhelm them because they tend to absorb other people's moods.

Not only are they able to sense the emotions of the people around them; they can even know when other people are having bad thoughts about them.

They may be uninterested in watching any type of violence or tragedy. They may be uninterested in watching TV or reading newspapers because watching and hearing too much bad information can make their mood drop too low.

Most of the time, they know very quickly, when anyone is lying to them.

They may develop physical ailments, aches and / or pain when they spend time around other people who are ailing.

They are likely to develop physical ailments. Those ailments might include digestive disorders, lower back problems or stomach ulcers.

They tend to always look-out for the underdog. They feel sorry for the victims of bullies.

Many people try to dump all their problems on people who appear to have a lot of compassion and empathy for other people. Over time, Empaths can get so overloaded with other people trying to dump all their problems on them, that the Empaths get completely sick of having to deal with other people.

Some Empaths experience constant fatigue. They become completely drained from all the people who try to dump-on them all the time.

Some empaths turn to addictive behaviors, like, alcohol, drugs and / or sex, to block out all the negative emotions they have absorbed from other people.

They have a natural ability to be able to help heal people, but they may turn away from doing that because they may emotionally absorb other people's problems too much.

Empaths are likely to have a vivid imagination and a creative streak. They are likely to be artistic. They may be talented singers, dancers, actors, writers or artists.

Empaths are likely to have a strong love of nature and / or animals. Their spirits can be dramatically lifted when they are out in nature or with animals.

Empaths need ALONE TIME. If they do not get to spend time by themselves frequently, they will become extremely frustrated.

Empaths are likely to doodle or daydream; if their brains are not stimulated with something they are interested in. They get bored with school, work or their home lives if their brains are not properly stimulated.

Empaths can find it close to impossible to do things they are not interested in doing. When they are forced to do things, they do not believe in. They will be likely to become extremely unhappy.

Empaths hate things and people who are fake. They constantly search for the truth.

Empaths constantly search for knowledge. They love to learn new things if they are interested in what they are learning about. They do not like to have unanswered questions.

They tend to be free spirits. They love freedom, adventure and travel.

They hate clutter. Liking the environment, they are surrounded by is very important to them. They love to be surrounded by things that are attractive.

They can be blissfully happy when they are left alone and allowed to just daydream.

They tend to despise routines, rules and people who are trying to have control over them. When people try to take away their freedom; they can feel like they have just been poisoned and debilitated.

They tend to be excellent listeners. They typically do not talk about themselves much unless they are talking to someone they feel very comfortable with. They love to learn about other people, and they genuinely care about other people.

Even though they tend to be very tolerant of other people; they detest Narcissists. They cannot stand how cruelly Narcissists treat people.

They typically do not want to purchase antiques, vintage items or second-hand anything. They know that used items can have the energy of the previous owner and they do not want to deal with that. They will even purchase brand new vehicles or homes if they are able to do that.

Animal Empaths will be likely to not eat meat or poultry. They do not like it that the animals suffered or were killed so we can eat them.

Many people get the wrong impression of an Empath. People sometimes assume the Empath is moody, quiet, shy, aloof, disconnected, unsociable and miserable. This is a very inaccurate description of the Empath. An empath needs to always 'test the waters,' before they allow themselves to get close to anyone. They are always afraid of getting hurt. They are careful to not spend time with or form relationships with people they think will be insensitive or hurt them. They always want to make sure they feel comfortable around someone before they start to open-up to them.

Since Empaths pick-up on other people's negative emotions easily, they intentionally try to avoid a lot of people and / or situations.

TRAITS EMPATHS ARE LIKELY TO HAVE:

Absorb external energy
Bottle-up their emotions
Compassionate
Dramatically affected by violence & trauma
Forgive too easily
Generous
Great listeners

Moody

Overly anxious to be likeable

Peacemakers

Proverbial Giving Tree

Quiet Achievers

Repelled by people who are overly bossy, aggressive and / or not trustworthy.

Self-sacrificing

Sensitive

They are likely to put their own wants and needs on the back burner.

Understanding

Want to be unconditionally loved

Empaths are disappointed with other people's behaviors frequently. They are always wishing the world were pleasant, fair and just. They are constantly trying to avoid having to deal with unpleasant people. They can feel elated when they are in an environment they love. However, their mood can come crashing down very quickly when they encounter someone who is mean. When they encounter nice people, they are relieved to know there are still some nice people in this world. Sometimes, they think there are way too many people in this world who treat other people harshly.

IMPULSIVE BEHAVIORS

When someone has the tendency to act uncontrollably and fast to receive an internal or an external stimuli, they are behaving impulsively. People who have impulsive tendencies are people who tend to act before they think things through. When people are impulsive, their analytical judgement is flawed. They do not think about what the consequences of their actions will be. Impulsive people typically act the way they do because they are constantly seeking some type of emotional response. These people tend to be anxious to receive rewards without putting the necessary effort into earning the rewards.

Some people have a lot of difficulty with postponing rewards for their impulses.

These are people who tend to be in a hurry all the time. They try to rush-through everything they do, and they try to rush other people too. They do not understand that people who are not impulsive are not interested in being in a hurry 24 hours a day, 7 days each week.

Impulsive behavior is closely related to neurotransmitters and the amount of dopamine someone has in their brain. These people have receptor flaws in the frontal lobe in their brain, especially in the prefrontal cortex where executive functions oversee decision making and judgement. This means, the area of the brain that oversees making decisions, takes a detour and looks for the quickest way to receive a reward without doing the necessary work. Other research has concluded impulsive behaviors can be

221

caused from underactive dopamine receptors in the middle of the brain. That area of the brain oversees one's ability to make logical decisions. These underactive receptors also explain why impulsive people the tendency can have to become depressed.

Impulsive behaviors are like drug addiction and gambling addiction because in all those instances, the individual who is behaving impulsively feels regret later, yet, they are aware that their regret will not stop them from behaving the same way again.

It is also believed that some people have an inability to plan and prepare. Their actions are so driven by their impulses that they can only think about what they want right now and those desires over-ride any other desires they may have.

People who behave impulsively tend to have low self-control. It is hard for them to not eat more, drink more, smoke more, etc. They tend to think about what they want right now, too much.

Impulsive people also have the tendency to want everything to be exciting. Excitement dictates their next move. If something is not exciting, they do not want to do it. They tend to procrastinate doing things that are not going to be fun.

These people are likely to be driven by the positive and negative emotions they are feeling at a particular moment. They are unable to use cognitive skills because that area of their brain is underdeveloped. They may, for example, enter a dollar store and spend a lot of money, then get home and realize they do not really want or need most of the stuff they just purchased. They quickly lose interest in what they purchased and figuring out what they are going to do with all that stuff may seem like a boring task. Consequently, they will let that stuff accumulate where they live. Later, they will be likely to do the same thing again because they are constantly seeking the positive emotional surge they get when they purchase these types of items.

Some more things impulsive people tend to do is, they talk on top of other people. They talk more than other people. They try to get other people to pay attention to them so much that the people they are around frequently find it hard to get a turn to talk. They tend to be so demanding that they are usually people who take, take, take and do not learn how to give.

Having an impulsive personality can include, over-eating, stealing, breaking things and self-mutilation. Sometimes impulsive people do these types of behaviors even when they know these behaviors may place them or their loved ones in danger.

Impulsive behaviors can also include sexual compulsion, internet addiction, compulsive shopping and kleptomania.

Some things that can help lower impulsive behaviors are:
1.   Take 20 deep breaths as soon as you are about to do something impulsive. Oxygen helps lower anxiety levels.

2.   Decide that every time you are about to do something impulsive, slowly count to 50 first. That time will help you get calmed-down.

3.   Keep a log of your good behaviors and your bad behaviors. This will help you be more aware of whether certain things that are happening in your life are causing you to behave better or worse.

4.   Ask a trusted friend or family member to keep an eye on you and step-in if they recognize that you need help.

5.   If you think your impulsive behaviors are affecting your personal life or career life too much; see a Counselor, a Psychotherapist, or a Cognitive Behavior Therapist. Understand that the first Counselor, Psychotherapist or Cognitive Behavior Therapist you see may not be a good fit for you. Some Counselors have book smarts but no common sense. Some of them really do not understand what you are feeling or experiencing at all.

6.   Breathe in deeply while you count to 4 and raise your arms above your head. Breath out slowly while you count to 8 and lower your arms back down. This activity helps calm hyperactivity.

7.   Close your eyes and focus your attention on each part of your body one-by-one. I used to do this with my daughter when we were trying to get her to fall asleep. She lied in her bed and closed her eyes. I would say softly, your toes are relaxed, the tops of your feet are relaxed, the arches of your feet are relaxed, your ankles are relaxed, your heels are relaxed, your shins are relaxed, your calves are relaxed, your knees are relaxed, your thighs are relaxed, your hips are relaxed, your bootie is relaxed, your belly is relaxed, your belly button is relaxed,

your rib cage is relaxed, etc. She loved it when I did this with her. It really did help her relax.

8. Take a coin and balance it on the back of your hand. See how long you can do this. This activity helps you focus on balancing the coin instead of thinking about whatever else you were thinking about.

9. Breathe as much air as you can in through your nose, then open your mouth and blow out all that air. Repeat this 30 times. This will help you feel more relaxed.

10. Neurofeedback has been proven to help calm down brainwaves; but it is an expensive procedure.

11. Make sure you do not have food sensitivities. Some people become hyperactive after they consume certain foods.

12. Make sure you do not have Sensory Integration. Sometimes people have that and they think they have issues with being impulsive. Treatment plans for Sensory Integration are different from treatment plans for Impulsivity.

13. Make sure you do not have a magnesium or zinc deficiency. Both of those deficiencies can cause people to feel impulsive.

14. Take movement breaks throughout the day. Spend some time outdoors. Both exercise and the outdoors can help people feel calmer.

15. Consider how you would feel if someone did to you; what you are about to do to them. If you would not like them treating you the way you are treating them, do not do it.

16.   When you are trying to decide whether you should or should not do something. Close your eyes and picture a traffic light. Make the light turn red. Next, think about the consequences you will experience if you do the thing you are considering doing. Once you think you have carefully thought through whether doing this would be a good idea, make the light in your head turn yellow. Think about whether you have made the correct decision. If you are sure you have made a good decision; go ahead and make the light in your head turn green. If you have decided you are about to make a bad decision, make the light turn red again.

17.   Physical massages, chiropractors and acupuncture can help people feel calmer.

Our daughter is very impulsive and impatient. Some of the things she does because she is always in a hurry are:

As soon as I hand her something clean, she gets it dirty.

She sets dirty stuff on top of clean stuff and makes sure everything is dirty all

the time.

She leaves the refrigerator door open.

She does not turn lights off.

She does not put phones back on the hook.

She interrupts other people when they are talking

She interrupts other people so much; the other people have a hard time with

being able to accomplish anything, or even have their own
thoughts.

She talks on top of other people.

She changes the subject when other people are talking.

She lets food splatter all over the inside of the microwave every
time she uses it.

She spills liquids and drops crumbs on our stove daily.

She splatters stuff on the bathroom mirror every time she goes into
the
bathroom.

She drops crumbs all over the counter, chairs, floor and inside of
the refrigerator
every day.

She fills drink cups too full, then watches them overflow and does
not learn to
not do that again.

She spills lots of stuff and does not clean-up the mess.

Every time she cooks something on the stove; she gets the food on
the outside
of the pan and spills stuff on the stove.

She spends money as soon as she gets money.

She buys stuff she really does not need.

She will not put leftovers away.

She does not put lids on containers.

She takes more food and drink than she will be able to consume.

She sets wet objects on valuable wood.

She throws garbage on the floor all over our home.

She treats the inside of everyone's vehicle like it is a garbage can.

She will not carry a full garbage bag outside to our external garbage can.

Instead, she just throws garbage on the floor next to the garbage can.

She will not change a roll of toilet paper, instead, she rests the new roll-on top   of the old roll.

Recently, I had to go to a local hospital to have another brain MRI done. My appointment was at 8:00 a.m. on a Sunday morning. I arrived at this hospital at 7:40. There were not any other people waiting to use the self-check-in monitors. I arrived extra early, because when I do that sort of thing, I am not interested in being rushed. I wanted to be able to take my time. I chose to check myself in at the monitor that was the furthest away from the lady who was behind the counter. As soon as I started checking myself in, the lady who had been behind the counter got out of her seat and rushed toward me. That alone made me mad. I did not ask for help. I hate it when people hover-over me when I am trying to do something. I hate it when people try to rush me. My concentration is the best when I am alone. I do not understand why it is so hard for a lot of people to just leave me alone. Anyway, as soon as she was invading my personal bubble; she asked me if I had been there before. I responded, "Yeah, lots of times." I tried to keep checking myself in. She asked me, "Do you need any help?" I responded, "No." She jumped in front of me anyway and started pressing buttons on the screen. She tried to prove to me that she knew how to do this, and she knew how to do it real fast. I know that some people like to do everything quickly all the time. I could tell she was one of those people. I am not one of those kind of people. I was completely aware that she was not trying to upset me. She did upset me, though. I also knew that it was going to take me a long time to be able to get out of the bad mood she put me in. It was not fair that I had told her, "I do not need any help," then, she jumped in front of me anyway. When I got home, I sent an e-mail to that hospital and told them about the experience I had just had. They called me later that day and asked me to take a telephone survey. I explained on that survey exactly what had happened to me when I was trying to get checked-in that morning. I told the telephone survey that my check-in experience had put me in a bad mood for a long time and the next time I need to get a brain MRI, I will strongly consider doing that somewhere else.

From my point of view. I am the customer. I am supposed to get a brain MRI every year for the rest of my life. I would think the Hospital would try to make sure I will want to keep taking my business to them. When I was younger, I would not have reported her. Now, I am so tired of all the people who go out of their way to make me feel bad, that, I do report them. Now, I have the attitude that that person did not care about how they made me feel. Why should I be deeply concerned about how I make them feel.

Yesterday, I made one of those Red Lobster Biscuit Mixes. I buttered a cookie sheet. I formed the dough into 10 balls. I carefully arranged the biscuits on the cookie sheet. I smashed each ball, then created a concave surface. Next, I poured the melted butter that I had mixed with the packet of seasoning on each piece of dough. I preheated the oven to 350 degrees briefly, then, I placed the cookie sheet that had the biscuit dough on it into the oven. Of course, I had other things to do, so I dashed out of the room to quickly accomplish something else. Pretty soon, I heard our smoke detectors going off. I returned to our kitchen and saw smoke everywhere.

The reason there was smoke blasting from our oven was because someone had spilled something inside our oven and did not clean it up. It was some kind of juice. I keep an oven liner in our oven, so if anything like that happens, I can change oven liners instead of having to clean the inside of the oven. Whoever spilled something inside our oven managed to spill it so far to the side of the oven that the juice puddled under the oven liner. Both my husband and my daughter told me they did not spill anything inside our oven.

So, this morning, I had to spend quite-a-bit of time cleaning the inside of our oven again. This sort of thing has happened to me many times before. Every time this sort of thing happens; I clean the oven again. I was never able to finish baking the biscuits yesterday.

I know some of you are reading this and you are thinking. That sort of thing would never happen in my house, you must not be training your husband and your child to behave properly. You did not teach your child to clean-up after herself. This situation is all your fault. You could have prevented that from happening.

All you people who like to condemn other people before you even know all the facts can stop your bad-mouthing right now. I have spent an enormous amount of time trying to teach my daughter to clean-up after herself. I have spent an enormous amount of time trying to teach my husband to clean-up after himself.

My daughter has been improving. She has been learning how to clean-up after herself gradually over time. Cleaning-up after herself is not something that has been easy for her to learn but she has been getting better at it and I have hope that one day, she will get to the point where she will clean-up all the messes she makes right away. She is not there yet. I know that I must choose the battles I have with her. I cannot have fights with her about everything she does that I do not like. She is wired so differently from how I am wired that she and I are never going to act or think alike. I do not expect her to act or think like I do. I want her to become the best person she can be. For her be become the best person she can be I need to make sure I do not complain to her about everything she does all day long, day after day, year after year. She would not be able to be a happy person if I harped-on everything she does that I do not like. As of right now, she is a happy girl.

Unbelievably, my husband is much better at cleaning-up after himself than he used to be. When I first married him, he used to check his blood sugar frequently though out the day. He is a Type 1 Diabetic. He checks his blood sugar at lots of different locations inside our home. Sometimes he takes his shirt off when he does this. He used to throw his shirt down wherever he was when he checked his blood sugar. He used to smear blood on lots of surfaces when he checked his blood sugar. We had not been married very long when I told him, I was only going to wash the dirty clothes of his that I find in the laundry basket. About 3 weeks later, he did not have any underpants that he could wear. He was notable to wear his favorite pants or shirts. He did not even know where he could find his favorite pants or shirts. He finally did learn how to throw dirty clothes in the laundry basket, but it took a while. I did get him to stop smearing blood on surfaces every time he checked his blood sugar. He, however, will never be good at doing domestic chores. That is not one of the talents that he has, and I understand that.

I do not know who spilled a lot of juice inside our oven and did not clean-it-up, but I think my daughter will be more careful about not doing that in the future. I left the over door open so, it would dry faster, and I wanted both to be reminded about what happened yesterday. I tend to be thorough when I do things. My husband is very thorough when he does things in our yard. He is not thorough when he does domestic chores. Our daughter is not thorough when she does anything. She is one of those people who tries to do everything, including homework, fast. That is how she is wired. I am trying to concentrate on helping her learn how she can develop the talents she has. I want her to be the best person she can become. For me to do that, I must help her figure-out what her natural talents are. I need to help her figure out what kind of things she loves to do that make her feel happy. I need to help her figure out what kind of a career she should be trying to obtain that will allow her to not hate going to work every day. I think if I spent a lot of time criticizing her because she is not good at cleaning-up after herself, that would just make her mad and it would hurt the relationship I have with her.

One of the reasons dealing with impulsive people is frustrating is because they constantly interrupt everything you do. They are not capable of leaving you alone. They are not capable of believing you will make competent decisions.

NARCISSISTIC PERSONALITY DISORDER (NPD)

These are the people who constantly try to fix other people's problems; but they do not try to fix their own problems. They are extremely self-centered. They care very little about people other than themselves. They have an exaggerated sense of how important they are. These people have strong tendencies to take advantage of other people to satisfy their own goals. They tend to have little or no empathy for other people. Sometimes their inflated ego is their attempt to cover-up their low self-esteem or their inability to admit they have failed at anything. It is common for people who have Narcissistic Personality Disorder to not recognize they have a problem, consequently, experts who try to study them, have a hard time finding people who are willing to participate in their study.

People who have NPD constantly need admiration from others. They also have a need to surround themselves with people who they think are powerful and special. NPD is one of the most difficult conditions to treat. People who have it really struggle with seeing other people's viewpoints.

Narcissists tend to react very quickly with violence when they feel threatened in any way. They can be very viscous. They react negatively any time they think their superiority role is being threatened. They want to be the dominant one in any relationship all the time. They always need to feel like they oversee everyone else. They are not interested in being anyone is equal, and they are not interested in being subservient to anyone.

They constantly fear being abandoned. They desperately need to have people admire them, do things for them and treat them like they are important. They do not want any of their regular people to leave them, ever.

All narcissists are hypocrites. They pretend to have morals and values, that they really do not possess. Behind closed doors, they lie, insult, criticize, disrespect and abuse. They believe they can do and say whatever they want but how dare you say anything back to them or criticize them. They have a different set of rules for other people, than they do for themselves. They do not follow any of the rules they place on other people. They do not practice what they preach.

They love to interrupt people.

They love to waste other people's time.

They frequently waste other people's time with trivial and unimportant things to do.

They love to fight and argue.

It is very difficult to have a conversation with them because they are not really interested in listening to what anyone else has to say. If you try to tell them a story, they will immediately try to tell you a story that they think is bigger and better than your story.

They love to win.

The only time they ever cry is if someone hurts their feelings.

They love to be in charge and make all the decisions.

They constantly try to fix other people, but they do not try to fix themselves.

They think other people should follow lots of rules.

They think they should not follow any rules.

They love to be in the spotlight.

They think they are more important than other people.

They think they should have more than their share of everything.

They are materialistic.

They think other people are materialistic.

They think they can bribe anyone because they think everyone else is as obsessed with money as much as they are.

They are moody.

They are extremely selfish and greedy.

They are heartless.

They do not have remorse after they do things they should not have done.

They do not learn from their mistakes.

They treat people very harshly and have no clue that all their negativity causes

them to lose friends and gain enemies.

When other people become upset with them, they are clueless. They never

comprehend they caused the other person to get upset. They always think there is something wrong with the other person.

Narcissists do not think of their children as separate people. They think their children are extensions of themselves. They expect their children to have no wants and needs of their own. They expect their children to accomplish all the things they wished they could have accomplished themselves. Children of extreme Narcissists are extremely likely to be adversely affected. Those children will be likely to feel unloved, insecure and lack confidence. They will be likely to be constantly seeking approval and validation. Their Narcissistic parent was incapable of really loving their child or seeing their child as a separate person.

Healthy parenting involves loving and accepting your child just the way they are. Healthy parenting involves helping your child celebrate all the things about them that are unique and helping them develop all their individual talents. This helps the child learn to love who they are. Healthy parenting involves nurturing your child so he can become the best possible version of himself.

A narcissistic parent thinks of their children as their property. A narcissistic parent typically sees their children as a nuisance and/or they constantly try to figure out how they can use their children to their advantage.

The child of an extreme narcissist is never appreciated for who they are.

Narcissistic parents are only capable of offering phony love to their children. Their love is shallow and conditional. This type of love never even comes close to meeting the child's needs. This child will grow-up feeling empty inside and they will be needing validation.

Children of Narcissists typically take one of two paths. They sometimes become people pleasers. They do this because they are seeking love, approval and validation. These people tend to struggle a lot during their lifetime. They are constantly trying to find other people who will help them feel good about themselves. The other path they might take is becoming a Narcissist themselves. They intentionally inflate their fragile ego and may become as grandiose as their narcissistic parent was. The children who grow up and become narcissists just like their parents were will always feel a void where their self-love should be. They will never be able to admit they have a problem and will never be able to resolve their problem. They will seek external gratification their entire lives. They will see others as a source of gratification for them or an obstacle to them receiving gratification.

People pleasers can sometimes heal and move on with their lives because they admit they have an emptiness that needs to be filled. People who become Narcissists, will spend their entire life trying to fill their emptiness with exploitative relationships, money, power and influence.

Having a low dose of Narcissism is healthy because it helps people be assertive and have a healthy self-regard. Having a high dose of it is a personality disorder.

One study that has been done categorized people who have NPD in one of three categories. Those categories are:

GRANDIOSE (THE OVERT TYPE)

This study determined the people who have this style of NPD are the ones who are the most angry and hostile. These people are not likely to admit they need help or try to receive any treatment. These people are the 'Malignant Narcissists'.

FRAGILE/VULNERABLE (COVERT TYPE)

The individuals who have this type of NPD are likely to have trouble with depression and anxiety. They are likely to have extreme mood swings that bounce back and forth between high self-esteem to low self-esteem. People who have this type of NPD are much more likely to seek help than people who have the Grandiose style of NPD. It is not always obvious that these individuals have NPD because they do not make it obvious that they are overtly grandiose or lack empathy. They do, however, feel they are superior to everyone else, and they do constantly crave recognition. They are preoccupied with their own sensitivity and their own failures.

HIGH-FUNCTIONING (EXHIBITIONIST TYPE)

These individuals tend to have Narcissistic traits. They can appear to not be Narcissists when things in their world are going well. When they experience something that is difficult; they, can suddenly behave very Narcissistically. These people can be successful, and they can maintain ego stability most of the time. However, when things in their life are not going well, they can start to behave as if they have antisocial personality disorder, which is much worse. They can also become a bit sadistic when things are not going well for them.

Historical figures who have displayed High-Functioning Narcissistic Traits have been Hitler and Stalin. These people were morbidly successful. They were able to get large volumes of people to believe in them and follow them, then, they became responsible for the slaughtering of unbelievable #'s of human lives.

Some of the people who have NPD cause some, but not a great deal of harm to other people because they are manipulative, and they have impaired or no empathy for other people. However, some of the people who have NPD can do a tremendous amount of damage to other people because they have a very serious mental health disorder. These people are completely unable to control their dysfunctional patterns of behavior. These people have dramatic emotional processing deficits.

Genetic Predisposition has been proven to be a cause for Narcissistic Personality Disorder.

Experts who have tried to determine whether neurobiology could be a cause of NPD have had a very hard time with finding people to participate in their studies, however, they have determined, that people who have NPD have deficits in the grey matter in the prefrontal areas of their brain. The lack of grey matter in the prefrontal areas of their brains causes them to have a lack of control of their emotional reactions. MRI scans on the brains of some people who have NPD show a less than normal amount of activity in the anterior insular cortex area of their brains. That is the area of the brain that causes people to have empathy. These studies did prove that these people have an inability to feel or express empathy.

It has also been proven that two parenting styles can increase the risk that the people they have been parenting will develop NPD. Those two parenting styles are: Over-indulgent parenting and Neglectful parenting. Over-indulgent parenting includes the parent praising and complimenting the child or children so much that those children develop a false belief that they are extremely deserving of praise, and it can cause them to believe they are better than other people. The parents who parent this way tend to blame people other than their child any time something goes wrong in their child's life.

Neglectful parenting is when the parents criticize and ridicule the child excessively and the child eventually decides to try to prove his parents wrong by trying to prove he is better than everyone else.

Experts have tried to study groups of people who have NPD to try to determine whether men or woman are more likely to have NPD. Once again, few people who have NPD were willing to be analyzed and studied.

The studies that were performed proved there are more men than women who have NPD.

This study also proved that it is common for a lot of teenage boys to have some NPD tendencies. This study determined that when teenage boys who have NPD tendencies have their NPD behaviors encouraged, they are likely to still have NPD tendencies when they are adults.

Studies have also determined that when people who do not learn how to handle, the setbacks and failures that all us endure, those people will be more likely to develop NPD. One of the ways people become mature adults is by learning how to become resilient when they are faced with disappointments. When young people are taught that everything that goes wrong in their life is someone else's fault. Those people might never learn how to accept responsibility for anything and can develop NPD. People who have NPD like to believe the illusion that they are too special to have any failures in their life.

Since people who have NPD are not capable of understanding how other people feel or how they make other people feel; they frequently make other people feel bad. They frequently talk to people in a condescending way. They like to assume you are inferior to them and they need to give you a lot of advice. If you realize you have been having to interact with someone who insults you every time they talk to you and acts like you must live your life the way they tell you to live your life; realize that person has a very narrow view of people and this world. They are incapable of understanding that every person is in this world is different and is supposed to be different. We are all supposed to develop our strengths and follow our own paths. We are not supposed to let someone else try to force us to live the way they think we should live. If you are a competent adult and someone is still trying to treat you like you are a child; realize that person's mind is very limited, and you should limit the amount of time you spend with that person. People like that love to bring other people down and they try to keep other people from growing.

Some of us have a personality type that is not emotionally based. Some of us respond to people and situations by thinking, analyzing or doing other things. Some of us, however, do have personality types that are emotionally based. If you were born with an emotionally based personality type, you will have a hard time with interacting with the kind of people who love to criticize you, argue with you, fight you and constantly disagree with you. Sometimes, it is impossible to get those people to understand that you cannot stand to be treated the way they have been treating you and if they can't treat you respectfully or leave you alone; you will not interact with them at all ever again. Narcissists tend to be control freaks and they are not interested in hearing that. Control freaks want to control and manipulate other people all day long every day.

Some of the Narcissists I have had to deal with; disagree with me every time I say or do anything. They always act like everything I do is wrong. They act like everything I believe in is wrong and I must think and act exactly like they do. They do not understand that I am not interested in interacting with them at all, because they insult me every time I speak to them. I have never understood how any of the people who act like that can keep relationships going with any people. Somehow, though, some, Narcissists, do find people who will put all their wants and needs on a back burner every day of their life and constantly wait-on and do things for the Narcissist. I do not understand how anyone can live that way.

I have learned that my emotions drop very quickly when I must interact with someone who treats me negatively. I am not interested in interacting with those kind of people. I am not going to intentionally spend time with people who make me feel bad. I have also learned that I cannot teach those people how to interact with other people positively. I understand that some people really do not have the ability to care about how they make other people feel. Some of those people have an under-developed brain and the area of their brains that controls empathy and compassion for other people is not fully developed. Those people will never care about how their words and actions impact other people.

I now understand that I need to get away from the people who put me in a bad mood right away. Next, I need to do things that put me in a good mood as soon as possible, so, I can get my mood back up to normal again. Listening to great music is an example of something that puts me in a great mood. In my world, how people make me feel is the most important thing there is. I try to spend time with people who put me in a good mood and avoid the people who put me in a bad mood.

OPPOSITIONAL DEFIANCE DISORDER

It is normal for children to defy their parents when they are experiencing their terrible 2's stage of their life. It is normal for them to defy their parents occasionally during the rest of their developmental years. It is not normal, however, for a child to defy their parents or other authority figures regularly during all their developmental stages.

ODD (Oppositional Defiance Disorder) describes a child who is uncooperative, defiant, hostile and annoying toward people who have authority regularly throughout their infant, toddler and teen years.

It is common for children who have ODD to also have ADHD, learning disabilities, mood disorders (such as depression) or anxiety disorders. Some children eventually develop a more serious disorder referred to as Conduct Disorder.

- ✓ Some common symptoms of ODD are:
- ✓ Throwing repeated temper tantrums
- ✓ Excessively arguing with adults
- ✓ Actively refusing to comply with requests and rules
- ✓ Deliberately trying to annoy or upset others or being easily annoyed by others.
- ✓ Blaming others for your mistakes
- ✓ Having frequent outbursts of anger or resentment
- ✓ Being spiteful and seeking revenge
- ✓ Swearing or using obscene language
- ✓ Saying mean and hateful things when upset

Children who have ODD are more likely than other children to start abusing alcohol and illegal drugs.

The cause of ODD is believed to be a combination of biological, genetic and environmental influences.

When children have ODD, they are likely to have many tantrums all in the same day. They are likely to have violent tantrums every day. Their tantrums can last for hours. Their tantrums are aggressive and violent. They are likely to hit their brothers and/or sisters, their parents, and other authority figures. They are likely to knock other kids blocks down for no reason. They are likely to punch holes in walls. These kids are likely to refuse to go to school. They are likely to steal things from other people. They will be likely to refuse to do their homework. Perhaps, they will refuse to bathe and wear clean clothes. These kids will be likely to clash with police. They are likely to push those around them to the edge of sanity.

I reviewed stories from 2 Moms of sons who had ODD. I found their stories on the internet. One of these ladies lives in England. The other Mom lives in the United States.

THE MOM AND HER SON WHO LIVE IN ENGLAND

She is the author of the book, 'THE BOY FROM HELL.'
Her name is Alison M. Thompson
This lady who lives in England claimed she had the 'Baby from hell.' She claimed she could tell this baby was different when he was only 2 weeks old. She said he was a very angry baby. She said he was always in a bad mood. She said he was very demanding, and he never slept. This Mom claimed her older daughter had a charming, easy and relaxed personality. She

said, she initially thought her son was acting very differently from his sister because he was a boy. As he became older, she realized her son acted very differently from other boys.

Once her son was in nursery school, his teacher pulled her aside and told her, the tantrums your son has are not normal tantrums. I think you should discuss this situation with his Doctor. She did discuss this situation with his Doctor. That Doctor told her, "Your son has ADHD, and it isn't severe enough to even label him with a formal diagnosis." Two years later, her son was expelled from school after he threw a chair at his teacher. At that time, the same Doctor was quick to diagnose him with ADHD, ODD and some autistic traits. Ten years later, this same boy was diagnosed with Asperger's syndrome.

The school told her they thought expelling him would be the best way for him to get the help he needed. This Mom, however, was feeling extremely overwhelmed. She said she had been struggling with managing him. She said he could be lovely, then, he would snap and suddenly have dramatic, over-the-top tantrums.

Next, she got him enrolled in a school that Britain called a 'pupil referral unit'. This was a school for children who had behavioral or developmental issues and are unable to attend mainstream public schools. These schools had a low student-teacher ratio. This school strived to accommodate each child's needs. This school was a good fit for her son. About a year later, they moved. She once again, enrolled him in the local public school. Two years and 4 months later, he was expelled again. She loved this school and its staff. When they expelled him, however, she understood. He had a violent meltdown at the school. He had been trying to kick his way out of the Principal's office. The school had to call the police.

She said, at that point, her son was 10 years old, and she was beginning to think, perhaps she should not be parenting him. She thought, maybe she should hand him over to someone else. She felt like her efforts of trying to parent this child had been failing.

She also thought at that time, when he is in a good mood, he is fun to be around. She admitted that she did enjoy his company much of the time but every time his mood changed, he became violent. She said, "We did not have that much money but when he was in a good mood, we did have a happy life."

She said she was very angry. She said she was not angry with him. She was angry with whatever was causing him to behave this way. She said she was very concerned he would never be able to fit into 'normal' society and do 'normal' things. At that point. She knew she was done with sending him to normal schools. She enrolled him in another 'pupil referral unit.' This time, he stayed there until he graduated at the age of 16.

At one point, her son was prescribed Ritalin and equasym (this is the UK's equivalent of Metadate). He experienced positive effects immediately. His mom said, it seemed like all-of-a-sudden, her son had been replaced with a better-behaved boy.

She said, it was not a cure, we still had problems. She said his meltdowns continued at school and at home. The medication helped him calm down enough to learn strategies to stay organized, follow directions and most importantly, cool down when he got angry.

This Mom stated formal behavioral therapy was rare in the U.K. The 'pupil referral unit', however, did establish a system of supports to help him with his temper. This school gave him a card to hand to his teacher when he knew he was starting to get angry. They gave him a different type of card to hand to his teacher when he felt like he was about to blow-up. He was rewarded for good behaviors. This school even paid him quite-a-bit of money when he graduated that was earned from the positive points he had accumulated for good behavior.

This Mom stated that whenever he had handed a card to a teacher to let them know he was getting angry or feeling like he was about to blow-up, he was taken to a quiet place where he had a chance to re-group. She said, she thought that was exactly what he needed. She said, placing him in a calm and quiet place really helped him get calmed down. She said, she knew that anytime he was getting upset, intervening in anyway made things get worse. This Mom said she, her son and this school all knew that him having occasional outbursts was inevitable and they all learned how to stop his tantrums before they became severe.

Once her son learned how to use tools to stop his tantrums from becoming so severe, his defiance diminished because he felt like he had some control over the situation. Once he was older and in more control, he realized that when he was younger, his tantrums not only frightened the people who were around him. They frightened him too.

Now, her son is 18 years old and works at a restaurant. His Mom wrote a book about her struggles with ODD. As her son became older and learned how to manage his anger better, he became less hellish. She started to see his potential. He and his Mom became involved in Europe's current refugee crisis. They both traveled to France to distribute aid to refugees. He had never been a social butterfly, yet he became close with many of the displaced people, and he discovered he had skills he did not know he had. He discovered he can lead people; he can motivate people and he can adapt to new situations. Realizing that has given him a huge confidence boost.

THE MOM AND HER SON WHO LIVE IN THE UNITED STATES

She is the author of the book called, 'The Whipped Parent.'
Her name is: Kimberly Abraham

The Mom who was living in the United States and was enduring a similar situation stated: My son tried to battle me throughout his childhood. By the time he was in middle school, he refused to go to school most days. His Mom usually tried to drag him to the car while he was still in his pajamas. She hoped he would get dressed on the way. He stole things from his brother. He broke his father's tools. He did not do his homework. When he was in the 8th grade, he refused to wear clean clothes for weeks at a time.

She eventually learned her son had ODD and ADHD. ODD includes backtalk and occasional tantrums. It is a persistent and excessive pattern of negative behavior against authority figures.

His Mom said, when this son was young, he tried lots of different activities; but he lost interest in everything right away. He loved to push boundaries and break rules. When he entered middle school he admitted he was constantly in trouble. He also said, "He concluded that since he was always in trouble already anyway; it wouldn't really matter if the things he did just kept getting bigger." He loved to work on cars; so, he frequently stole his Dad's tools, then, either lost the tools, or left them lying around.

Eventually, his Dad and Mom put a lock on the toolbox. They locked-up everything that was valuable in their garage. Their son broke into the locked-up objects anyway. He kept antagonizing his older brother. He infuriated his teachers by refusing to do anything they asked him to do.

When he was 14; if his Mom told him he was grounded; he would respond, "No, I am not, then he would walk out the door.

She then took him to see a Doctor who diagnosed him with ODD. She suspected he had ADD or ADHD also but was not as concerned with having him diagnosed with that as she was with getting him diagnosed with ODD. She knew her son's defiance had been running her life.

Next, she saw a therapist. This therapist told her, "Boys like yours usually end-up institutionalized." She decided to not see that therapist anymore.

Next, she saw another therapist. This next one told her she needed to be dispersing more consistent parenting. She knew she had been dispersing very consistent parenting. She knew her son did not care about consequences. She knew her son was not interested in doing anything she asked him to do.

Traditional discipline does not typically work for kids with ODD. Kids who have ODD ignore punishment and enjoy upsetting everyone who is around them. To help someone who has ODD improve their behavior. Positive reinforcement is usually dramatically more effective than negative reinforcement. When dealing with these kids; you need to try to refuse to engage in arguments. Instead, focus on rewarding their good behaviors and help them build their self-esteem.

She took her son to see many different therapists. None of those visits had a positive effect on him. His behavior just kept spiraling out of control.

This Mom said there were times when she really hated her son. She said, she loved him and hated him at the same time. She said he was really putting their family through an unbelievable amount of turmoil.

She started earning a master's degree in psychology and social work. She was determined to find a solution to figure-out how she could get her son to finally behave well. Once she completed earning her master's degree; she started implementing a program for her son that she had created on her own. With this plan, she would have 100% of the control. The main concept behind her plan was, 'If you do not do anything for me; I'm not going to do anything for you.'

For example, if she asked him to wash the dishes by 6:00 and he did not do it. She washed the dishes; then, the next time he asked her to do something for him, she told him, 'No.' and reminded him, you did not wash the dishes for me, so, I am not going to drive you to where you want to go.

She also convinced her husband and son to stop doing things for her son who had ODD too.

When she first started this program; he became more defiant than he had ever been before.

Eventually though, he did do something her husband asked him to do. He did not do it right away. He started to ignore his father and kept walking; but then, he did turn around and do the simple task his father had asked him to do. His Mom felt like she had just had a breakthrough. She had never witnessed her son do anything like that before.

She said she was determined to teach her son that no one in the real world is going to do things for you if you do not do things for them. She was not sure whether her program was going to work. Her son, however, did slowly start to do things he was asked to do. She admitted they had setbacks. Now, though, he is an adult. He is a roofer, and he has children of his own. She said her relationship with him is not perfect, but it is dramatically better than it had been.

This Mom also said, when he was a teenager, she thought he was going to end-up in prison or dead. She is amazed by the transformation her son has made.

Experts have estimated that about 40 – 60% of children who are diagnosed with ADHD, also have ODD. About 68% of those who have been diagnosed with ODD also have ADHD or another impulse control disorder. About 25 percent of the children who have ODD later become diagnosed with conduct disorder. About 25 to 40 percent of teens who are diagnosed with conduct disorder later become diagnosed with antisocial personality disorder.

It is difficult to measure whether ODD has been on the rise. If you just measure how much social security payments have risen to children who have been diagnosed with ODD, there has been somewhat of a rise among low-income people. It is thought that if there has been an increase in ODD, it is due to the fact that divorce rates have increased, economic hardships have increased and how many single parent mothers there has increased, especially among the lower social economic levels. When parental stress increases, children are more likely to develop defiant behaviors.

Children who have a negative temperament from birth and are unusually fussy babies may have ODD. Children who are very impulsive may have ODD. Children who are impulsive tend to have abnormalities in the amygdala, pre-fontal cortex and anterior cingulate areas of their brains.

It is also believed that children who are living in families where there has been a divorce are more likely to become defiant. Children who are growing-up in families that are poor and have access to fewer resources will be more likely to become defiant. Negative patterns in the parent-child relationship can cause a child to become defiant.

A situation where a child was a mild-mannered baby and toddler, then, became defiant around the age of 12 or so, is completely different from a child who has been defiant and doing a lot of screaming and having a lot of tantrums ever since they were born. If a child was born defiant; their brain is not operating within a normal range.

Our daughter did a lot of screaming from the time she was born. My husband and I were extremely familiar with her screaming. She did not behave that way when other people watched her, and we were not around. One time, my husband, myself and our infant daughter were at my parent's house all day long because I was making and installing some homemade curtains for my parent's bedroom. While I was at the top of the ladder, and I was trying to get the curtain rod that had heavy curtains hanging from it to rest on some hooks; our daughter started screaming. I do not remember how old she was, but I know she was notable to crawl yet or get out of the 'baby carrier with a handle,' she was lying in on the floor, on her own yet. Our daughter started crawling when she was 7 months old. Once I heard the screaming, I decided to ignore it. I knew she did not need a bottle, a diaper change or sleep. I knew she should have been content because I had just tended to her. My husband did not jump-up and tend to her either. We were both tired of tending to all her needs all the time and having no time left to take care of our own needs. It always seemed as soon as we started to do something we really wanted or needed to do, she would start demanding our attention one way or another.

The screaming did not slow down. A few minutes later, my Mom rushed into her bedroom and asked, "Are not you going to do something about that screaming?" I responded, "I can either work on the curtains or I can tend to her. I cannot do both at the same time. Which do you think I should do? Someone else can tend to her." My Mom could not stand the screaming. Eventually, I had to get off the ladder and hold our daughter for a while. That was the only thing that got her to stop screaming. I knew darn well, however, that as soon as I was once again at the top of that ladder, she would start screaming again.

Also, our daughter had a lot of trouble with sleep. It seemed like she was overly-wired all the time. We know other people have driven their kids around in a car to get them to fall asleep; then, they would drive home, carry their kids into the house and put them to bed. Every time we tried that, our daughter would wake-up as soon as we turned the car off. As a baby, she always woke-up every time we stopped at an intersection, a light, a toll booth or in our driveway. She would not stay asleep. She has always fallen asleep very late and woken-up very early.

When she was a baby, she would only drink 4 ounces of formula at a time when I was feeding her. Two hours later, she would be demanding a bottle from me again. All the other babies I knew-of drank 8 ounces of formula every 4 hours. When she was 3 months old, and I started leaving her at a Sitter's home when I worked; I explained to her Sitter that she will only drink 4 ounces at a time, and she wants to be fed every 2 hours. When I picked her up at the end of that day, the Sitter told me she drank 8 ounces for her just fine.

When our daughter was young; I was regularly reading articles about what to expect your baby to be doing at the age she was at. I remember that when she was about 5 months old she was already making a lot of noises with her mouth, and she was trying to act like she was going to talk. When she was 6 months old, I read an article that said, soon your child will probably start making a lot of noises with her mouth and that is what your child should be doing. That is going to help her develop all the muscles in her mouth that she will need to be able to talk. When I read that I thought, first, with all the screaming this child has done, how could she not have all those muscles developed in her mouth already and secondly, she started doing that about a month ago. When I told my husband about the article I had just read, he responded, "I can't wait for her to start talking." I responded. "I have read an article that said, do not be in a hurry for your child to start talking; once they start, you may wish you could get them to stop talking." WOW, that was an accurate statement. Our daughter did start talking way ahead of time. Once she started talking, she did not stop. She always had diarrhea of the mouth. She was always trying to get us to pay attention to her or get us to do something for her. We had to get ourselves completely away from her to get the non-stop demands from rolling-in. As soon as we returned she would do whatever it took to get us to wait-on-her. Our daughter was not acting like that because we were catering to her needs too much and we were jumping every time she wanted something. I was doing the opposite of that much of the time. I was not trying to cater to her every whim. Never-the-less, it was obvious to me that this child is extremely bossy and demanding and she was born that way.

Our daughter went to the same ladies home every time we were both working until she started going to school. This lady told me many times. As soon as your daughter arrives here; she drags all the toys out of their home and places them all over the floor and she does that about 10 times faster than any other kid I have ever seen drag toys around.

That explained to me why, sometimes, I felt like I was raising 10 kids. We only had 1 kid. Our daughter has always had to touch everything. It was very difficult to take her inside any stores. She tried to touch everything she saw. We had heard that you can tell your child before you enter the store, "I will give you a quarter as soon as we leave this store if you do not touch anything while we are in the store." We tried that. Our daughter never earned a quarter from doing that. That strategy did not even slow her down. It had absolutely no impact.

When you try to explain these types of behaviors to other people or Counselors. Those people often act like you are at fault if your child is not behaving properly. We even had a Counselor tell us that it sounds like the tail is wagging the dog and we must not be parenting her correctly. If you had been parenting properly, your child would not be acting that way. There was no reason for us to keep seeing that Counselor. Eventually you realize, you cannot talk to anyone about what you have been going through. I started reading a lot of books about parenting. I tried lots of the strategies the books suggested. One of them said, "Just count-out-loud, to 10 every time your child starts doing something they should not be doing. If they do not stop the bad behavior by the time you get to 10. Take something away from that child. I tried that strategy for about a month. That strategy never worked.

Ever since our daughter has been about 3 years old, I have thrown her shoes down the basement stairs every time she leaves her shoes in the middle of the floor where someone could trip over them. Now, she is 16, she still leaves her shoes on the floor where someone could trip over them. I still throw her shoes down the basement stairs when she does that.

Since we had an EEG done on our daughter's brain and the Doctor who performed that procedure told us our daughter's brain operates about 9 times faster than the typical female her age and that Doctor handed me printouts of the results from that test. I know that our daughter has been behaving outrageously because of the brain she was born with.

When you have been putting dramatically more effort into parenting than all the other parents you meet and some of those parents have the nerve to tell you; your child would be behaving much better if you parented them properly; you can become angry.

Our daughter has thrown lots of wild tantrums. She breaks a lot of stuff. I must tighten the screws on many of the kitchen cabinet doors periodically. If I did not those doors would fall. Our toilet seats become loose frequently. I have had to replace our doorbell about 5 times. She is not careful or cautious. Even though she is not supposed to take food anywhere in our home other than the kitchen and the breakfast nook. She carries food all over our home. I find food crumbs all over the place. Most of her friends carry their dirty dishes to our sink and have been doing that for many years. Our daughter did not start carrying dirty dishes to the sink until she was almost 13. However, she sometimes carries them sideways and drops food and crumbs all over our floor on her way to the sink. Luckily for us, she does not behave that way when she goes other places. Yes, she goes to the bathroom and the nurses office way too frequently when she is at school, but she has not become violent when she has been at school. She dumps on us as soon as she walks in the door at the end of a frustrating day at school. Luckily, for us, she has that much self-control. Our daughter tried to get out of having to go to Religious Education Class every week. She tries to make us late for church every week and she usually does. This morning, My husband and I were ready to drive to church at 10:10. He went and sat in our vehicle. I stayed inside and gently tried to encourage her to get ready a little faster. We did not leave to go to church until 10:30. Church starts at 10:30. It is a 5-minute drive to our church.

She does have a lot of challenges because she was born with a brain that is extremely overactive.

When she was about 3 years old, my husband and I were trying to get us all ready for bed. He poured her a drink in a sippy cup. She told him, she would only drink it if it was in her favorite sippy cup. He told her, "No, it is already in this cup. You are going to must drink out of this cup. She refused and started screaming. Since we had been down this road many times before; we knew that if we decided to battle her; it would be a very long battle. It was about 10:00 at night when this battle started. My husband was going to need to wake-up to get ready for work at about 5:00 the next morning. Her screaming had him so wired already that he knew if he even tried to fall asleep now; he would not be able to fall asleep. He decided he was going to win this battle. He told her if she did not drink out of the sippy cup the drink was already in, he was going to get out his saw and saw her favorite sippy cup in half. She screamed and refused to drink out of that sippy cup for about an hour. Eventually, he got his saw out of the basement. He took her favorite sippy cup out to the garage. She followed him out there. She watched him saw her favorite sippy cup in half and throw it in the garbage. After he did that; she finally calmed down. Of course, then, it took all us a long time to be able to fall asleep. It sure is fun to fall asleep at 1:00 a.m. and wake up at 5:00 a.m. and get ready to go to work; isn't it?

Of course, if you try to explain what just happened in your house to someone who is now parenting or has parented children who are easy to parent; they, will probably tell you something like, "Well, when I was parenting I always had the upper hand. I never let my kids tell me how things were going to go. You must get that under control now because she is just going to get worse as she becomes older. You cannot let her run your life." They will one way or another act like you have created this situation. Your parenting style is not good, and you need to start parenting the way they parented immediately because they are experts regarding the topic of parenting, and you obviously know nothing.

So, you have just been slammed with a double whammy. Your child is treating you horribly and the people you try to confide-in when you are just needing to vent, or you are hoping someone will be at least a little understanding and hopefully give you a constructive idea regarding where you can find real answers.

Recently, a man told me his first 2 children, a son and a daughter were well-behaved kids. They did not need to child-proof anything for their first 2 kids. Both of those kids were adorable and easy to parent. He said they had heard other parents tell them stories about how difficult one of their kids was to parent and they did not really comprehend what those other parents were talking about. Then, they had a 3rd child. This 3rd child of theirs had to touch everything. He had to pull on every knob, open every door and drawer. He must approach and interact with everyone and everything he sees. He just cannot leave anything alone. This 3rd child has been extremely difficult to parent. Now this family has a 4th child. Their 4th child is calm and mild-mannered. She does not need to touch everything and interact with everything. She seems like she is going to be easy to parent.

Sometimes when I go to my eye Doctor's office I talk to one of the ladies who works there. She tells me she has 2 daughters. She is divorced because her ex-husband is a Narcissist. He was extremely difficult to get along with. She was not aware of what an extreme personality he had until after she was married to him. She told me her oldest daughter has a personality that is very much like her ex-husband's personality. Her older daughter is now almost 40 years old and has never been married. She told me this daughter was dating a guy for quite-a-while and she was really hoping this guy would marry her. One time she asked this guy if he thought he would ever marry her daughter. He responded, "No, never, she is too demanding. She is high maintenance. There is no way I could be married to her." She understood where he was coming from completely. She also told me her younger daughter is very mild-mannered and easy going. She admitted her younger daughter has no problem with having quality relationships with people that last a long time. Her younger daughter is married.

There are a lot of people in this world who have mental health issues. They have never been diagnosed with mental health issues and they do not want to admit they have mental health issues. Sometimes we must interact with these people. Sometimes these people have occupations that allow them to oversee other people even though these people are not even capable of forming good relationships with any other people.

I think when experts say, how much of someone's adult behavior is a result of their environment and how much is a result of their genetics. Those results change if someone has mental health issues. If someone has a Narcissistic Personality Disorder, ADHD, Anxiety, OCD, Oppositional Defiance Disorder, or any type of a difficult personality; their behaviors become much more difficult to shape and mold and even if those people are growing-up in a perfect environment. Those people are never going to behave completely normally.

MOST PEOPLE NEED TO RECEIVE MORE POSITIVE REINFORCEMENT THAN NEGATIVE REINFORCEMENT

Among the 16 Myers-Briggs Personality types, only 2 of those personality types (the INTJ and the ISTP) do not really crave positive feedback. The other 14 personality types all do need to receive positive reinforcement, however.

It seems obvious to me that this world seriously needs to teach everyone how to appreciate and compliment other people.

A lot of people treat other people negatively more often than they treat other people positively. We all must encounter people who treat us negatively.

Lots of us have positive thoughts about other people but we never let those people know we have positive thoughts about them.

Lots of us crave being appreciated and complimented but we rarely receive appreciation or compliments.

Many of us are very familiar with being corrected, criticized, degraded, ridiculed, made-fun-of, poked, prodded, rushed, treated like we are inferior, or like we do not know anything. Some people treat us like all our ideas are bad ideas.

Some people scold us when we have not done anything wrong.

Some people constantly need to act like we are incompetent so they can feel like they are superior to us.

In my opinion, how negatively lots of people treat other people is what is causing a lot of the problems we have in this world. I think making other people feel bad is very destructive.

I think if everyone in this world treated other people well, lots of our world-wide problems would dramatically decline or disappear.

Currently, we are all preyed-on more now than ever before by people who are trying to steal our identity. We are all preyed-on more now than ever before by people who are trying to sell us things and over-charge us for things than ever before. We all have less privacy now than we have ever had before.

I keep feeling like I need to get out into nature, do some photography, gardening, dancing, watch movies or sitcoms that I love to watch or listen to great music just to be able to escape from all the people who intentionally try to put me in a horrible mood. Doing the activities, I just mentioned puts me in a good mood.

I keep finding myself trying to escape from all the negative people. I can even think of times I have been doing something nice for someone; and they responded to me by being very mean to me. Time after time, I have been disappointed by how mean some people are capable of being. During my entire lifetime, I can only think of a few times when I have been mean to someone and the only reason I was mean to those people was because they made me so furious; I had to do something to get them to leave me alone. Some people do not know when to quit. They do not even know when they have pushed other people too far. Some people act like they need to treat everyone roughly all the time.

They do not comprehend that sensitive people cannot handle being treated roughly. I have an extremely sensitive personality. I get my feelings hurt easily and I cry easily. When people are nice to me, I am likely to knock myself out for them.

I do a lot more than most people would do for people when people are nice to me. In my world, how people make me feel is what matters most. When people are mean to me, I am not interested in doing anything for them. I cannot spend much time with the kind of people who intentionally make other people feel miserable. Those people put me in a terrible mood every time. Any time I am around those types of people, I feel like all my creative juices have stopped flowing. I feel like there is no reason for me to say anything to those people because I know they will immediately try to criticize anything I say. I cannot have any type of a relationship with those types of people. Anytime I am around one of those types of people, I cannot wait to get away from them, so, I can relax and be myself. No one has ever accomplished anything good by being mean to me. Frequently, I am surprised by how many people act negatively and aggressively. I find it hard to believe that those behaviors have been getting them any good results. I have witnessed pushy salespeople have higher sales, though. I have witnessed aggressive people convince people to do things they do not want to do.

When I have witnessed that, I have wondered, "Does that aggressive person not have a conscience. Does that person not care about the fact that they just made that other person feel bad and uncomfortable. It seems to me like the negative and aggressive people really do not care about how they make other people feel. I get the impression that some of those people really do only care about themselves and no one else. Some people think other people should be doing things for them all the time and they should not do anything for other people.

PHONE #'S YOU CAN CALL IF YOU NEED HELP OR IF YOU NEED TO REPORT SOMEONE

Sometimes when you are being bullied; you will need to report the bully secretly. Calling one or some of the #'s listed here may be a place where you can get some help. You may want to ask whoever answers the phone to make sure the bully does not learn who reported them. If you want to make sure the bully never learns you were the one who reported them; you may choose to send an anonymous letter instead.

9-1-1   Call if you need immediate help

1-800-448-3000   24-hour National Crisis Hotline

1-810-412-6109   Abuse / Violence Child Protective Services

1-888-982-0210   Better Business Bureau

1-800-821-4357   Alcohol and Drug Helpline

1-800-232-4636   CDC.gov/violence prevention

1-703-482-0623   Central Intelligence Agency (CIA), (they investigate international problems)

1-800-233-4357   Anorexia & Bulimia, National Crisis Line

1-202-514-4713   Civil Rights Division, U.S. Department of Education

1-202-514-3831   Complaints of Employment Discrimination (involving a group or class of individuals)

1-404-562-2313   Complaints of Employment Discrimination (involving Service Members)

1-800-669-4000   Complaints of Employment Discrimination (involving individuals)

1-800-799-SAFE   Domestic Violence

1-800-669-4000   Equal Employment Opportunity Commission (EEOC)

1-800-255-7688   Immigrant and Employee Rights Section Worker Hotline

1-866-488-7386   LGBT Youth

1-800-321-6742   Occupational Safety and Health Administration

1-202-514-4609   Place to Worship Initiative (Civil Rights Division)

1-202-353-1555   Prosecuting and Preventing Hate Crimes

1-202-307-7272   Protecting rights of Service Members

1-800-292-4517   Runaway RAP Line

1-800-Dont-Cut   Self Harm

1-844-380-6178   Sexual Harassment Housing Initiative

1-800-273-8255   National Suicide Prevention

1-202-514-4713   U.S. Department of Justice

1-866-4-USA-DOL   U.S. Department of Labor (call this number to learn your local 1-202-606-1800   U.S. Office of Personnel Management

To discover the phone # for your local FBI, visit:

http://www.fbi.gov/contact/fo/fo.htm (they investigate problems within the United States)

Tell someone; if no one knows, no one can help !!!!!!!

Report bullying to an adult. If that adult does not help; keep reporting it until someone does help. Documenting the bullies offenses can be very helpful.

Adults you may want to report bullying to may include:

A Teacher

A Counselor

A Principal

A Superintendent

Your State Department of Education

A family member

A friend

A Professional Psychiatrist

A Professional Psychologist

stopbullying.gov

Someone at a local Church

IDEAS REGARDING HOW YOU MIGHT WANT TO RESPOND TO A BULLY

A Hater's opinion is very much like an expired coupon. It is not worth anything.

There are lots of different types of bullies. Some bullies are so extreme; they are sociopaths, and they are dangerous. If you are dealing with a sociopath or any type of extreme bully; try to avoid contact with them. Try to avoid communicating with them completely. If you do find yourself having to deal with someone who is an extreme bully; try to show minimal reaction to their bullying, then, try to walk away from them and stay away from them.

Sociopaths are clinically incapable of empathizing with or connecting with other people. They lack having a conscience. They have no problem with harming or hurting people. Do not try to fight a sociopath.

Sometimes bullies behave the way they do because they have sensory issues or other neurological problems.

Among bullies, there tends to be 1. Taunting Bullies, 2. Emotional Bullies & 3. Aggressive Bullies. Among the various types of bullies, you should figure out if you are dealing with a dangerous bully or a bully who is just trying to do emotional damage to their victims. You need to figure-out if you are going to be able to handle their backlash. Even among the bullies who are only trying to do emotional damage; those bullies can cause such severe emotional scars that their victims will never be able to completely forget the attacks that were placed on them.

If you decide you are ready to deal with all the backlash the bully will spew at you; you may proceed with doing some things to fight back.

There are bullies who love to fight and argue. They love to criticize and attack people. They especially like to ridicule good people who are always trying to improve things. They are constantly trying to prove to everyone they are better than everyone else. They act like they are superior to everyone in the world, and they act like they know everything. They constantly try to walk all over other people. They are always desperate to be in the spotlight and get attention. Avoid trying to fight them; they will always fight back harder. They pride themselves in trying to win every battle. They do not care at all about how annoying they are. Their main goal is to have more power than everyone else all the time and they will do whatever it takes to not be dethroned. Some of these people are not dangerous. They are incredibly annoying, however.

Feel you inner strength.

Try to go places with other non-threatening people instead of alone.

Realize that if you are being bullied; you are probably an interesting person.

Outsmart the bully. That is typically easy to do. Bullies tend to have poor problem-solving abilities. They lack imagination and assume other people do not have an imagination. They think they should be able to make and enforce all the rules and everyone else should follow all their rules. If you have an imagination. You will be able to find ways to be able to fight the bully secretly.

Fighting a bully secretly can include:

Calling the police on them, using someone else's phone, so they will not know you are the one who reported them.

Writing an anonymous letter, then wearing gloves when you are handling the paper, envelope and dropping the letter in the mailbox.

Realizing you can report the bullies to organizations such as: stopbullying.gov,

OSHA, EEOA, State Labor Law Organizations, Security Officers, Police Officers.

Realizing you can sometimes report bullies to their Superior(s) and their

Superior's Superior.

Find an authority to report the bullies to.

Realizing there are a lot of Government phone #'s you can call to report illegal   activities.

Being aware that bullying is illegal in most states, and you can refer to   stopbullying.gov to learn what the laws are in your state.

Understand that bullies hate to be ignored. You can use that as a weapon.

Sometimes ignoring them infuriates them.

Understanding that bullies are not used to anyone standing firm against them and that is exactly what you should do if the bully is not dangerous.

Understand that cyber-bullying is just as real as face-to-face bullying.

Do things that increase your self-confidence. For example, learn Ju-Jitsu, Judo, Karate, Kung Fu, Self-defense and/or Tae Kwando.

Bullies really hate it when the person they are jealous of loses weight or has any type of success in their life. The more successful you are the more they will think of you as their enemy. You should understand that if the bully is

spending a lot of time hating you. The bully is just wishing they were succeeding

instead of you. If you have been doing things that will help you move forward

with your life, the bully will try to find new ways to criticize and demean you. If

someone keeps trying to bully you more, that, really is a backwards compliment.

If the bully is not dangerous, you might want to tell them you know that their

bullying tendencies stem from their insecurities and their need to pick on other

people really come from them being unhappy.

Tell the bully their behavior will not be tolerated.

Tell the bully, you realize that people who are truly confident and comfortable

do not feel the need to bully or demean others to feel good about themselves.

Tell the bully; you realize all their malicious targeting of other people is just

one of the things they do to hide all their insecurities.

Tell the bully; you know that bullies typically feel threatened by the people they

choose to bully.

You can improve the way you react to bullies by confronting them.

Keep a log of all the bullying you witness, including the dates and the times.

Realize that most bullying occurs when there is an audience present.

Realize that 'hurt people.............................hurt people'.

Help raise awareness about bullying and spread the word.

Try to encourage other people to report bullying.

People who are being bullied should not be quiet.

People who are being bullied should be aware; they are not alone.

Get a buddy and be a buddy.

Stand-up for yourself.

Do things that help you calm yourself or put you in a good mood.

Do not expose your feelings to the bully. The bully wants you to feel bad. Do not let them know that they made you feel bad. That will make them feel good.

Bullies always look for traces of panic in their victims. Bullies want you to feel like you are helpless.

Understand that the bully does not control you.

Understand that the bully cannot affect you unless you let them.

Talk to someone about it (someone who wants you to be happy).

You might want to seek professional help.

You might want to contact www.betterhelp.com/start/ to obtain online counseling. At this website, there are more than 2000 Licensed Counselors. If you would prefer to meet with a Counselor in person, this website can help you

find a Counselor who is located close to where you live. The Counselors at this

site can be contacted 24 hours a day, seven days each week. You do not need an

appointment to talk to any of these Counselors.

If you are unable to fight against a bully; you will be more likely to be a target

for a bully. You, especially, may need to travel with someone who could help

you protect yourself. Do not be socially isolated.

Realize that most bullies are filled with fear and if you do stand-up to them; you

might make them so embarrassed; that they will be afraid to ever try to bully

you again.

If a bully insults you in public and you respond to them with a better insult.

That bully will be humiliated. That is not the kind of attention any bully wants.

Realize that bullies actions might not have anything to do with you. Some

people are negative all the time and they want to dump all their negative

feelings on other people. They constantly try to make themselves feel strong by making other people feel weak.

If you are being bullied; do not let that define your future. You are capable of

Accomplishing great things. Rise above the haters.

SOME PHRASES YOU MAY WANT TO SAY TO A BULLY

Unfortunately, there are a lot of people in this world who treat other people badly. There are a lot of different reasons why these people behave badly. Most of the time, the reasons these people behave badly has absolutely nothing to do with the people they are dis-respecting. It does not matter how good of a person you are or how well you treat other people; you will encounter people who try to treat you badly at least occasionally. It is difficult for some people to know how to respond to mean people. It can be difficult to know what to say to these people at the right time. The following is a list of phrases you might choose to say to someone who is not treating you respectfully. I suggest you choose 5 to 10 of the following phrases. Memorize them and be ready to say them to anyone who tries to treat you badly. People who do not fight back and stand-up for themselves tend to be likely to be targeted again by the same bully. The following phrases are intended to be used to get annoying people to leave you alone or treat you decently.

Anyone who is trying to bring me down is already below me.

Be an encourager, the world already has enough critics.

Behind every successful person, there is a pack of haters. Either walk beside me or get behind me.

Being mean is destructive, being nice is constructive. When you are ready to be nice to me, that is when I will allow you to spend time with me.

Bullies are the people who are the most insecure.

Bullies cause depression. Depression causes suicide. Are you a murderer?

Congratulations on your ability to create drama out of absolutely nothing.

Dear hater, there is so much more about me that you could be mad at, just be patient.

Did your brain take a laxative? There is a lot of poop coming out of your mouth right now.

Do not be a hater.

Do not hate me because you are not me.

Do not talk when your mouth is full of lies.

Every time I do 99 things correctly and 1 thing incorrectly; you try to tell me I am a loser because I did 1 thing incorrectly. Just stay away from me. I have no use for you.

Everyone is entitled to act badly some of the time; but you abuse the privilege.

Friends are like boobs. Some are big. Some are small. Some are real. Some are fake.

Gossiping about people is unhealthy for you and for your targets.

Haters are people who think you are better than they are.

Have a nice day. Somewhere else.

I am an acquired taste. If you do not like me; you should acquire some taste.

I am returning your nose. I found it in my business.

I am tired of people being ugly to each other.

I avoid certain people because I am wise.

I could eat alphabet soup and poop-out better comments than you have stated about me.

I did not mean to push your buttons. I was just looking for the mute button.

I did not order a glass of your opinion.

I do not care about what all those other people have been saying about you. I

think you are all right.

I do not let toxic people rent space in my head. I raise their rent and force them to move out.

I do not like people who go out of their way to make other people feel miserable.

I do not spend any time with mean people. I do not have any time for you.

I do not spend time with people who degrade me. I spend time with people who inspire me.

I do not spend any time with toxic people.

I function much better when I do not receive unsolicited advice.

I heard there is a new app called sense of humor. Go ahead and download it.

I stay away from negative people.

I stay away from toxic people.

Your drama is largely self-created.

I understand that when people treat me badly, there is something wrong with them, not me.

I walk away from people who will never see my worth.

I wish I had a dime for each of the times you have criticized me. I would be filthy rich.

I wish you would shut that convenience store mouth of yours; but I have noticed it is open 24 hours a day, seven days each week.

If all the stuff you have said about me was true; my life would be a lot more interesting.

If drama follows you everywhere you go. Maybe you are the drama.

If I wanted to listen to a butthole. I would fart.

If you are waiting for me to care; you should pack a lunch. It is going to be a while.

If you need to hurt people to feel powerful, you are weak.

If you ran as much as your mouth runs; you would be in great shape.

If you say you do not like me; yet you watch everything I do; let us face it. You are a fan.

If you want to screw me over; you will buy me dinner first.

I am not Willy Wonka. I do not sugar-coat stuff.

Is your drama going to have an intermission soon?

It is against the law for you to bully me. Shall I call the Police?

It is too bad that running your mouth is not a legitimate calorie-burning exercise.

It is better to let someone think you are an idiot, than, to open your mouth and prove to them that you are.

It is OK if you do not like me. Not everyone has good taste.

I have been wondering how you are able to comb your hair, so your horns do not show.

Jealousy is a disease. I hope you get well soon.

Mean people are destructive. You are a mean person. That is why I need to stay away from you.

Meanness is a sign of weakness.

My feelings are not your playground.

My life is not your game.

My name must taste good. It is always in your mouth.

Normal people do not try to destroy other human beings.

People who know the least about me seem to be the ones who have the most to say about me.

People seem to feel better when you are not around.

Remember that momentary time you shut up? I do not either.

Right now, I would rather have no friends than be friends with you.

Sanity is highly over-rated.

Since my skills and intellect are superior to yours; you really should not try to bully me.

Since you are bossy, demanding and unconcerned about other people's feelings. I am not concerned about your feelings.

Since you are a mean person, I do not value anything you must say.

Since you are a negative person who thinks it is a great idea to find fault with me all the time. Just stay away from me.

Since you know-it-all. You should know when to be quiet.

Suicide does not end pain. It passes pain along to other people.

The only things I fight for are my destiny, my dreams, my ideas and my visions.

The only thing that is wrong with me is that I am talking to you right now.

The spotlight is not supposed to be on you all the time. Give someone else a turn.

The Zoo called. They said you are due back by 6:00.

Those who are at war with others are not at peace with themselves.

Unless your name is Google; stop pretending you know everything.

When I hear people talking about me, I realize, 'Birds peck-at the best fruit'.

When so much poop comes out of your mouth all at once. I do not know if I should hand you a roll of toilet paper or a breath mint.

Where is your off button.

Winners focus on winning. Losers focus on winners.

You are like a bag of pampers. Self-absorbed and full of doo doo.

You are emotionally abusive.

You are like a hemorrhoid. You are a pain in the butt that just will not go away.

You do not like me. That is a shame. I will pencil in some time to cry about it later. Right now, I am just going to continue to enjoy my life.

You have the rest of your life to be mean. Why not take today off.

You never look good when you are trying to make someone else look bad.

You should learn how to treat people well enough that they want to spend time with you.

You should try to spend an entire day, not criticizing anyone.

Your opinion is not my problem.

When people throw stones at me, I pick them up and build something with them.

HOW CAN WE RECOVER WHEN SOMEONE MAKES US FEEL MISERABLE?

This world is a very difficult place for sensitive people to live. It does not matter what we say or do. It does not matter what we look like. Lots of people treat us badly. It is impossible for a person to be alive in this world and never be treated badly. Sensitive people have higher highs and lower lows than the people who are not sensitive. Oh, sure, the insensitive people cry occasionally. They do not cry nearly as frequently as the sensitive people do.

The insensitive people are not trying to make sure they do not upset anyone. The insensitive people roam around this world and try to figure out how much other people can do for them. They do not care about how they make anyone feel. Yes, they suffer consequences because they treat people harshly. They never learn how to treat people better. They do, however, learn how to adapt their behaviors when they learn they might incur horrible losses if they do not. Not emotional losses, materialistic losses, loss of power and/or loss of status. They do some changing when they receive threats and ultimatums. They think if they dump threats and ultimatums on other people, those people will adapt their behaviors. That is not true. When most people are treated badly repeatedly over time, they tend to fight back or leave. Sometimes they do both.

The insensitive people love to:

Accumulate materialistic things

Act like they are better than and more important than everyone else

Act phony

Badmouth people

Be in the spotlight

Be selfish and greedy

Blame other people for everything that goes wrong in their life

Boss people around

Brag

Criticize people

Dump their problems on other people

Have everything their way all the time

Have horrible listening skills if they can listen at all

Have power and control over people

Interrupt people

Poke and prod people

Scold people

Scream at people

Show-off

Talk down to people

Talk on top of people

They try to dress-up and decorate themselves and the parts of their home that people can see while everything people cannot see is a complete mess.

They think they can make a mess everywhere they go, and other people should clean-up after them

Use threats and ultimatums

In other words, they kind of act like they are going through their terrible 2's stage their entire life. It does not matter how much a sensitive person tries to explain to them that they cannot tolerate some of their behaviors, the insensitive person will not mature. They will not change their behaviors. They will not care that they are damaging the people with whom they are interacting. The insensitive people think using all the immature behaviors they use all the time is how they will get more of the things they want. Since lots of the insensitive people want to oversee people they do whatever it takes to get promoted. Once they oversee people, they are very mean to the people they are supposed to be Supervising. Being mean to decent people is a very unwise thing to do.

When you consider what percentage of the people in this world are Narcissistic; the ones who have been diagnosed with Narcissism by Psychological Professionals is around 6%. You can assume the percentage who have Narcissism is higher than 6% because they do not all seek help or get diagnosed. We all encounter people who are Narcissistic.

The sensitive people in this world must learn how to feel better every time someone upsets them. The sensitive person's moods are what is behind all their decision making. They are constantly thinking, 'What kind of a mood will that activity put me in. What kind of a mood will interacting with that person put me in.' They try to avoid the activities and people who they know will put them in a bad mood. When people really upset them, all a sudden, they are not able to think clearly, concentrate or be productive. Sometimes they start crying every time someone treats them harshly. This world has lots of people who think treating people horribly will suddenly make those people become more productive. Treating sensitive people horribly backfires every time.

Treating people who are passive-aggressive, badly, tends to backfire too. The insensitive people should be very careful around the passive-aggressive people because they never know when or how the passive-aggressive people will respond. The passive-aggressive people are very capable of staying mad for a very long time. They are very good and creating elaborate plans regarding how they will respond to people.

As soon as a sensitive person starts crying or becomes really upset. The insensitive person tries to list all the things that are wrong with the sensitive person. That immediately makes the situation worse.

Sensitive people must learn how to make themselves feel better. Sensitive people are the ones who are the most likely to commit suicide.

It does not matter how much the sensitive people try to explain to the insensitive people, 'You are driving me crazy, I can't take it anymore,' the insensitive people keep doing all the things to the sensitive person they always do that drives the sensitive person crazy.

I was recently talking to a friend of mine who has been working with a lady who is very mean and Narcissistic. She told me working with this lady was so difficult that she was starting to have thoughts that she wished she could kill this co-worker. The lady who said that is a lady who is a very nice person. She has a lot of compassion and empathy. She is a gentle person. She has been pushed too far. She had told the management several times about how badly this coworker had been treating her and the problem never got resolved. Recently my friend was invited to transfer out of that location and work at a different location. She immediately transferred and started working at the other location. She told me she is so glad she transferred. Working at this other location is so much better than having to work with that horrible woman. She wished she had transferred out of there much sooner.

Sensitive people must figure-out what puts them in a better mood and do those things as soon as they can.

If a sensitive person feels much better when they listen to music they love, they should turn on the music they love as soon as they can.

If going outside helps them feel better, they need to go outside as soon as they can.

If crocheting helps they feel better, they should start crocheting as soon as they can.

If talking to a close friend helps them feel better, they should do that right away.

In other words, negative thoughts can start filling the sensitive persons head and those thoughts will not go away until they can do something that will lift their mood.

If the thoughts you have in your head are negative most of the time, you need to start having better experiences.

If interacting with insensitive people is more than you can tolerate, you must get away from those insensitive people.

Some of us must work with or for people who have an extremely insensitive personality.

Some of us must live with someone who has an extremely insensitive personality.

The insensitive people will never admit they are a problem. They will never apologize.

The sensitive people must become good problem solvers. The insensitive people will never improve their bad behaviors unless they are forced to.

Sensitive people are sometimes extremely artistic. Sometimes they have incredible gifts and talents that most people do not realize they have. Frequently, the sensitive people are much more intelligent and talented than the bullies who treat them badly all the time.

Sensitive people must find ways to overcome having to deal with the people who treat them cruelly.

Recently, I was walking through a public place. There was a girl who works there who was leaning against a wall and she was crying. I have had a few small conversations with her before. A while ago she told me she is autistic. When I have talked to her before, I could tell that she is very kind and very sharp in a lot of ways. Her autism, however, causes her to be a very emotional person.

I explained to her that I have a non-cancerous brain tumor in my left thalamus. One of the things the left thalamus controls is emotions. I told her, "I understand how you are feeling." I told her, "I have cried in public lots of times." I told her that when I start crying in public, I will not be able to stop until I do something that takes my mind off what has upset me. I told her I have cried in public for 4 continuous hours before many times and I want to help her get out of this bad mood. I started asking her what her hobbies are. I asked her what kind of things put her in a good mood. I was able to get her to start talking about things she enjoys doing. She stopped crying. Soon another employee walked up to us. I told her this girl was crying because another employee had treated her very badly. The employee acted like she was going to try to solve the problem. I walked away. About 10 minutes later the girl who had been crying walked past me and she said, "Thanks for talking to me, you really helped me."

Insensitive people typically do not have the ability to improve any situation, yet they love to announce to lots of people that they are very important. They do not know how to make people feel good. They frequently try to bribe people. They think if they give people threats and ultimatums, they will suddenly behave better. They do not understand that they cause people to feel bad time after time and they do not understand that doing that is destructive.

The bottom-line is. The sensitive people must rise to the challenge and learn how to recover from the emotional damage people do to us. We must be the problem solvers.

We must learn:

How to find the people in this world who we will be able to have good relationships with. Doing that might include joining groups of people who participate in the same hobbies we have, joining online chat rooms where there are people who share our interests. Joining online chat rooms that are for people who have our same personality type.

Lots of people will suggest you do certain things with your time, but you are the only one who can really comprehend what types of activities make you feel better. Once you figure-out what those activities are; that is when you will really learn how you can have better thoughts in your head and better moods.

Sensitive people should understand that there are lots of people in this world who you could have a great connection with, but you will probably need to put effort into finding those people because the people who are kind and gentle are harder to find. They typically are not loud and obnoxious. They are not asking people to help them and do things for them all the time. Since they tend to be self-sufficient, they are quietly walking past you and you do not notice them or remember them.

Sometimes we must find a different job or career.

Sometimes we must give people the mushroom treatment (keep them in the dark and feed them B.S.) Any information the insensitive people have about you they will probably try to use against you.

Sometimes we must limit how much time we spend with the insensitive people.

Sometimes we must remove certain people from our lives.

We need to spend a lot of time doing the things that put us in a good mood.

The insensitive people will never understand our point-of-view, they will never understand what we think or feel, and they really do not care about what will help us feel better.

There may be people who you must interact with regularly who you hate, and you will need to figure-out how you can spend dramatically less time with those people. Those people might be family members, they might be people you live with, they might be people you work with or for. You might go to school with people you hate interacting with. They might be neighbors. You will need to find ways to spend less time with those people.

Your personality type will not be a good fit with everyone. There is only a small percentage of people in this world who you will really be able to connect with.

Sensitive introverts need to have as much alone time as they need. If they do not spend enough time alone, they will become extremely frustrated.

As I have aged, I have become completely sick of having to deal with mean people. I have had to find solutions. I have learned lots of ways to report the mean people. I have gotten some of the mean people to leave me alone.

I believe if all the sensitive people in this world started reporting the insensitive people every time the insensitive people treated us badly, lots of the bad behaviors would stop.

Everyone is born with a personality type, and everyone is born with a temperament. You cannot change someone's personality type or their temperament.

About 20% of the people in this world have a sensitive personality type. About 30% of the people in this world have emotional disorders.

Among the 30% who have emotional disorders, some of those people are sensitive. Some of them have downs syndrome. Some of them have autism, some of them have depression.

Some of the people who have emotional disorders are people who treat people very badly. Some of those people are narcissists, psychopaths, sociopaths or they have oppositional defiance disorder or bi-polar disorder. Some of those people have such an extreme personality that they will never be nice people. Some of those people really do need to be taking prescription medicines for their emotional problems, yet they refuse to take the prescription medicines that have been prescribed for them. Reporting these people to authority figures may not get these people to change their viewpoints, but sometimes they do stop verbally attacking people when they realize they may get demoted or lose their job if they continue to behave the way they have been behaving. What motivates these people to change their behaviors is completely different from what motivates sensitive people to change their behaviors.

The average person walks past about 7 Psychopaths every day. Sometimes the people who get promoted to oversee large groups of people are Psychopaths. Many people think Psychopaths are locked-up in a jail cell somewhere. That is not true. Many Psychopaths are high functioning. They manage to stay out of jail. They can fool a lot of people. They have no problem with treating people cruelly. Treating people very badly helps them feel better.

Here are some examples of the things you can do to report the mean people.

I was shopping in a grocery store; the cashier was so rude to me before I even had the chance to speak to her. Once I was on the front sidewalk, I was hyper-ventilating. When I got home I sent an e-mail to that store. I used a fake e-mail address, and I did not tell the store my name. I told them how that cashier treated me. I told them, "I will not be shopping at this store again for a very long time and I will never be interacting with that cashier again." It was a couple of years before I ever shopped at that store again. I never did see that cashier again. I do not know what became of her, but I am confident someone spoke to her about how she treated me.

I was entering a store. There was a girl who was trying to sell me something before I entered the store. I politely told her I was not interested and kept walking. She followed me into the store and yelled at me. As soon as I got home, I sent an e-mail to that store. This time I did use my correct e-mail address. I told them how that girl had treated me. I quickly received an e-mail back. I was told that girl was immediately spoken to and asked to leave and never return.

I was approaching a different store. One of the employees was standing outside of the entrance of that store. He started yelling at me and telling me I was trying to enter through the wrong door. There were no signs stating this was the wrong door to enter. I was so shaken-up from how he had yelled at me that I could not think straight. I could not stop thinking about that incident for a long time. As soon as I got home I sent an e-mail to that stores Corporate Headquarters. I explained how that employee had treated me. I used a fake e-mail address. I had to keep returning to that store. I never saw that employee again. I do not know if he transferred to a different store, if he quit, if he was fired or if he started working a different shift. I never saw him again.

I have spent some time working with the public. I have learned that any time someone treats me badly, I should get their name if I can. There are a lot of agencies you can report badly behaved individuals to if you know their name. Sometimes it is customers who have treated me very badly. Sometimes it is people who are supposed to oversee me. Some of those people have treated me so badly, that I have reported them to different agencies. I have reported people by sending anonymous letters. When I do that, I wear gloves before I handle the paper, pull the paper away from the printer, handle the envelope, write on the envelope and place the stamp on the envelope. I do not take my gloves off until after I have dropped the anonymous letter in the blue mailbox.

Some of the places you can report badly behaved people to are:

A company's Corporate Headquarters. Frequently, when you report that someone has been treating you badly to the Management who is working at that location, those people really do not care and do not do anything to correct the problem. You may need to go over their heads.

Department of Human Services

EEOC (Equal Employment Opportunity Commission)

OEIG (Office of Executive Inspector General)

OSHA (Lots of Companies break basic safety rules. You can report them to OSHA)

State Department of Labor

United States Department of Labor

Your States Department of Human Rights

Unfortunately, I have needed to contact some of these agencies to report people anonymously. These agencies do respond. All a sudden, those places are getting visitors. People do show-up to learn what has been going on. They try to get the problems corrected or at least improved. Even when you report the evildoers anonymously to these agencies, the problems do get addressed.

When I report people who treat me badly, I feel like I am helping protect other people from being abused.

I think if everyone in this world was reporting the abusers to the proper agencies, the amount of bad behavior in this world would finally start to decrease.

I think reporting the evildoers to these agencies is an excellent thing to do because the people who have chosen to work for these agencies are people who have chosen to interact with the insensitive people in this world. If they do not mind doing that, go ahead and let them. Interacting with the insensitive people in this world is more than most of the sensitive people can handle.

Many of the sensitive people are able to report these people without anyone ever suspecting they are the ones who reported them because sensitive people tend to be the opposite of the hot heads. They are typically people who think everything through before they react to anything. If you never react to the abusive people, the abusive people will not have any idea you are ready to challenge them.

I have needed to report some of the people who treat people very badly repeatedly. These people who treat people badly every day do change their behaviors after they get reported. They usually become very afraid that another anonymous letter will get sent-out to report them. Some of the people who I have reported do not have a life outside of their job. Their job is their entire life. They are obsessed with having power and control over people. They live alone and some of them will probably spend the rest of their lives living alone because they do not know how to have a good relationship with anyone. They crave having power and control over people so much that they destroy every relationship they start to create.

When a Narcissist's brain is MRI'd it is always discovered that the area of their brain that controls empathy and compassion is dramatically under-active. These people are truly not capable of caring about anyone in the world other than themselves. If they do have children, they will always think of their children as extensions of themselves. They will not think of their children as separate people. They will expect their children to accomplish all the things they wish they could have accomplished. Narcissists can be very capable of being fake nice to try to attract people and to get people to do things for them. Once they think they have those people hooked, they will start to treat those people badly. Some people are fooled by them in the beginning because they can be very charming when they are trying to attract people. Sensitive people need to learn how to recognize the Narcissists immediately and get away from them.

Narcissists are attracted to sensitive people. They are constantly looking for people who are kind and interested in helping people. They look for people who they think they will be able to treat like slaves.

Since sensitive people can become targets for Narcissists, the sensitive people must learn how to not only recognize the Narcissists. They also need to learn how to report the Narcissists and get away from them. The sensitive people will feel miserable all the time if they must keep dealing with the Narcissists.

The Narcissists have no clue that when they constantly boss people around and expect people to think and act like they do all the time, they are creating big problems.

Many of the people who are promoted and placed in charge of people are not capable of fixing anything. Many of them are people who have diarrhea of the mouth. They must hire people to do things for them all the time. They are not doers. Many of them are not good at planning for the future, they tend to only think about what is going on today. Many of them desperately want to oversee people, yet they do not have a clue that lots of people would do things for them if they appreciated people. They do the opposite of appreciate people. They are very good at making people feel miserable. They frequently have huge egos. Sometimes these people are so focused on overseeing people that they do not care about how many problems there are in their environment. They do not care that everyone is fighting all the time. They just want to be the Boss. Sometimes the environment they are in is completely rancid and they will do absolutely nothing to try to improve the environment. Situations just continue to get worse. People who behave like this typically will not ever behave better until someone forces them to behave better. Since most sensitive people hate conflict and do not want to have any more confrontations with the difficult people in this world any more than they absolutely must, they need to learn how to REPORT THE EVIL-DOERS.

I have the Irish complexion. I must see a dermatologist regularly. The Dermatologist Office I was going to hire a lady to collect payments from people who was so aggressive that she made me furious, and I was hoping she would not be employed there anymore when I returned in 6 months. I have a high credit score and I have always paid all my bills on time. No one in this world should be giving me a hard time about me paying for things. When I returned to this office 6 months later, I told the lady who was making sure I did not have any skin abnormalities that I was never going to return to this office again because of how that lady treated me 6 months ago. She looked at my chart and she said, "You are all paid-up." I responded, "I know." When I was leaving that office that day, I quickly walked past the lady who had bullied me 6 months earlier. She was yelling at me to come back. I kept walking very quickly. I never returned to that office. I found a new Dermatologist office.

One day the Dentist Office I had been going to called me at home on the day of my Dental appointment. The lady who called me was so rude to me that I was crying all day. When I arrived for my Dental appointment, I eventually told the Technician how the lady behind the front desk had treated me. I told her I was never going to return to this office. I cried some more while I was in that office. The Technician felt bad. Another lady took the lady who worked behind the counter to a back room. I never returned to that office. I found a new Dental Office that is very nice to me.

Before I make appointments with any Doctors Offices I do searches online to see how that office is ranked. I read the comments people have written about these Doctor's Offices.

I am always trying to improve the likelihood that I will not encounter mean people.

Sadly, I have another example of a time I was feverishly trying to solve a problem when some insensitive people chose to be mean to me. The fact that those people were mean to me solved nothing. Their behavior created more problems.

My husband and I were unable to have children. We adopted a girl. We were at the hospital when she was born. We have an open relationship with her biological family. We have gotten together with them lots of times.

When she was a baby. We spent lots of time with her. We spent at least 30 minutes with her in her bedroom before she went to sleep every night. We built blocks with her. We played lots of games with her. We read to her. We played music for her.

We tried to make sure she received a lot more positive reinforcement from us than negative reinforcement.

When she was in kindergarten she was supposed to read the words on a word ring the school gave her. She refused to read those words every night.

When she was in the first grade, she took a test that compared her with the other 1st graders in the United States. She scored 93% in her ability to read. The score she received for math was 52%.

She did well at school.

All her teachers had lots of positive things to say about her.

The only negative things any of the teachers said about her was, "She finishes tests and quizzes very quickly and she starts trying to talk to the other kids who are around her while they are still trying to complete their work."

She has always been very sociable and had lots of friends.

Yes, we knew she had some issues because she had horrible temper tantrums any time she got upset about anything.

She seemed to require a lot more attention from us than other kids seemed to need from their parents.

It was obvious to us that she had ADHD. She has moved the furniture around in her bedroom more than 300 times.

She has never had regular sleep patterns.

There had been signs that she had emotional issues, but she was doing so well at school that it seemed like she had lots of great qualities that might help her overcome her issues and have a successful life.

When covid showed-up and she was an 8th grader at the Junior High, the school announced the students would not be attending school anymore when there was about 6 weeks left in that school year, she decided she was not going to do any schoolwork from home either.

She stopped doing schoolwork completely.

When she was in the 9th grade and she was supposed to start attending a good high school, she refused to go to school most days and she did not do much schoolwork from home either.

During the 2nd semester of her freshman year, the school decided they would have her go to a room near their offices at the front of their school and work on her schoolwork there while teachers were keeping an eye on her. She did not do much schoolwork when she did go there.

When she ended her freshman school year she had 5 F's and a D- on her report card.

Before she became a Sophomore, the school called me and told me they thought she should be bussed to a different high school and be in a classroom with other students who had fallen behind with their schoolwork. I agreed we should try that.

Once that schoolyear started she refused to go to school almost every day. She started getting caught-up with some of her classes a little bit. It was obvious that this program was not a good fit for her. She hated going there.

I am going to refer to our daughter as Abby even though that is not her name.

A few months after she had started that program, I received a certified letter in the mail from her high school that stated, if we (Abby's Parents) cannot get her to go to school every day, we will be sent to a courtroom, and we may be sent to a jail cell for up to a year or severely fined.

This certified letter we received was so disturbing and insulting. We could not believe we had received it.

I had been communicating with the staff at both high schools well.

I had been really trying to get our daughter to go to the schools and everything we were trying was not working.

We had been taking her to see Psychiatrists and Counselors even though it was very difficult for us to get her to do that.

The school was aware that we were really trying to get her to go to school.

Trying to punish us was completely the wrong thing to do.

Thankfully, our daughter's biological grandmother called me one day, soon after we received that certified letter and she told me, "My youngest sister acts a lot like Abby does and she just had her DNA tested. The results from her DNA test suggested which prescription medicines are compatible with her. She started taking new prescription medicines and she started behaving a lot better. I think Abby should have her DNA tested, I am going to e-mail you information about where Abby can go to have her DNA tested.

We did take Abby to see a new Psychiatrist. He tested her DNA. The results from that test stated she has:

ADHD

Anxiety

Depression

Oppositional Defiance Disorder

The Psychiatrist told us right away. I am not going to tell the school she has Oppositional Defiance Disorder. If I do, they might try to send her to one of those schools where the kids behave very badly. I will tell the school she has Social Anxiety instead.

The school received this Psychiatrist's diagnosis.

The school told me they were going to mail paperwork for me to fill out and for Abby to fill-out about how she behaves, and we were supposed to mail it back to the school. After the school received our paperwork, they called me and scheduled a time when my husband, Abby and I could go to the school and have a meeting with many of the staff members. They told us they had some other programs they could place her in, and they were trying to figure out which program would be a good fit for her.

The 3 of us did attend that meeting. At that meeting there was a guy there who oversees a school in the same community that has about 70 students. All those students have been diagnosed with some type of an emotional disorder. These are students that do not have behavioral issues at school they all have trouble with learning for one reason or another. The school he oversees has a time-out room where the kids can go if they need to get calmed down. These kids can get up and walk around during the middle of the class if they feel like they need to get up and walk around. There is a park right next to this school and when the weather is nice the kids are allowed to do their schoolwork while they are at the park with a teacher. These kids earn points throughout the day for good behavior. At the end of the school day, they get to trade their points-in for cookies.

The guy who oversees this school asked us if we would like to go to this school and get a tour of it.

The 3 of us did go to this school and we toured the building after the meeting.

We were told if we signed the paperwork and transferred Abby to this school, we could always transfer her back to the regular high school any time we wanted to.

We did sign the paperwork and we transferred her to this school during March of her Sophomore year.

She likes going to this school. She likes all the teachers at this school. None of the teachers are mean to her at this school. By the end of her Sophomore school year, she had most of her classes caught-up.

As of now, she has been attending this smaller school for 2 months during her Junior year and she now has A's in all her classes. She goes to this school almost every day she is supposed to go there.

This is a classic example of how when you treat people decently, they usually respond favorably. When you treat people roughly, expect the results you receive to vary.

Our daughter is thriving at this smaller school.

We did not know if she would ever do well at school again. We did not know if she would ever graduate from high school. When she finally got transferred to a school where the teachers are nice to her, and they adapt the environment to suit her needs she started doing well at school again.

Every time we drive past the high school she used to attend, she says, "I hate that school, I hate that school." Not all the teachers and staff members at that school were nice to her.

She needs to be treated kindly and respectfully. When she is not she probably will not cooperate. That is how she thinks.

When Sensitive people are treated badly repeatedly over time, they usually develop physical diseases that continually get worse over time.

Can you imagine what this world would be like if everyone in it was nice? Can you imagine what this world would be like if no one owned a gun and people did not feel like they never know when they are going to need to protect and defend themselves?

Parenting experts say newborns and children should receive positive reinforcement much more than they receive negative reinforcement. Yes, it is necessary to use some negative reinforcement some of the time, however, parents should try to use positive reinforcement about 4 times more often than they use negative reinforcement.

Adults also need to be treated positively much more often than they are treated negatively. Lots of people are not good at all at treating people positively.

Everyone in this world needs to learn how to understand that everyone in this world thinks and acts differently and everyone in this world is supposed to think and act differently.

This world should not have only:

One style of decorating.

One type of art.

One type of music.

Only people who are good mechanics.

This world needs people who are:

Artistic

Good at being Doctors

Good at Cooking and Baking

Good at Counseling

Good at doing physical activity

Good at Engineering

Good at Teaching

Good at Singing.

Our world needs lots of different types of people. We all need to think and act differently. We are all born with strengths and weaknesses. Everyone needs to learn how to develop their strengths and overcome their weaknesses.

People need to focus on taking care of themselves and improving themselves, not trying to bring other people down.

We really need to get the insensitive people to stop scolding people, stop criticizing people, stop treating people like everything they do and say is wrong, stop interrupting people, stop hurting people, stop treating people like they are worthless. Sometimes all the garbage the insensitive people dump on the sensitive people is more than the sensitive people can handle.

We really need to stop creating new rules and laws that make life harder for everyone. Currently, I feel like a lot of people treat me like I am probably a criminal. I get insulted every time that happens to me. The law-abiding citizens are getting treated worse as time goes by.

Instead of treating everyone badly, we should be empowering the decent people and helping them get the indecent people discovered. We already live in a society that makes it close to impossible for anyone to ever be able to relax. People harass us everywhere we are these days. Even when we are at home, we keep getting harassed by phone solicitors, internet criminals and shady people who knock on our doors.

Even when some of our neighbors have loud parties until 5:00 a.m. and we call the Police, the Police show-up but the party never stops. Many of our neighbors told us they have called the Police about the loud parties that disrupt lots of our neighbors all night long too. We cannot even get the Police to stop the loud parties during the night.

I do not know why the Police have not gotten the loud parties that go on past the noise ordinance time in our community to stop. I do think if enough people call the police every time that happens, perhaps, that obnoxious behavior will finally stop.

Yes, many of the Police Officers do an excellent job. Many of them are extremely helpful. They have helped us solve other problems.

We have a neighbor who likes to scream at us when we are in our yard. She is abusive. I have decided, "If she screams at us one more time, I will tell her, "I am going to call the police and try to get them to stop you from harassing us." I will call the police. Every time I am in my yard, I am always wondering if she is going to start screaming at me. I should not have those kind of thoughts in my head every time I am in my yard.

Currently, I am sitting in front of my computer. My phone just rang. The person on the other end of the line stated, "Hi, my name is Sarah, I am with Medicare Benefits, How are you doing today?" I responded, "I do not accept phone solicitations." I hung-up the phone. I have spent a lot of time and effort trying to get no phone solicitors to call me and it keeps happening. I have blocked lots of phone solicitor's phone #'s. I cannot believe how many phone solicitors still call us. I will keep fighting it. Those phone calls cause my mood to drop.

I sincerely believe what we need is to give the victims of the crimes lots more ways that they can report the evildoers and we need to have Police Officers and people who have authority to get the evil doers to stop doing the evil deeds. We need to make it a law that BULLY BOXES must be installed in all the bathrooms at every school, every church, every library and possibly in large corporations where people work, so the victims will know where they can easily and safely report crimes.

The internet has caused bullying to be much worse than it used to be. Bullying now happens 24 hours per day, 7 days per week because of the internet. The rate that people commit suicide is getting worse as time goes by.

We must get these problems turned around.

I believe all the people who do have empathy and compassion for other people need to start reporting all the people who treat people very badly. I have started reporting people and I have helped lots of people get treated much better. I know that reporting the people who wander around this earth and torment other people every day, all day long need to be stopped. I am surprised there are so many people who see bad behavior happen frequently and they do not report the bad behaviors.

Please start speaking-up and try to get the negative people to stop their bullying.

If this world would concentrate on helping people become more positive, kinder, better listeners and people who appreciate and compliment other people. I think that would solve a lot of the problems we have in this World including physical and mental health.

Some supplements that can help improve your mood are: 5-HTP, St. John's Wort and Dopa Mucuna.

CONCLUSION

Dogs are only capable of learning new things for about the first 6 months of their lives. Human beings are capable of learning new things almost their entire lives.

Many human beings, unfortunately, are not interested in learning new things. Many people think they are already experts on every topic. Some people think they could not possibly learn anything new from another human being. That is absolutely the wrong attitude anyone should have.

All us are born with a unique personality. Yes, most of us fit into personality categories but there are not 2 people anywhere in this world who think exactly alike. We all have things we are good at and things at which we are not good. We should all try to see how we can improve ourselves by learning new things. We should all try to learn how to be kinder and more appreciative of others. No one should expect other people to act and think exactly like they do. I strongly believe that we could dramatically improve this world if everyone in it strived to be more positive and less self-centered.

I think everyone should learn to be less critical and condescending when they are interacting with others. Everyone should learn to stop scolding and hurting others. Everyone should be aware that they can motivate people much more effectively by using positive reinforcement most of the time.

Because I have a sensitive personality; most of the time, I feel like I am getting overloaded with negative vibes from other people. I have always felt like I have finely tuned antenna is that detect all the negative comments and gestures other people send-out. All those negative vibes I detect accumulate over time and the more I get to know the people who frequently emit vocal and/or physical garbage, the more I feel like never interacting with those people again.

From what I have heard people say, many people get lonely. I think, because I have a non-cancerous brain tumor in my left thalamus, I react to negative vibes very much like an autistic person who has sensory issues reacts to lots of noise and commotion. I understand that other people can handle being corrected and insulted frequently. I cannot handle that. I know that there are lots of people in this world besides myself who cannot handle being treated badly repeatedly over time. There are a lot of sensitive people in this world who cannot handle what I am describing. I have been so disgusted by how some people have tried to treat me, that, I have decided to fight back. I have decided that I can help raise awareness about bullying and I am capable of helping countless other people who are being treated badly all the time and they do not know how to stand-up for themselves.

All the people in this world who constantly think they should belittle other people at a level 10, when belittling other people at a level 3 would have infuriated most other people, need to be stopped. All these bullies need to be educated and policed. They are causing a lot of damage in this world. I understand that a large portion of these people desperately feel like they need to have power and control over other people; but they do not even understand that they are pushing people away from them all the time. These people who are so power hungry would be much more effective with getting people to want to spend time with them and do things for them; if they would learn how to be nice to other people and appreciate other people.

If you feel like you need to make-fun-of other people all the time, then, you need help. It is very sad that so many people feel like they need to put other people down to feel better about themselves. These people who repeatedly try to control and manipulate other people keep making sure they do not have a close relationship with any of those people. These master manipulator's become increasingly lonely over time, and they act like they can't understand why no one wants to spend time with them. If you are a control-freak; a lot of people will not like you. These people who have aggressive personalities would have much better lives if they understood that they need to be positive people. They should spend at least one hour, with a pen and a piece of paper. Every time they have a negative thought, do something negative or say something that is negative, they should draw a small x on the page. Every time they have a positive thought, do something that is positive, or say something that is positive, they should draw a small circle on the same page. At the end of that hour, they should analyze how many x's they have on the page compared with how many circles they have on the page. If they have dramatically more x's on the page, than circles, they seriously need to learn how to become a more positive person.

When you have negative thoughts, actions and words, you are hurting yourself and you are hurting other people. Oh, sure, you act like you have it all together, you are better than everyone else and you know more than everyone else, but you do not, and you are lying to yourself repeatedly. The more you insult other people, the more you hurt them and yourself.

It is normal to have some negative thoughts, but you should not be having negative thoughts all day long every day. If you are saturated with negative thoughts all the time, you need to learn how to become a happier person. You need to figure-out what kind of things put you in a good mood and spend time doing those things. Those things could be spending time out in nature, spending time doing your favorite hobbies, watching movies or sitcoms that you love, reading a book that you love or visiting an arboretum. People tend to be the happiest when they spend about 1/3 of each of their days doing things that they enjoy doing.

You will benefit dramatically if you can learn how to not dump all your problems and worries on other people.

Everyone in this world should try to learn how to be better listeners. Lots of people love to talk about themselves; but lots of people are not good at listening to what other people must say. Learning how to be a good listener is exactly what helps people develop strong relationships with other people. If you talk about yourself and all your wants and needs all the time, and never care about what other people's wants and needs are, you will alienate those people eventually. Even if they are not consciously aware of what you are doing, they will subconsciously realize that you make them feel bad. They may not understand why you are making them feel bad. They will, however, know that you make them feel bad and over time, they will try to avoid you. The only way you can form a great relationship with another human being is if you treat them respectfully and they treat you respectfully.

I know that I am constantly craving having a great and fun relationship with other human beings, but most people do not make me feel good. Lots of people make me feel bad and I know right away that I do not want to interact with them. I am always hoping to find intellectual stimulation, but I cannot find that with people who are condescending. Time-after-time, I am disappointed when people start talking and I learn right away that they have a lot of negative things to say. I am always amazed that a lot of people think being negative will help them get the things they want. There is a saying that I heard a long time ago. It said something like: 'People will not always remember what you did or what you said. People will, however, remember how you made them feel.'

I do remember how people make me feel. Any time I am walking toward a group of people who I have walked past many times, I have random thoughts in my head. I think things like:

'He is probably thinking, 'Why do not you ever smile'

'He is a negative person; I am sure he has something to complain about'

'She loves to insult me'

'She is a nice and fun person, but she is a very simple person, it is a shame I can't have a stimulating conversation with her, because she is probably the kindest person in this building right now'

'That guy is mean, I need to get away from him, I hope he did not see me'

'Oh, yeah, there is someone who actually acts like he appreciates me, he is capable of listening to what I must say, I can talk to him, he will probably put me in a good mood'

'Oh no, here comes the girl who is always rude to me, she is really friendly with all the guys, she smiles at the guys, but every time she sees me, she looks at me like I am the worst person in this entire world'

'Here comes a nice person. She seems like she is very pleasant, but she is kind-of clueless, from comments she has made to me before, I can tell she is living in a completely different world than I am living in'

'There is that guy who's life revolves around rules. He does not care about how he makes anyone feel, he loves to tell everyone what all the rules are, and he doesn't care about how harsh he sounds, he just loves to boss people around'

'There is that lady who sounds like she is a robot, she says and does exactly the same things all day long every day'

I have a strong hunch other people's thoughts are nothing like mine. I know that a lot of the people in this world make most of their decisions according to logic. Some people, including me, make most of their decisions according to their emotions. As I move around every day, I anticipate how people will make me feel and I try to decide who I should avoid. I even eyeball all the cashiers before I decide which checkout lane I will stand in. For me, I do not just choose the checkout lane that has the shortest line. If the lane that has the shortest line has a cashier working there who has gotten on my nerves in the past, I will not stand in that line.

I realize that the people who let logic guide them through their lives really have no clue that they sometimes hurt other people because they are too bossy. I do not know what kind of thoughts those people have as they walk around but because of the things I have heard those kind of people say, I am guessing they think things like:

'She isn't wearing a collared shirt, which is against the rules, I am going to write-her-up'

'He is making a mess; he is going to must do a much better job of cleaning-up while he works'

'She is too slow; I am going to scold her and make her work faster'

'He looks like he found the buffet, I look better than he does'

'If I get promoted, I will earn more money, I need to do everything I can possibly do to get promoted'

All the thoughts I listed above were thoughts that did not have any concern for how the other people think or feel. They were all bossy thoughts. All these thoughts would be likely to hurt other people's feelings if they were spoken out loud. One time, I heard a person who is extremely bossy and logical say: 'All students should wear a uniform all the time when they are at school. That would cut down on the need for families to spend lots of money on clothes. That would keep children from making fun of other student's outfits. That would keep children from wearing inappropriate clothes to school. That would solve a lot of problems, so let us do that.'

Rules like that do not make sense for everyone to adhere to. Rules like that are not a good idea for every student.

Some kids have sensory issues and would be miserable if they were forced to wear a uniform that had an uncomfortable fabric.

Some kids get cold easily and would be uncomfortable if they were forced to wear a uniform.

Some kids get hot easily and would be uncomfortable if they were forced to wear a uniform.

Some kids are artistic and would be extremely frustrated if they had to wear the same thing every day. Wearing a uniform would keep them from being able to express themselves artistically through their clothes.

Anyway, one of the points I am trying to make is that there are a lot of people in this world who love rules, schedules and routines. Some of those people act like everyone should act, think and dress the same all the time. Some of those people act like having lots of strict rules and laws will fix everything. They are wrong. Some people love strict rules, and some people hate strict rules. Some people prefer to have loose rules and schedules because they like to keep their options open regarding what they will be doing, when they will be doing it and where they will be doing it. Some people love to have flexible schedules. Some people love to try new things and learn new things and they do not want to be tied down to a lifestyle that seems like it came from a military base. The people who have extremely bossy and rigid personalities really get on some other people's nerves. Some of the bossy people have such tunnel vision that they cannot see the big picture. They do not know what is best for everyone, but they act like they do. Across-the-board, bossy people, in my opinion, are a group of people who really do not care about how they make other people feel. They seem to like rules more than they like people.

It you are someone who thinks there is not a problem in this world with people being inconsiderate. Go to any grocery store or department store on a Saturday. Look down the aisles. Look to see how many aisles are blocked by people and their shopping carts. Sometimes it is one normal-sized person and 1 shopping cart and the person who is pushing the shopping cart does not have the sense to stay to the left or to the right. They park themselves and their cart in the middle of the aisle. From my experiences, it seems like about 50% of the people who shop in stores do not even try to not get in other people's way. It seems like those people are so focused on what they are doing and what they want that they never stop to think, 'Can other people travel down this aisle?

I do not think all the people who do that are mean people. I think a lot of them do not have common sense. Some people are not good at figuring things out on their own. They really do need to have simple concepts explained to them. I also think some of those people have never really learned to think of other people as equals. I think some people really do think they are more important than everyone else. They think all their wants and needs should be tended to first.

Some people say, "The bullies are people who need more love."

Some people say, "The bullies are people who have been bullied."

The truth is, there are a lot of different reasons why bullies bully. There is not one solution that will get all the bullies in the world to behave better.

Some people have personalities that are so self-centered, those people are not interested in caring about anyone in the world other than themselves. They do not care about how they treat other people. They only care about what other people can do for them. Because those people, time-after-time make other people feel bad, they push other people away from them. Ironically, they tend to have unhappy, unfulfilling and lonely lives. These people tend to have poor problem-solving abilities and these people tend to try to dump all their problems on other people.

Some people become bullies because they were parented by one or two parents who were bullies and that is what they are familiar with. They never learned how to behave any differently.

Some people become bullies because they love being the center of attention so much that they would rather get into trouble than be ignored.

Perhaps our prisoners should be required to receive neurofeedback treatments. Neurofeedback treatments help calm down over-active brains. Perhaps the neurofeedback treatments would be less expensive than housing and feeding these people in jails.

Some people become bullies because their emotional needs are not getting met at home. They know they need to have relationships with people, but they do not know how to have healthy relationships with people. They are just trying to figure out how to relate to other people and they have not figured-out a good way to relate to other people. If you are unsure of how you should treat other people, you could try asking those people, "How would you like to be treated?" In other words, do not assume other people want to be treated the same way you like to be treated. Different people have different wants and needs.

There is a guy who I see frequently when I am working. He sometimes says things that put me in a bad mood. If he would just say to me, "How has your day been going today?," "How has life been treating you lately?" or "It's good to see you." All those comments would be good comments for him to make. Lots of people cannot figure out what the proper things to say to other people are and what the improper things to say to other people are. It seems like people from a very young age should learn at school what kind of comments are appropriate to say to other people. Some people never do learn what types of words, phrases and sentences will be likely to upset other people.

There are a lot of guys in this world who want to talk to females, but they do not have any idea what they should say to them. It is quite simple. Be a good listener. Ask her to tell you stories about herself. Ask her about what her dreams are and what she wants to accomplish during her life. Try that and I think you will be amazed by the great reaction you will receive.

I think the United States Government should designate one Television Station to broadcast lots of different types of educational and self-help programs. This Television Station should be viewable in all 50 States, and it should have helpful programs aired for long hours every day of the week. That Television Station could teach people how to not become bullies, how to stand-up to bullies, how to learn to do karate, self-defense, Tai Kwan Do, how to stop smoking, how to stop drinking, how to stop using illegal drugs, how to handle sex-addiction, how to deal with your parents getting a divorce, what you should do if the parent you are living with moves someone else into your home that you do not feel comfortable around, what to do if a gang is trying to get you to join them, what to do if you feel like you are in danger, how to manage money, how to plan for your retirement and countless other programs that would help people learn how to improve their lives.

Bullying tends to be the worst among kids who are in the 6th, 7th & 8th grades. At that age, the front part of their brains is not developed that well yet. The front part of the human brain does not get fully developed until someone is about 26 years old. The front part of the brain enables people to be able to make good decisions, be able to reason, be able to understand what the consequences of their actions will be. The front part of the brain helps people have organized thoughts. Even kids who do well academically at school can be kids who make a lot of bad decisions.

Anyway, most of the time, when bullying occurs, the person who is doing the bullying is trying to get something. Sometimes they are trying to get power and control over their victim. Sometimes they are trying to get attention. Sometimes they are trying to prove to people they are capable of intimidating people. Sometimes they are trying to make sure everyone understands, no one should question them, and everyone should just obey their every demand.

Regardless of why the bullies bully. All the people in this world who bully other people do a lot of damage to other people. There are a lot of victims who are getting treated very badly every day.

We all need to learn how to help each other. We all need to learn to not hurt other people. Hurting other people does not help anyone.

Some people bully because they were born with a difficult personality type. People cannot change their personality type. Some people have a very rigid and stubborn personality. They do not want to admit that anything they do is wrong. They want to blame all their problems on other people.

To make positive changes in this world, we need to change the way people think.

Empathy should be taught in schools. Some people do not learn empathy at home.

People should not be forced to be so busy that they become extremely stressed-out and feel miserable all the time. Americans need to learn how to have Siestas. Many of the other Countries allow their employees to take a lot more vacation time, than the United States does.

During the 1960's it was very common for families to be able to live a comfortable lifestyle when only the father was employed. During that time, Companies used to take a lot better care of their employees. It was common for Companies to offer their employees decent benefits and decent 401K plans. Now, most families need to have both of their parents working full-time jobs for their family to live a comfortable lifestyle and be able to pay all their bills.

Now, it is common for employers to not offer their employees much regarding planning for their retirement. Employers keep trying to figure out how they can take things away from their employees and they frequently replace their employees with less expensive employees. This is one more example of how a lot of people treat each other badly. When employers treat their employees decently, their employees are much more likely to treat their employers decently. When employers treat their employees badly, their employees are a lot more likely to not care about their employers. This is a very simple concept that a lot of people just do not comprehend.

Now, it is common for students to incur an enormous debt from getting student loans, then, lots of those students are not able to find a job that pays well   enough for them to be able to pay-off their student loans once they graduate from college. Colleges have become ridiculously expensive and there is no good reason for it. When I graduated from college with a 4-year bachelor's degree in 1985. I had paid $13,000.00 for my 4 years of education and boarding. I had acquired a $9,000.00 student loan that I was able to pay-off within a reasonable time after I graduated. Now, it is common for students to graduate with hundreds of thousands of dollars of debt and they are not even able to find a decent job after they graduate.

About 80% of all Americans have big financial problems. Among the 20% of people who do not have big financial problems, about 3% of those people are filthy rich and the other 17% are doing OK but lots of those people are stressed-out all the time because they must work all the time.

Women who are pregnant should be extra careful to not smoke, drink or use illegal drugs when they are pregnant. It is strongly believed that the # 1 thing that causes adverse outcomes for babies, is when a woman smokes while she is pregnant. When women smoke while they are pregnant, their developing baby does not receive as much oxygen as it would have, the mother did smoke while she was pregnant. Her baby will be dramatically more likely to:

Be born prematurely

Be born with a low birth weight

Be born too small

Die before they are born

Their lungs may not be ready to work on their own when they are born

They may need to be on a respirator the first few weeks of their life, even if they

were able to breathe on their own when they were born.

Experience sudden infant death

Have asthma

Have a heart defect at birth

Have lifelong effects on their brain

Have behavioral problems

Have a low IQ

We need to be much more understanding that we all have brains that think differently and we are supposed to think differently. We should not expect other people to think and act like we do.

We should learn to appreciate other people for the things they are good at and understand that their strengths add value to our lives.

We should try to develop the things we are good at and help other people develop the things at which they are good.

We are all flawed. We all have things at which we are not good. Do not criticize or shame people because they have weaknesses. No one is good at everything.

People need to learn to not to take their frustrations out on other people.

People need to learn when they should stand-up for themselves and report people to try to stop those people from doing the same type of behaviors again in the future.

There should not be a negative stigma attached to people needing to seek mental health. If someone is not feeling well mentally, they should seek help.

Seeking help for mental health issues should not be as expensive as it is and insurance companies should cover those kinds of treatments.

There is proof that neurofeedback treatments can dramatically calm down over-active areas of the brain and help people behave better. Since these treatments can dramatically help people who have behavioral problems behave better. I think these treatments should be dramatically less expensive and I also think Insurance Companies should cover these types of treatments.

Every school should have a quiet room that people can go to when they are feeling overwhelmed. It should be a place where people can go to help get themselves calmed down.

Schools should teach everyone what they should do if they are feeling over- whelmed.

Schools should understand that lots of kids have emotional health problems that make it hard for them to learn the way most students learn. Some of those students need more positive reinforcements, more rewards for good behavior, the opportunity to get up and walk around during the class, the opportunity to go outside during the school day, lots of opportunities to talk to someone who is a good listener because some of them really need to have someone to whom they can talk.

Schools should understand that the students who are introverts do get extremely emotionally drained when they are in public all day long. Introverts need to have privacy and they need to be in calm environments frequently.

Frequently, when our society is trying to figure-out how to solve a problem, like how many school shootings we have had in America. People start talking about raising money and enforcing more rules and beefing-up security, but no one talks about changing the way people think or feel.

Quite frankly, I am completely sick of the fact that a lot of people treat me like I am probably a criminal and I need to be checked out to make sure I am not a criminal. Just because a small percentage of people do horrific crimes, the rest of us must get treated like we are suspicious characters everywhere we go.

There are a lot of people who get bullied every day and lots of people watch it happen and they do nothing to try to stop the bullying. People who have special needs get bullied very frequently. Some of the people who get bullied are not able to defend themselves. If you can help someone not get bullied, do that. Do not watch violent acts and let them happen.

Seriously consider being the person who stops people from bullying. If more of us would stand-up for ourselves and for other people, the world we are living in would improve dramatically.

I did a search on the internet for, 'Are the people who have shot people in schools, people who have been bullied?' I was surprised to learn that those people, for the most part, were not people who have been bullied. The article talked about how the people who have done that are Narcissistic people who really do not have any compassion for other people. I have learned enough about Narcissistic people to know that Hitler and Stalin and some other people during our history who performed horrific acts were people who had absolutely no compassion or empathy for other people. People who are high-functioning extreme Narcissists can hurt other people and they enjoy hurting other people.

Our society should learn how to discover which people in our society have brains that think that way and remove those people from our society to protect the rest of us. Sometimes our society is completely unaware that some people can do lots of harm to other people and they like to have those types of people oversee lots of other people because they are convinced that mean people who enforce lots of strict rules are doing what needs to be done to get people to do what they are supposed to do. Some people think there is no way to get people to behave, other than by treating people harshly.

Most people spend about 95% of their time thinking about themselves. Some people have brains that cause them to spend about 100% of their time thinking about themselves and what other people can do for them. Those people who have very extreme personalities should not oversee lots of other people.

I have had a strong dislike for the kind of people who treat other people harshly my entire life. I have never liked people who are mean, people who bully other people, people who are overly strict, people who love to criticize and correct me, people who talk to me like I am stupid, people who talk to me like I do everything incorrectly, people who try to fight and argue with me all the time, people who refuse to listen to me when I tell them they are doing something that is getting on my nerves, people who try to force me to do things I do not want to do, people who try to rush me and people who constantly interrupt me and try to hover over me when I am doing things.

Time after time, I have been amazed that there are so many people who stick their noses in my business and cannot seem to not try to control and manipulate me. I am also shocked by how many times people have thought they were doing something good, when they were scolding me. I am a good person. My entire life, I have been doing good things. I am a productive person. I am a hard worker. I am punctual and dependable. When people are nice to me, I will do a lot for them. When people are mean to me; I am not interested in doing anything for them. Lots of people have been mean to me during my lifetime. I am completely amazed that so many people have treated me badly. I am shocked that so many people have tried to treat me like I am a bad person. I do not do anything to try to get on other people's nerves but lots of people go out of their way to try to make sure they make me feel miserable. Unfortunately, I have a good memory for how people have made me feel during my lifetime. It does not matter how much someone tries to bribe me. People who go out of their way to make me feel miserable do not deserve to be in my life. I am not interested in spending time with people who treat me negatively.

Apparently, there are a lot of people in this World who can handle being treated badly time-after-time, because it keeps happening. I think we would start to see lots of positive changes in this world if people would finally learn how to treat each other much better.

Employers need to learn how to treat their employees much better.

Parents need to learn how to treat their children much kindlier.

Children need to learn how to treat their parents much kindlier.

Married people need to learn how to treat each other much kindlier.

Parents need to be a lot kinder toward other parents. There are a lot of times when people accuse parents of parenting badly when their child or children are misbehaving. Sometimes parents are parenting very well, yet, their children still behave badly. Some kids behave a lot worse than other kids. Some kids are a lot more challenging to parent than other kids. Parenting is a very difficult job. Why do so many people accuse other parents of doing a bad parenting job, when those people do not even know how that parent has been parenting.

We should all be treating other people positively much more frequently than we are treating them negatively. Unfortunately, most people treat other people negatively much more frequently than they treat other people positively.

Everyone has stories to tell about their lives, but most people are better talkers than listeners. When people can tell stories about their lives, that helps them feel better. Great salespeople learn how to let people tell them stories about their lives, at least while they are leading up to making the sale. After, they have made the sale, very few salespeople will spend time with listening to other people tell their stories. If we could all learn how to be good listeners and encourage other people to talk about how they are feeling and talk about things they have been through, people would, then be helped and be able to start to heal.

I think the selfish attitudes most people have are hurting our society. I think if everyone could learn to be less selfish and learn to care about other people more, that is when we will be able to have a lot less violence and problems in this world.

Imagine how much better this world would be if everyone in it had opportunities to talk about the experiences they had that day, at the end of each day. Being able to talk about the things they have been through helps them heal. Our society is so hectic that people finding time to talk about their day does not happen nearly as much as it should. When no one ever listens to what you must say, you will be likely to become very frustrated. Even the quiet people who do not talk much need to be able to talk about the things they have been through and they need to be able to talk about their dreams and their aspirations but sometimes, the quiet people do not talk much because they get their feelings hurt easily and they are not interested in talking to anyone who is going to be likely to make-fun of them and criticize what they must say.

Even the people who have extremely controlling and manipulative personalities soften and melt when you ask them to tell you stories about things that have happened to them during their lifetime. Most people love to talk about themselves but how often does anyone ask other people to talk about themselves? Oh sure, people ask, "How are you?" when those people are in a busy environment, like a grocery store checkout line, and they do not really have the time to talk and tell stories. How often, though, do people ask other people to tell them stories about their life when they are sitting across from them at a party or a picnic. Most people do not ask other people to talk about themselves. Most people talk about themselves. A lot of the people who talk about themselves do not even try to talk about a topic the person they are talking to is interested in talking about, instead, they just talk about the things they like to talk about.

Many people, including myself, have personality types that are very emotional. They feel lots of emotions that most people cannot understand. I and many others must strategically plan our lives to try to avoid all the people who are likely to really upset us. Even though I have earned 2 college degrees, I have ended up doing a job that allows me to get in my car and drive away anytime someone really upsets me. Yes, people make-fun-of me because I am doing the kind of job I have been doing. Those people act like I should be doing more with my life. Those people make me want to not spend time with them at all. I can tell they will never understand how I feel or how they make me feel no matter how I explain it to them.

The people in this world who think if they keep poking and prodding people and making fun of people, their targets will suddenly accomplish more. Those insensitive people are so wrong. They have no clue how much damage they do to people. Those people are damaging the sensitive people repeatedly over time. The sensitive people will not forget about how you keep making them feel and one day the sensitive person will probably react in a way you do not want them to. They may react violently. They may react in a sneaky way. They might write a book about their experiences, and have it published; they might run away. They might commit suicide. The insensitive people tend to get on the sensitive people's nerves repeatedly over time.

We all need to do a better job of reporting people who bully people. We all need to stop putting-up with bad behavior. This problem is not going to go away unless we all put a lot of effort in trying to get the people who are harming people to stop. Bullying is an epidemic that has been getting worse. We cannot watch it happen and ignore it. Please help get this problem turned around.

BLURB FOR THE BACK OF MY BOOK COVER

Perucca has invested a tremendous amount of herself in the researching of all aspects of the subject matter - cyber bullying.

It is fascinating - the ideas on how to learn to have the courage to retort back to trolls and cyber bullies.

To hone those skills in written back-chat, down to how to answer someone who she calls 'mean'.

Although not an easy read for lovers of chick-lit, romance or general fiction genres, it can drive those with an interest in the subject.

It gives those people who are familiar with the subject, somewhere to find out about the emotion, and that 'you' are not alone; traumatic accounts of those who have been victimized; and heartwarming stories of those who have conquered their fear of bullying in this new digital age.

In Scotland, some young people call those who troll others as 'Keyboard Gangsters'. Bullies who - given the opportunity to confront people face-to-face, would stay silent. Not brave at all - in fact - cowards.

Bullying back in 'the day', when at high school in the 60s,70s and 80s, would come up against someone who thought they were 'hard' - whose family perhaps had a reputation for being gangsters and doled out violence to some poor person in the wrong place at the wrong time. But at least - given the opportunity and willingness of a victim to tell, they could be brought out into the open by authorities, whether in schools, colleges, universities, workplaces, communities or in detention centers and the like.

Now in this 21st century era - they hide behind their glaring screens in their bedrooms, living rooms, dorms and even in the workplace, seemingly with nothing better to do.

Now, do we analyze and categorize these folk and tar them all with the same brush, or do we give them the benefit of the doubt, and just feel sorry for them, or try understanding their circumstances and reasons why they do what they do. Perhaps they think it is just a laugh, a prank, a one-off jibe. Or is it chronic, on-going, and never-ending. This is where the danger lies, in the young, vulnerable and people who do not know how to respond, nor act, so they opt for the finality of suicide.

This is where Perruca is at her best. She knows.

It is also difficult, through text alone, to see and believe that a message is full of cruel intentions or typed with a light-hearted sway. We cannot tell.

When face to face, we as human beings can see and tell whether a phrase is meant as tongue-in-cheek, or whether their facial expressions show other emotions like, anger, hatred, disgust, belittling, and have an exhilarating effect on the bully. They can show signs of aggression, they body language can show them gearing up for an attack - making them feel supreme and in total control.

Behind the screen, it is difficult to tell what the intention is of the bully. They could be a normal everyday person that goes to work, comes home and spends time on the laptop - unbeknown to their own family and friends. Or, they could be very sinister, and someone who should be investigated by police and other authorities.

She believes in the concept that there could be a correlation between cyber-bullying and suicide.

She provides sources and quotes from various authorities, Perruca has also brought her own experiences of bullying and cyber-bullying to the forefront of a subject that is millennial-old. When the words damage, hurt, terrify, threaten, stress and consume the victim, is where Perruca's knowledge, understanding and forward-thinking ideas to stop it come to bear fruit.

Her ideas include, forming online communities, forums in educational establishments, with boxes to place thoughts and worries, and ideas in patrolling cyber-bullying.

She has also put together a list of do's and do nots in layman's terms. Phrases to say back to a cyberbully, that would be suitable for most age groups to understand without the use of complex jargon. This could put people off from coming forward, as they could think that it is too complicated to get involved in, and there is always the fear.

There is critical advice, plans of action and preventing them from seeking that reason to live and fight on, and impart the knowledge and solutions that suicide is not their only option - under the knowledge that things do get better.

If this book saves one single person from committing suicide due to bullying, then the years of hard work, research, proofing, editing and publishing has been worth it.

This book has so much content, information, empathy, it is refreshing to read something that has been put together with so much grit and passion.

Kind Regards

By Sandra Walls

Published journalist, author, academic and poet.

Works and Publications:

Lapidus Press: Three pieces of poetry published in Anthology: Words Work Well.

University of Glasgow: Advanced Fiction Portfolio of Work inc. Short Stories, Flash Fiction, Poetry and Monologue.

Media Scotland: Published News & Features, in weekly newspaper The Hamilton Advertiser.

Authorhouse: Author of Book - Love, Grit, Blood and Spit - By Pen Name 'Sandra Reid George'.

United Press: Author of Poem called No Regrets - in anthology The Heart's Content.

Hieton Press: Author of shorts stories and poetry in various anthologies.

University of Strathclyde; Academic Paper - Dissertation on 'Domestic Violence and the Role of the Community Worker.'

My academic credentials are: (Most Recent First)

Dip HE in Creative Writing (December 2019)

Cert HE in Creative Writing and English Literature (2018)

BA Journalism inc. Broadcast (2005)

Dip HE in Journalism inc. Criminology (2004)

BA Community Education inc. Counselling (1996)

SVQ Social Sciences inc. Psychology (1993)